"Skepticism about biblical truth clai
forms. For some, no amount of evidei   .... their
zeal to deny God. Their will is set against even the possibility
that they might actually be accountable to God, and they're
therefore more interested in dreaming up ways to disprove
the evidence than to prove it.

But there are other skeptics who are genuinely convinced
that biblical truth claims are mistaken while remaining open
to be convinced. This is a type of skepticism that those of
us who are firmly convinced of the truth and importance of
biblical truth must learn to address.

Jason B. Ladd makes an admirable contribution to this
end. An accomplished fighter pilot in the U.S. Marines, his
life story is itself an adventure worth reading about. Few are
vouchsafed the types of experiences Jason Ladd has lived
through. But as Ladd makes clear, there's a far more exciting
adventure to which everyone, including skeptics of all
stripes, is invited—the discovery of God's original blueprint
for humanity. Ladd is a sure guide in this adventure. If you
have ever wondered how to speak to a seemingly self fulfilled
skeptic or if you are skeptical about Christian truth claims
yourself, Jason Ladd's book is the place to begin. I highly
recommend it."

— **John Njoroge,** speaker and host of RZIM's radio
programs *Let My People Think* and *Just Thinking*

"In One of the Few, Marine fighter pilot Jason B. Ladd takes
you on a thrilling mission to make life's most exciting and
impactful discovery. You'll really enjoy being his wingman
(and the rewards are eternal)!"

— **Frank Turek,** author of *Stealing From God* and *I Don't
Have Enough Faith to Be an Atheist*

"Marine fighter pilot Jason B. Ladd describes his journey from atheism to become a disciple of Jesus Christ. The narrative moves along in a manner that captures and keeps one's attention, describing how his journey to Jesus and afterward caused Ladd to wrestle with common misconceptions about Christianity and various issues that often pit Western culture against the teachings of Jesus. This book is recommended for those seeking truth and those who need encouragement in their Christian faith. It is also an encouragement for all of us believers to keep praying for our friends who do not know Jesus, no matter how negative they may be toward the gospel. For one of them may be the next Jason B. Ladd!"

— **Michael Licona,** author of *The Resurrection of Jesus: A New Historiographical Approach* and Associate Professor in Theology, Houston Baptist University

"Jason B. Ladd explains why we should be 'skeptical' about skepticism in relation to biblical truth in a powerful story of moving from atheist to skeptic to committed servant of Jesus Christ. In a moving testimony, he debunks fallacies and clarifies truths, effectively challenging the notion of glamorous atheism by depicting the Christian journey as life's greatest adventure. I highly recommend it for seekers and saints alike!"

— **Steven Garofalo,** author of *Right For You, But Not For Me: A Response To Moral Relativism* and President of Reason For Truth

"One of the best works I have ever read, bar none."

— **Sandra T. Lloyd,** writer

"WHAT. A. READ. Here I am on the edge of my chair, white-knuckling my Kindle Reader, and I'm still in the Prologue for Pete's sake! If Jason B. Ladd flies as well as he writes, then both America and the kingdom of God are blessed to have him on their side."

— **Ray McClendon,** writer, minister, and Police Chaplain

"Strap into your favorite chair. Lock and load the coffee pot, and prepare for your greatest mission in the battle for your soul! Supremely crafted, this book engages life's most difficult questions with a compelling and insightful view from the heart and soul of a warrior. Like adding hot sauce to grits, this is not your average bowl of theology! High praise for this mix of love, loss, war, and peace. You will be stirred to the point of action."

— **John M.,** husband, father, and Marine

"This book will transform your heart and strengthen the heart of your family."

— **Susan Irene Fox,** blogger and teacher

"One of the few books that gets down to business. Real, honest, and authentic."

— **Andrew Tuttle,** writer, MotoSport.com

"A masterful story blending military life, family, faith, and the life-changing power of God. A must read for Service Members, parents, and their children."

— **Michael Silva,** pastor and former USMC Captain

"One of the Few is both a fascinating glimpse into the world of a Marine fighter pilot and an intriguing conversion memoir that is destined to reach an under-served readership. Ladd's account of his journey has a sharp authenticity about it; it is honest and intellectually sound, but without affectation. I have already begun recommending it!"

— **Melissa Cain Travis**, M.A., Assistant Professor of Christian Apologetics, Houston Baptist University

"Jason uses the events of his life, from the seemingly mundane to the life-changing, to show us something about the Father and about Jesus Christ, and to draw out deeper spiritual points. In this way, he uses his own journey from agnosticism to Christianity as a spiritual roadmap for those at various places on their own journeys."

— **Joseph Heschmeyer**, blogger and Seminarian at Roman Catholic Archdiocese of Kansas City

"A personal journey with a convincing rationale for conversion from agnosticism to saving faith in Jesus Christ and full confidence in the Word of God. Contrasting quotes to start each chapter, word pictures and vivid illustrations throughout made it a joy to read."

— **Clarke Holtsberry**, retired missionary

"An insightful exploration of what it takes to live in today's culture. A must read."

— **Elizabeth Ellis,** poet, artist, and IT professional

"Jason B. Ladd offers a unique look into the life of a soldier, a son, and his Savior. With the same precision that he uses as a jet fighter pilot, he unpacks a rationale for why he lives by faith—and why he passionately invites others to join him. It's the adventure of his lifetime—one that I've been invited into as his pastor and his friend. If you read this book, you will be better because of it."

— **Steve Wyatt,** Lead Pastor, Christ's Church at the Crossroads

"I highly recommend this book to anyone looking for a strong resource for Christian growth; especially young men who have a heart for God and seek support from men who demonstrate strong, moral character. Jason B. Ladd balances story, with worldview comparison, and apologetics. This combination provides powerful insight for understanding how to live in a dark world without conforming to its mold."

— **Scott Steiner,** Minister of Music, First Baptist Church Middleville

"I was first drawn to this book because of my connection to loved ones in the military. What I discovered is that the subject is deeply meaningful to anyone who desires to live a life devoted to the Lord and desires to live uprightly before the world. This book is engaging, fresh, insightful, and exciting. It really lifts my spirits, but more importantly it compels me to lift up Christ in my interactions with my world. I identify with Jason's passion for God and how he sees everything through the eyes of faith. I wish everybody could read this book, especially those in the military!"

— **Kathryn W. Armstrong,** blogger and teacher

"Jason tells an engaging story of how we should see the world with Christian eyes, and his experience in the Marines provides an intriguing backdrop for addressing the struggles of walking in faith. Jason's story goes from mere existence, to Christian discovery and growth. He shares his lessons and thought-provoking questions with his readers using an inheritance of common sense, ethics and integrity, providing a fresh perspective and using language that is easy to understand. I would recommend One of the Few to anyone wanting to look at the world with new eyes. It will touch the heart and mind of the civilian, service member, child, parent, spouse, teacher, student, friend, and the faithful and faithless alike."

— **Anita VanderMolen,** Public Affairs Journalist, Army National Guard

"I consider it a privilege as a pastor, missionary, Vietnam vet and a former infantry officer to commend this book for the way in which Jason skillfully parallels military service with discipleship principles. This will resonate with all who have served and is certainly in keeping with the many Biblical references to the struggle believers must endure to achieve victory in Christ. I was surprised however by the unique way in which the author so engagingly covered important topics for believers, especially males, such as marriage and pornography. Jason reflects on the obstacles to accepting Christianity and ably reveals the heartbeat of the book—how Christ provides the only sufficient worldview. This book presents apologetics in a winsome and inviting manner. Read it together, and allow the Spirit to bring you closer to God and encourage you to help strengthen others in the Faith."

— **Bill Vermillion,** One Mission Society

"Drawing from the depths of his own experience, knowledge of others, and the wisdom of God's word, Jason B. Ladd has written a survival guide for today's Christian. Of the estimated 50 books I have read in the past year, there is none that parallels the learnings I received from One of the Few. Using an extensive scope of credible resources, Jason paints a broad stroke, covering the foundations of living a Christ-filled life at any age. He writes with deep conviction on why the world needs God and how to be part of the remnant that seeks to honor God and serve His kingdom with spiritual boldness and integrity."

— **Jane Anderson,** Insite Skill, Chief Communications Officer

ONE OF THE FEW

ONE OF THE FEW

A MARINE FIGHTER PILOT'S RECONNAISSANCE OF THE CHRISTIAN WORLDVIEW

Jason B. Ladd

BOONE SHEPHERD

One of the Few: A Marine Fighter Pilot's Reconnaissance of the Christian Worldview

Copyright © 2015 Jason B. Ladd
Cover design by TVS Design Craft
All rights reserved.

ISBN: 0996538402
ISBN 13: 9780996538404
Library of Congress Control Number: 2015913380
Boone Shepherd, Wasilla, AK

Published by Boone Shepherd, LLC
        P.O. Box 871943
        Wasilla, AK 99687

The views presented are those of the author and do not necessarily represent the views of the DoD or its Components.

TABLE OF CONTENTS

This book is dedicated to the women in my life:

Mom, for the mother you've been;

Karry, for the wife that you are;

Ainsley, for the woman you're becoming;

And for *Nana:* I'm sorry.

INTRODUCTION

EVERYONE DIES. YOUNG OR OLD, whether by accident, murder, natural disaster, or illness, death comes to every human being, and only rarely does the dealer show his hand. When the flame of life is extinguished, we exit the realm of time and enter into eternity.

For centuries, the great thinkers have labored to understand man's purpose.

Can there be true meaning and significance in our lives now if there is no ultimate, objective meaning and existence after death? If our species is just a cosmic blip of evolved energy and matter, then will it matter what we were when our energy runs out? Human beings are either very special or very deluded. What do you believe about God? Your answer will lead to a worldview that shapes your thinking about humanity, the world, and what exists beyond. This question is a matter of life and death. A life pursuing the answer is well spent.

While this book will connect strongly with parents, it will benefit a wide group of readers. It will help the student struggling to make sense of the world. It will encourage men on a mission to find their faith and women desiring to share their convictions. It will help seekers exploring the concept of faith and Christians struggling with doubt. It will help older Christians understand the new generation of skeptics and the youth to understand the faithfulness of their elders. It will help anyone tired of floating through life without direction, purpose, or hope.

"Part I" offers a look into my childhood as a military dependent, and chronicles my journey as a spiritual seeker. It provides a glimpse of Marine Corps training, flight school, and combat in Iraq and describes how being raised in a military family groomed me to pursue the Marine Corps values of honor, courage, and commitment. I welcomed the opportunity to join the band of brothers dedicated to protecting America in times of crisis.

Although I believed in the existence of right and wrong, I never thought about where morals or values came from. I grew up in a loving family, but I never knew of a God to love. Some Christian parents fear their children may be "already gone." I was never there.

Abraham Lincoln has been credited with saying, "It's better to remain silent and be thought a fool than to open your mouth and prove it." A fool is a person who acts unwisely. Despite succeeding in most endeavors, I realized I was foolish on a higher level—a macro-fool. I lacked the ability to understand the world around me. I had no moral compass, no working framework, and no worldview. I had no way of deciding whether or not it was okay to hurt bullies, hunt deer, or support a woman's decision to abort her baby.

Young love, a Christian family, and the grace of God nudged my disposition on spiritual things from apathy toward inquiry while the Marine Corps taught me about glory, discipline, and suffering. As I learned how to fly for the Marines, my list of questions about life grew, and I started learning about a man glorified through suffering on a cross.

Being a fighter pilot is everything you think it is and more. Compared to training for aerial combat, there is no greater thrill. Measured against supporting ground units in danger, there is no greater responsibility. In serving a grateful nation, there is no higher honor. By day I studied tactics and flew sorties to prepare for combat. By night I studied the Bible and devoured books written about Christianity, atheism, and apologetics.* With the (mistaken) notion that I was beginning with a clean slate, I strived to discern whether the truth lay in materialism, in the supernatural, or somewhere in between.

A deployment to Iraq, away from my wife and children, gave me time to reflect upon these topics. I watched men perish and wondered about my own fate. Scenarios at home and abroad challenged my resolve to live by the Christian values I was exploring. As I studied the art and science of Basic Fighter Maneuvering (BFM), Air-to-Air employment, and Close Air Support, I realized that principles based on fighter pilot fundamentals could help me in my search for truth.

"Part II" explains the importance of having a worldview capable of filtering out false teachings, harmful doctrines, and all the trappings of a sinful world. Armed with an adequate worldview, I explore the concept of sexual sin, the sacredness of marriage, and the danger of pornography. After recognizing my sin and accepting the truth of Christianity, I learned how a worldview affects every facet of life. Figurative scales fell from my eyes, and the brain-fog obscuring the view from my unexamined life lifted like a cloud. I was no longer paralyzed by spiritual apathy, and misguided notions about faith and God were discounted by reasonable arguments from credible sources. I was relieved to learn that you do not have to reject science or education to believe in God, and I soon agreed with Dr. Norman

---

* The branch of theology that is concerned with the defense of Christian doctrines.

Geisler and Dr. Frank Turek: it really does take more faith to be an atheist.

"Part III" uses my background in peace, war, and defense to help you prepare for spiritual warfare as I discuss searching for peace and struggling with doubt before, during, and after my decision to follow Christ. Every believer has doubts, and I explain how to successfully engage the enemy when he attacks.

Jesus is looking for all to enter his kingdom, but he knows that few will answer the call. He has his eye on you, and it is my hope that this book will encourage you to take a closer look into him.

PART I

SEEK AND YOU WILL FIND

PROLOGUE

Somewhere over Death Valley
August 14th, 1990

THE NAVY PILOT LOOKED DOWN toward the fast approaching earth speckled with desert brush. He was drifting towards the side of a ridge covered with rock outcroppings and perilous vegetation. *So that's what it is like to eject.* There was little time to reflect on what went wrong. He recalled the procedures from his egress training and put them into action. *Oxygen mask – off. Gloves – on. Steer into the wind. Eyes on the horizon. Brace for impact.*

Whether or not to eject from an F/A-18 is one decision a "Hornet" pilot hopes never comes but is always prepared to make. The Martin Baker ejection seat has a broad ejection envelope, but getting out too low, too fast, or too late can be fatal. Descending with consciousness, a good chute, and air between your feet and the ground is one of many small victories in the fight to survive an ejection.

A parachute that fails to fill with air, known as a "streamer," will lead to excessive sink rates and bone-shattering landings. Water landings bring danger of entanglement and drowning. High winds can drag survivors at dangerous speeds over rough terrain. Low winds and bad luck could have you floating into your own fireball. God forbid one ever ejected over a remote desert mountain range with steep cliffs covered with jagged trees and deadly reptiles.

The pilot's wingman overhead assumed the duties of on-scene commander, and a loud repeating noise blared over the emergency radio frequency. The emergency locator transmitter automatically activated upon ejection and squawked like a staccato siren into the headsets of nearby aviators.

An instant before the pilot felt twenty g-forces compress his spine, the Weapons and Sensors Officer (WSO), pronounced "whizz-o," rode his own rocket seat out of the Navy grey jet into God's blue yonder. He floated toward the southern slope of a steep ridge somewhere near Hunter Mountain, California. Black smoke rose from a forest fire ignited by the downed aircraft while dark clouds surrounded the valley and signaled an advancing thunderstorm. The sun would be down in a few hours. A bad day could be an even worse night. These "Rough Riders" from VFA-125 needed help, and they needed it fast.

A small beeper went off inside a base housing unit on Ticonderoga Ave. *The squadron. Here we go.* This was not the first time Arnold was on call. He was involved with several other rescue missions involving downed aircraft since moving to the small base in the Mojave Desert. The streets of Naval Air Weapons Station China Lake were named after famous admirals, ships, and battles. Neighborhood kids rode bikes up Leyte Road, over across Kearsarge Avenue, and back down Midway toward the local elementary school where they traded Transformer stickers and memorized the lyrics to "Ice, Ice, Baby." Arnold had just arrived home and was still wearing his green flight suit when he got the page. He called the Operations Duty Officer (ODO) back at the squadron. It was 1730 military time (5:30 p.m.).

"It's Arnold. What have you got?"

"There's an aircraft down over Panamint. We need you here right away. I'll brief the rest once you get here."

"I'll be there in five minutes." He kissed his wife and gave his boys a hug. "Gotta go, babe. They called me in."

"When will you be home?" she asked, already knowing the answer.

"Not sure. I'll be home as soon as I can."

"Be careful," she reminded him.

Arnold was a Marine's Marine. He majored in physical education and had the physique to prove it. His call sign was pronounced "Ah-nuld" and came from excessive time spent at the gym aboard the USS *Inchon* while deployed with his AH-1 squadron to the Mediterranean Sea. The allusion to the famous Austrian bodybuilder was fortunate in light of the mostly less than desirable call signs traditionally dished out in the Naval Aviation community. "Bullet Bob" got his call sign from accidentally discharging his pistol during a squadron formation. "Morty the Mortician," in spite of resistance, never escaped the moniker he earned for being negative.

Arnold was the number one Marine and honor graduate of his Officer Candidate School (OCS) class and garnered respect from all he led and served. He loved the Marines and he loved to fly. He loved his country and was ready to go whenever the nation called. Twelve days earlier, Saddam Hussein's forces invaded Kuwait sparking international condemnation and economic sanctions, and he wondered if his future would include combat in the Persian Gulf. Trained as an attack helicopter pilot, he was an expert at providing assault support for Marines on the ground. Marine Cobra pilots are more like airborne grunts than your stereotypical "flyboy." They are close to the ground, close to the ground-pounders, and close to the enemy. When they shoot, or get shot at, it's up close and personal.

China Lake was a change of pace from the high operational tempo of a Fleet Marine Force attack helicopter squadron. During his three years there, he participated in weapons development and testing and flew the HH-1K and TH-1L helicopters (Vietnam era "Hueys") in search and rescue (SAR) operations. He already had several SAR missions under his belt as a co-pilot, and responding to the beeper was a normal part of his routine.

At the squadron, the ODO shared what little information they had. The downed aircraft's wingman was still on the scene and provided them with a rough estimate of the crash site location. Two good chutes were observed which meant there was a good chance of recovering two survivors. He expected to find the aircrew somewhere in the Panamint Valley—a wide swath of flat desert wash and dunes. Arnold could land the SAR bird anywhere in that kind of terrain. So far, it sounded like a piece of cake.

After a quick flight brief, they loaded up with a mission crew of pilot, crew chief, and corpsman along with approximately 200 pounds of rescue equipment. The co-pilot seat was occupied by the base Safety Officer instead of another helicopter pilot. That meant Arnold would be on double duty as the pilot and Mission Commander—he was in charge. They launched at 1800 hours and flew across the desert terrain at three thousand feet wondering what challenges they would face. Everything changed when they rounded a mountain ridge and turned north to reveal the Panamint Valley. They saw smoke but not from the nearby desert floor. The tiny cloud rose in a thin column far in the distant north of the valley in high mountainous terrain.

All wrong, he thought to himself. *Too high. Too heavy. Steep terrain. Not enough power.* The image of cake crumbled. It was 1840 with the sun getting low on the horizon, and the mishap site was at seven thousand feet on a forested mountain. The mishap pilots were on the southern slope of a steep ridge with one 75 meters below the crest and the other 80 meters further below. The downed aircraft started a forest fire burning three to four hundred meters south of the pilots. A northerly wind blew the flames away from the crash site, but the blaze continued to creep in their direction. The fire was not an immediate concern, but the potential shift in the winds and the setting sun made a rapid rescue imperative.

Arnold learned during the briefing that one of the survivors had smashed his leg on a tree during his parachute landing. In scanning the area, he determined there were no suitable sites nearby to land. They would have to use one-skid and hoist operations for the pickups. Arnold made calculations and conducted power checks to determine the performance he could expect from his aircraft at the current elevation and weight. It was as he suspected—they were too heavy.

He found an adequate landing zone with a steady wind to use as a staging area one thousand meters away on top of a ridge. He dropped off the co-pilot and rescue gear which lightened the load by 400 pounds. That put them at the maximum weight for the "hover out of ground effect" operations needed for the rescue. Hovering close to the ground, in ground effect, yields better performance for the aircraft. After climbing out of ground effect with the additional weight of the rescued pilot, lift capacity would decrease. If available power was already approaching limits in the hover, Arnold would have little power left to maneuver. There could be no mistakes.

The worst thing a SAR pilot can do is crash over the rescue site. He remembered the cardinal sin of SAR pilots. Crashing would be even worse than not trying in the first place. One crash site becomes two, and the rescuer needs rescuing. The worst-case scenario would not be a fast plummet, but rather a slow settling into the trees, an eventual impact with the ground, and a breakup of the helicopter.

This is why I get flight pay. I need 40% torque, and I have 41% available. It's gonna be close. He maneuvered to the injured pilot's location and worked the collective while he kept the aircraft balanced with the stick and rudder pedals. He targeted a rock outcropping 70 meters from the injured pilot and maneuvered toward the ledge until a skid made contact. Half landed and half flying, one skid hovered in the air while the rotor blades struggled to create lift. The corpsman jumped out and began treating the mishap pilot's injuries while Arnold flew back to the uninjured pilot's position and prepared the hoist.

Having the co-pilot seat empty added several unusual risks. First, it adversely affected the ability to provide rotor clearance and general lookout doctrine during hillside hovering. Second, there was no one to actively monitor the engine instruments while the pilot prevented blade strikes and maintained a stable position over the ground. Third, having an empty seat on that side affected the center of gravity shift during hoist operations. Finally, they could not use a belay rope during the hoist—there was no one to tend it.

As he hovered above the site, he repeatedly pushed the left rudder forward within an inch of the mechanical stop to keep the nose from yawing to the right. Powerful rotor wash bent the tops of the trees downward as they swayed in the melee, and gusts of wind required full throw of the left rudder just to maintain control of the aircraft. There was no extra power, no extra nose authority, and things were about to change with the additional weight of the mishap pilot on the hoist. As soon as the winch lifted the mishap pilot, the combination of increased weight and adverse right shift of the lateral center of gravity caused the nose of the aircraft to yaw to the right in spite of full left pedal. He glanced at the torque—41%—and pulled the collective harder against the stop. They began to sink.

"Get him up!" Arnold commanded. He looked through the window under his feet; the branches were getting bigger.

He fought to keep the aircraft steady while the winch reeled the pilot in. "Where is he? We gotta go!"

"Almost clear of the trees!" the crew chief yelled back.

A gust of wind pushed the nose to the right and Arnold slammed his left foot forward. The helicopter continued to settle and yaw to the right. Arnold was out of control…

CHAPTER 1
THE WORST DAY

Phoenix, Arizona
March 2015

"...it is faith that keeps the whole terrible edifice of religious certainty still looming dangerously over our world."[1]

—SAM HARRIS

"Keep your protection of your wife strong and know in your hearts our Lord will carry you through whatever happens."[2]

—RAVI ZACHARIAS

"THIS IS A HORRIBLE, DREADFUL day. No good news at all."

The words came after a quiet entrance with little eye contact. The dimly-lit ultrasound room had already grown old since we entered it over an hour prior. The time between the technician's departure and the doctor's arrival was enough to worry ourselves to death.

The doctor extended his hand to my father-in-law and asked his last name. He assumed I was the husband. The doctor was dressed in a purple shirt with a plaid design mixed with grey, split by a paisley tie of purple swirls and flowers. His hair was grey and slightly waved, moving from front to back, slightly rising to form an almost-pyramidal cap to an overall solid structure. On his left hand, a gold ring, a black ring with silver trim on his right. I stared at his face, but my thoughts were already somewhere else.

My wife Karry remained sitting on the examining table. I stood beside her, holding her hand. This is where we would all cry.

For ten years I had been developing my faith in Christ. And in ten years it had never been tested. Karry and I had five beautiful children and a strong marriage. Life was so good, we wondered why we had been so fortunate.

"Aren't you afraid that one day the bottom is going to drop?" Karry would ask.

"No," I would say. "That's not going to happen."

But the bottom was slowly dropping.

Our doctor began listing all the indicators seen on the pictures from the ultrasound: too much amniotic fluid, bone measurements indicating stunted growth, a heart defect, and perhaps the most recognizable indicator for a possible chromosomal anomaly, clinched hands.

Clinched hands.

The first indications were good. The shape and form of our 27-week baby was clearly seen. His spine looked straight, his legs and arms looked normal. He even granted us a clear picture of his nose and mouth, indicating no cleft lip or palate. His brain looked normal and free of excess fluid. She pointed to all his parts, calling them by name. His kidneys appeared normal.

Then they were looking bad.

A cyst on the umbilical cord was easy to see. Shaped like a circle and appearing black on the screen, it would become the least of our worries. The umbilical cord is supposed to have three vessels. Our baby's cord appeared to be missing one. Too much amniotic fluid dampened the feel of every kick and indicated a possible problem with the baby's ability to swallow. The technician spent a long time on his heart. I guessed that she was searching for any way to tell us it was normal. But in the end, she couldn't.

Karry often confessed an ominous feeling about the pregnancy. Now it was all coming true.

"I suspect your baby has a chromosomal condition known as Trisomy 18," the doctor informed us.

Also called Edwards syndrome and referred to as a "lethal fetal condition" in the medical community, it has a grim prognosis.

What do we do? What should *we do?*

Before our baby was born, we began preparing for him to die.

Oh my God. This is it.

---

[1] Sam Harris, Th*e End of Faith: Religion, Terror, and the Future of Reason* (New York: W. W. Norton & Company, Inc., 2005), Kindle ed., loc. 3656.

[2] Ravi Zacharias, e-mail message to author, March 18, 2015.

CHAPTER 2
RISING SON

Naval Air Weapons Station China Lake, California
July 1991

*"I've begun worshipping the sun for a number of reasons.
First of all, unlike some other gods I could mention, I can
see the sun."[1]*

—GEORGE CARLIN

*"I believe in Christianity as I believe that the sun has risen,
not only because I see by it, but because by it I see
everything else."[2]*

—C.S. LEWIS

PLENTY HAVE WARNED MY LIFE is not remarkable enough for a book. I've decided not to believe them. I have lived an extraordinary life. Some would call it luck, others, karma, but I call it the grace of God.

I didn't always believe that. For years, I lived on autopilot doing what I thought you were supposed to do. It wasn't until I became a father that I realized my secular worldview was inadequate. And it wasn't until I established a Christian worldview that my life was truly transformed. Your life can be transformed, too.

We'll get to that. For you to appreciate where I am now, you must first see where I've been.

MY FAMILY

I had a happy childhood and was raised by two loving parents. But as too many children know, sometimes the love runs out. A word of warning to the future architects of perfect lives: the wrecking ball of divorce has no less momentum when the children it smashes are grown.

THE WRECKING BALL OF DIVORCE HAS NO LESS MOMENTUM WHEN THE CHILDREN IT SMASHES ARE GROWN.

My childhood was safe from the trauma of every-other-weekend visitations. But the aftershocks of divorce visit every day—a reminder of the challenges ahead, where I see attempts to comfort my children with the promise of a stable future met with a depressing skepticism.

Man and wife are equal partners in the venture to create a family, and they share equally in its dissolution. Angry for a time, I have made my peace, and I see no more folly in my mom than in my dad. I see only a man and wife, both confused about where life was taking them, and each unable to help the other—both with problems they couldn't help each other fix. But let's leave the world as it is and go back, for a moment, to where it was.

My father joined the Marines in 1976, and his career took us to places like Pensacola, Florida; Camp Pendleton, California; Jacksonville, North Carolina; and a small base in Japan shared by the United States Marines and the Japanese Maritime Self-Defense Force. He loved the outdoors, physical activity, and spending time with us. He never suggested we break the rules or approved our requests to bend them.

My mother fostered imagination and creativity. As an artist specializing in calligraphy and watercolors, she gave us plenty of help with school projects, and our homemade Halloween costumes were first-class. She was always present and involved, finding ways to keep us entertained and out of trouble.

The military provides a wealth of benefits and services for spouses and dependents. However, service members also know the mission comes first. My mother learned sacrifice is not a word reserved for the rifleman on point or the pilot in harm's way. I am sure many Soldiers, Sailors, Airmen, and Marines agree that the spouse makes the greater sacrifice.

My brother, Kevin, is my only sibling and elder by two years. We were close growing up and spent hours playing Nintendo, watching television, and re-watching our favorite movies. We loved *Star Wars, Indiana Jones,* and anything with Arnold Schwarzenegger. Something about the unchanging nature of movies forever preserved on VHS cassette provided consistency in a life of changing scenery. Quoting movies remains one of our favorite pastimes.

One summer, Dad prepared us to move from Camp Pendleton to Okinawa, although there was a small chance of moving to a small town in the Mojave Desert. Dad was so certain we were going to Okinawa that he promised dirt bikes if we ended up in China Lake instead. Not long after the promise, his orders were changed. That is how it goes in the military. You never really know when or where you are going until the last minute. Even then, it is subject to change. Goodbye, Japan. Hello, dirt bikes!

THE DESERT

I was 10 years old when we moved to China Lake—new house, new school, and new wheels! Ten is a big deal when you're a military brat. You finally qualify for a government issued Identification Card. This is the key to the city— unaccompanied gymnasium entrance, commissary credentials, something cool to put in your wallet, and most important: access to movie rental privileges. We ran paper routes, raked leaves, mowed lawns—anything to make a buck. Then we would watch movies and gorge on Skittles until we felt sick.

If we were not launching model rockets in the desert or swimming at the local pool, then we were out on the dry lakebed. Located a short distance from our on-base housing, it was the perfect place to open up the throttles on our 4-stroke, single cylinder, off-road dream machines. After dismounting our dirt bikes to walk them across a single paved road (after all, they were not street legal), we blazed through the sandy trail that led to the dry lake bed, feeling invincible in our blue jeans and dirt biking garb. I glanced at the speedometer: 55 mph.

This is awesome, I thought as we headed toward the perimeter entrance to the track. I had come a long way from my first lesson with Dad behind our house. The foot gears, clutch handle, and kickstart took some getting used to. He taught us how to keep our balance, work the handle and foot brakes, and kill the engine using the kill switch. We headed toward the jumps.

The track was a short, loopy course carved out in the desert adjacent to the lake bed with small jumps and tight turns. Once, I lost control on a landing, bounced high off the seat, and unintentionally ripped open the throttle. This caused the bike to rear up like a mustang bucking its breaker and slip from my grip. I survived the short fall into the sand as my two-wheeler's short-lived attempt to fly came to an end. The bike bounced on its back wheel, kicked up a rooster tail of sand, and flopped onto the desert brush. From then on, I rode with the understanding that recklessness has consequences.

One early weekend morning, we raced across the baked dirt and headed for the entrance to the track. It was easy to spot. A large mound of dirt about four feet high marked its position—the first jump of the day. Kevin led the way and hit the jump first. The bike flew through the air and leaned to the left before landing on top of him and bouncing off to the side. I hit the jump after him, blind to his wreck on the other side. Fortunately, I landed clear of his crash site, and I stopped to survey the damage. He

IT WAS UP TO ME.
I HAD TO GET HELP.

sat in the sand, propped up by his hands with his legs extended. Everything looked okay to me, but Kevin knew something was wrong.

"It's broken! Don't touch it!" he yelled. He was not crying, but his winces and inability to move indicated it was serious. He started to shiver from a combination of shock and the cold morning air. "Go get Dad!" he commanded.

It was up to me. I had to get help. I sprinted to my bike, lifted it up, and kicked the starter. Nothing! I tried again and again, but it refused to turn over. I felt tears coming, the kind that remind you of the moment's significance. *C'mon, start!* Panicked, I threw the bike down and started for Kevin's. Then I remembered: the kill switch! I spun around and checked the yellow rotary switch that cut off the flow of gas to the engine. Sure enough, I had used the kill switch on shutdown—one of our standard operating procedures. This would not be the last time distraction would lead to a breakdown in proper procedures. I would re-learn this lesson 15 years later over the skies of Iraq.

I flicked it back to the starting position, jumped up, and descended upon the kick starter with 70 pounds of desperation. The engine gave out a glorious whine. I raced home at mach-one and returned with Dad in our '91 Chevy Blazer.

Before leaving, he rummaged through the garage and grabbed a few rags and some plastic oars from an inflatable raft. We reached Kevin and Dad assessed the situation.

"We'll have to splint his leg," he said.

I spun away in horror, "I can't look." I had seen movies where bones were set, and it looked painful. I envisioned Dad taking the plastic oar, raising it above his head like a lumberjack and slamming it down leaving Kevin's leg in not one piece, but two. I tried not to faint.

"No, we're not going to split it. We're going to make a splint. Get over here and help me."

With some convincing, my fears were assuaged and we lined up the two oars and used the rags to secure them to his leg. We lifted him up into the back of the Blazer with the seats down and made for the hospital. X-rays confirmed his leg was broken. His recovery required metal pins through his bones; traction for six weeks; a body cast that traversed the length of the broken leg, crossed his midsection, and continued halfway down the other; a lift for his shoe to counteract the new height differential; and, later in life, leg shortening surgery on the good leg. Soon after, we bid farewell to our dirt bikes.

I learned to respect the unforgiving nature of physics in the California desert. Understanding the forgiving nature of the Spirit would come much later.

I became accustomed to moving every few years; it was an exciting opportunity to travel the world. The novelty of a new home lasted a few months until routines eventually bred familiarity.

But there are some drawbacks to the nomadic way. Parents experience most of them, but children have their own to endure. I once heard someone say it takes six months to really get to know someone; I think it is more like a year. Once you are finally settled (your relationships mature, you are in full stride with your job, your house has been made a home, and your life has gained a modicum of stability), it is time to pack up, move again, and start all over. But as you will see, starting over in Japan turned out to be a very good thing.

JAPAN

I arrived in the "land of the rising sun" a high school student 13 years before returning a Marine. The monsoon had begun, and rain pounded the roof of the white Toyota as Dad drove us around the air station. I looked around to get my bearings; it wouldn't take long on a base just six miles in circumference. As a fifteen-year-old entering his junior year of high school, it was sad to leave our previous duty station in North Carolina and the relationships I spent three years fostering.

Iwakuni lies on the coast of southern Honshu. It is about an hour drive south of Hiroshima or 45 minutes by train. It rained non-stop since our arrival two weeks prior, and we grew suspicious of this supposed rising sun.

I was thankful we were moving into a three-bedroom detached housing unit as opposed to one of the monstrous "towers" on the base. The six-story mid-rises contained two and three-bedroom units and housed the bulk of base residents.

I daydreamed as Dad entered through the industrial-steel door and went down the checklist to survey existing damages before he signed for acceptance. *What will this duty station hold? What are the girls like here? What will the school be like? Will I make any good friends? Will I have a girlfriend? Do they have football? What's the food like? Will there be any cute girls in my classes?* You get the idea. Dad snapped me out of my daydreaming.

"I heard a Navy Commander is moving here in a few days," he said.

No big news there. *What's a Navy Commander? Is that like G.I. Joe?* I was aloof regarding most military matters. My dad has always been miserly with conversation, so when he speaks, you listen. I failed to see where this was going.

"And he has two sixteen-year-old twin daughters..."

My heart skipped a beat. *Stop the press! Why didn't you say so! This is the kind of information a kid needs immediately! Did you forget? Were you held against your will from the time you were informed until now? How you are just now telling me this!*

"Oh yeah?" I casually replied, "That's cool." When you're fifteen, it is all about being cool. Our adventure overseas gained huge potential. I devised a test to serve as a harbinger for things to come: if the girls were attractive, then it would be a great two years. It was settled. I had only to wait for their arrival. In the meantime, I hit up the racquetball courts with Kevin.

THE SUN ARRIVES

A few weeks later, the rain finally let up and we saw the sun. New neighbors were moving in behind our house. The Japanese workers scurried to and from the moving truck, unloading box after box into the neighboring house while taking their shoes off, putting them back on, and taking them off again. From our living room, I opened the standard government-issue vertical blinds and peered through the sliding glass door. My dad entered the room.

"Guess who's moving in next door."

I looked back at the neighbor's house as the patio door slid open. A light-brown cocker spaniel ran out and began sniffing around the yard. Then I saw a girl. She stepped onto the patio and waited patiently for the dog to return. She wore a red collared shirt with short sleeves, jean shorts of moderate length with the hem upturned, and tennis shoes. Golden-blond hair fell past her shoulders and danced off delicate skin. I may have forgotten to breathe. She was the most beautiful girl I had ever seen. Hanging from a decorative torii in their front yard was a placard:

CDR Mark E. Babbitt, United States Navy
Officer-in-Charge, Branch Medical Clinic

The Navy Commander! The twins had arrived and things were looking up. My dad said she brought the sun. All I knew was I had to meet that girl. What I didn't know was that she would change my life forever. Her example would lead me to study about a new land and another rising Son.

---

[1] George Carlin, *Brain Droppings* (New York: Hyperion, 1997), 20.

[2] C. S. Lewis, "Is Theology Poetry?" in The Weight of Glory and Other Addresses (1949; repr., New York: HarperCollins, 2001), 140, quoted in Ravi Zacharias, *Has Christianity Failed You?* (Grand Rapids: Zondervan, 2010), Kindle ed., loc. 232.

CHAPTER 3
HE'S GOT THAT LOVING FEELING

Marine Corps Air Station Iwakuni, Japan
July 1995

"The secret of attraction is to love yourself."[1]

—DEEPAK CHOPRA

"My command is this: Love each other as I have loved you."

—JESUS

KARRY WAS THE YOUNGER SISTER by three minutes, and her twin, though fraternal, shared many of her striking features. Their personalities were distinct, and I was immediately attracted to Karry's meek and quiet spirit.

One of our first dates was spent inner-tubing down the Nishiki River just outside the base. We drove with a group through the mountains and launched upstream of the historic Kintai Bridge. Karry walked down to the bank trailing pockets of perfume, unaware of its intoxicating effect. The river meandered through the valley and the August sun shone on her skin.

Rounding a bend, the famous wooden bridge came into view. The unique five-arch design and location beneath

Iwakuni Castle draws tourists and photographers looking to capture the beautiful marriage of man and nature. Sakura trees line the river bank, bound by the code of Nature to guard each cherry blossom until their unveiling in the spring.

We floated beneath the arches and continued downstream past a bend where a hidden rope swing waits for adventurous swimmers. My gaze kept coming back to her face, the way her bangs slalomed around her temple, down past her cheekbones and raced toward her clavicle. I felt like Kevin Arnold from The Wonder Years with the beginning of "Good Vibrations" setting the scene.

Another summer night, we biked along the air station perimeter seawall looking for a place to be alone. The seawall ran about two-and-a-half miles along the seaside portion of the airfield. The top was wide enough to accommodate walkers, bikers, and joggers. Toward the end, just beyond the flashing runway lights, the steady row of streetlamps ended. It's hard to find privacy on a base that small, but the seawall was relatively remote—it would have to do.

I MOVED CLOSER AND GAVE HER A SINGLE KISS.

We sat a few feet apart as mountains rose up from the Sea of Japan to witness our meeting. My heart pounded and I wondered what the summer would hold. *Will she become my girlfriend?* My last girlfriend lasted two recesses in eighth grade, and then I checked the box marked "yes" on the note asking if I wanted to break up. That night on the seawall, anything was possible. I moved closer and gave her a single kiss. We breathed sighs of relief and scooted closer together.

In the distance, we heard a faint and rhythmic sound. It was approaching and getting louder. I gradually made out a silhouette bouncing up and down with each stride—a lone jogger. A slight distraction, but no matter; he would pass by momentarily and we could resume our magical moment despite minor embarrassment from the intruder. As he approached, I recognized a familiar sound—something about the way he was breathing. And those shorts—were those silkies?* The Marine turned his head as he ran by, and his face registered shock as realization hit.

"Dad?" I stammered.

He tactfully kept on running.

She and I shared a laugh and headed back home. It was a small base indeed. My father's presence in the darkest corner of that air station foreshadowed my Father's presence in the darkest reaches of my soul. For the next two years, Karry and I were inseparable. On occasion, I accompanied her to the base chapel for the morning Protestant service. I had neutral feelings about going, and I enjoyed the music (though I never sang). I did my best to listen to the pastor's message, but wafts of Karry's perfume kept me distracted.

If church was something I didn't understand, then prayer was inscrutable. *Oh, boy. Here we go. Everyone's supposed to bow their head, right? Am I supposed to bow too, even though I don't really believe what's going on here? Who is the pastor talking to? God, or us? Is God really there? Is he listening? Does he have any obligation to answer our prayers? What if he doesn't? Does that say something about us, or God?* I wondered about these questions until the prayer was over, and then they vanished until the next uncomfortable round of "let us pray."

My relationship with Karry's parents was a source of friction. She was raised in a Christian home, and her parents rightfully guarded their youngest daughter's virtue at the hands of a sixteen-year-old boy.

My parents were good by my standard but her parents were good by some other standard. My relationship was stifled with Karry and strained with her parents. Something had to be done. We decided to have a meeting.

---

* Extremely short olive-drab-green silk running shorts.

To say the meeting was awkward would be an understatement. My parents talked about our need for space, and the Captain (her father) spoke of balance. In the end, little was accomplished short of creating an experience forever known as "The Meeting." Today I see the meeting as an orchestrated accident with two families speeding toward the intersection of secularism and faith. I never imagined the enormity of wreckage created when worldviews collide.

A FATHER'S NUDGE

My two years in Japan flew by, and I had to decide where to attend college. My brother was accepted into the University of North Carolina at Chapel Hill while my dad was stationed at MCAS New River as the Executive Officer of HMLA-167. I visited the campus several times and liked the idea of being close to my brother. I applied as an out-of-state student with a solid GPA, a decent SAT score, and a boatload of extracurricular activities and was rejected. Without a backup plan I was out of ideas. My dad, on the other hand, was not.

"Have you ever thought about an ROTC scholarship?" he asked. I had never considered military service. I decided to apply for a scholarship from the Naval Reserve Officers Training Corps (NROTC) under the Marine Corps option and join the military. A father's words are powerful. So powerful that since my dad was a pilot I decided I would be an aviator, too. I contacted the Marine Officer Instructor (MOI) at the Chapel Hill NROTC unit and explained my desire to attend the school and my previous admissions rejection.

He encouraged me to retake the SAT and submit the scholarship application. A few months later, I received a call from the MOI. I was awarded the scholarship, and my admissions letter was in the mail. I was going to Chapel Hill.

A BULLET TO THE HEART

Karry was making plans to become a nurse. After a two-year relationship and high school graduation, we were facing a four-year long-distance relationship with 1,300 miles of separation.

The death-hour arrived on the platform of the *shinkansen* (bullet train) station in Iwakuni just around the bend from the Kintai Bridge. We fought back tears and said our goodbyes.

The train eased forward, the intercom chimed, and a female voice crooned its recorded announcement in Japanese. Life was moving on, but as far as I was concerned, it was over until I saw Karry again.

---

[1] Deepak Chopra, *The Secret of Love: Meditations for Attracting and Being In Love* (Play It By Ear Music, 2011), MP3, 0:20, http://www.amazon.com/Secret-Love-Meditations-Attracting-Being/dp/1937398005

CHAPTER 4

WHAT'S THE QUESTION?

University of North Carolina at Chapel Hill
November 1997

"I've decided to believe everything I hear. Why not? It's all unbelievable anyway."[1]

—SHIRLEY MACLAINE

"The lips of the righteous nourish many, but fools die for lack of judgment" (Prov. 10:21).

—SOLOMON

"MY AUNT SAID THAT YOU ARE GOING TO HELL," KARRY SAID.
I spoke with her on my new cell phone and paced the hallway of Mangum Dormitory. We kept the calls short after learning how much overtime-minutes cost, but this conversation was longer than usual.

"What?" I asked, taken aback.

"She said we were 'unequally yoked,' and since you don't believe in Jesus, you'll be going to hell."

That was exactly why I did not like religion. I was told something similar by someone at the chapel in Iwakuni. Karry's aunt was a Christian and outspoken about her faith. Though not technically her aunt, she was as close as any blood relative. We loved her like family, and she was fun to be around. I was irritated she would sling such an accusation. *Who is she to say something like that? Doesn't she know I'm a good person? How can she judge me? Why would God send a good person to hell? And what in the world is "unequally yoked?"* We brushed off the warning and moved on with our lives, but there was a tinge of discomfort during future visits. At the time, I was blind to her aunt's loving concern. Now I am thankful she had the courage to speak the truth.

UNC AND NROTC

While attending the University of North Carolina at Chapel Hill, I studied peace, war, and defense (PWAD) which included a variety of classes in history and political science.

I was also on the Battalion drill team, which sharpened our marching skills, honed our M-1 Garand rifle handling skills, and most important, brought us to the annual drill competition held at Tulane University in New Orleans. After the competition, the team marched in a parade and enjoyed two nights in the French Quarter during Mardi Gras. For four years straight, I was excited to witness this annual mass indulgence of sin on Bourbon Street. I would not have called it sin at the time. It was the country's biggest party. "Love and do what you will." "If it feels good, do it." "You only live once."

Is there any wisdom in these platitudes? Why are some people at ease with binge drinking, promiscuity, and illegal activity, while others are morally repulsed? How do we know who is right? My conscience steers me in one direction, but does the conscience really exist, or is it an illusory manifestation of an evolutionary process enduring only for its survival value? Is it even possible to know? Introspection like this usually ended with a shrug. Who am I to judge whether the actions of others are right or wrong? I did not want to become like Karry's aunt. If it's not affecting me, why should I be concerned? Different people have different values.

ONE TOO MANY

One evening in the dorms at UNC, people with different values showed me a new level of hospitality. It was the weekend; my roommate and I were milling about in our room with the door open. One of our suite-mates exited his room and crossed the

AND THEN IT HAPPENED: HE ASKED IF I WANTED TO JOIN IN.

hallway dabbing his forehead with a towel. Music from the other room played over the sounds of other individuals making recognizable sounds of passion.

Yikes! What's going on in there?

I was shocked at the orgiastic activity right across from my room. The suite-mate returned to his room and shut the door. A while later, the door opened again with a different suite-mate exiting for a breather. And then it happened: he asked if I wanted to join in.

I have been offered a lot of things—"Can I take your coat?" "Let me pick up that check," "Would you like some of my beef jerky?"—but at that moment, southern hospitality took on a whole new meaning. I backpedaled slowly and stuttered like Porky Pig hoping to hide my discomfiture.

I made it back to my room and shut the door. My roommate's jaw dropped when I told him what happened. An unthinkable act for the two of us seemed as normal as a night at the movies for the three of them. But if someone had asked me for the reason such an act was wrong, I would have been hard pressed to give an answer.

THE SIN OF SELFISHNESS

I did my fair share of shirking moral duties and was a terrible roommate at times. I once flaunted my lack of altruism when I prepared for my dreaded 8:00 a.m. class. I hopped off the top bunk of my home-made wooden bed and noticed my roommate lying disheveled on the floor just past our open door. I vaguely remembered his entrance in the middle of the night when I was momentarily roused by his moaning. He was in a bad state on the floor. Unable to right himself, he groaned for help while I shook my hypocritical head in disapproval and went back to sleep. When I left the next morning, he remained where he lay in vomit-soaked attire. Thinking only of myself, I made one long stride to avoid trampling him and moved through the odoriferous cloud surrounding his prostrate body. I was off to start my day.

How embarrassing it is to look back on this kind of response to a person in need. What kind of person lets a friend sleep on the floor in his own vomit? Who leaves a hurting person by themselves without the slightest sense of a moral duty to help them? My roommate wondered the same thing later that afternoon.

"Dude, why didn't you help me last night?" he asked. I didn't have an answer, and his question seeped into my conscience. He continued, "You could've helped get me to the shower and get cleaned up. You just stepped over me this morning as you went to class? Dude, that's messed up."

He was right. It was messed up. My roommate was clearly in need. But I was selfish, like I am today. I just didn't see it as clearly then. I didn't care for my roommate, or anyone else for that matter, as I should have. I wasn't burdened or impassioned, and I could not connect with people or groups that were.

IT BEGAN WITH ROLOS

One of my earliest memories is of breaking God's commandments. I was four years old and accompanied my parents to a grocery store. At the checkout counter, I gazed upon a wall of candy. Colorful packaging lured me closer, and I honed in on my target. Rolos—chocolate covered caramels wrapped in shiny foil. I wanted the Rolos, so I put them in my overalls pocket. We left the store and went home. After arriving at the house, I went to the bathroom and locked the door. I do not remember having malicious intent when I stashed the Rolos in my Oshkosh B'goshs, but the fact that I hid to eat them reveals my conscience at work. I unwrapped the chocolates and ate them, one by one. Someone knocked on the bathroom door.

"Jason, are you in there?" they asked.

"Yeah," I replied after a slight delay.

"What are you doing in there?"

"Nothing," I mumbled.

"Open the door and come on out," they commanded.

I opened the door to reveal chocolaty teeth and golden pieces of foil littered about the floor. The look on my mom's face confirmed my suspicion: I did something wrong. I took something without paying for it. Four years old and already a thief.

From then until now, I have made mistakes. I've done things I shouldn't have, and I have regrets—small ones and big ones. I was neither the best nor the worst—just a dumb kid doing what the world probably expects. I am thankful to know Christ, and I am a better person for it.

A Spectacle of Faith

When we lived as boys in the desert, we were amused by a preacher on television. He walked the stage and preached about God to a congregation of thousands. It was not the preaching we were eager to hear—it was the spectacle. "Be HEALED!" he would say and cast his open hand towards the congregant, and, "Take it in the Lord's name!" as his forceful touch sent prayerful bodies to the ground, seemingly overcome by an invisible power. We thought it was hilarious.

Is this some sort of show? What are these grown-ups doing, pretending to pass out at the touch of his fingers? What is the sickness for which they needed healing? Didn't Steve Martin make a movie about guys like this?

I didn't know anything about Pentecostalism, charismata, or being slain in the Spirit. All I knew was if these people really had a sickness, then they should probably go to a doctor instead of a preacher. People would say "Jesus is the answer," but I was

> THE SIGNIFICANCE OF JESUS' DEATH ON THE CROSS IS ONLY FULLY GRASPED AFTER UNDERSTANDING WHY HE HAD TO DIE.

with the skeptics who replied with a snicker, "What's the question?" Nothing better sums up the discord between those who recognize the brokenness of the world and those who do not.

Why would a good person like me need Jesus? I'm polite, well-mannered, slow to anger, and much better behaved than most. Life's going pretty well. I'm happy, loved by my family, and have enjoyed a respectable amount of success. I'm glad you found something you feel you need. I simply don't see why I need it.

That's how you think when you are given a cure without knowing you have a disease. This blunder when sharing the Gospel has led thousands into false conversions that, like a flare decoying a heat-seeking missile, burns brightly for a moment and then fizzles out. The significance of Jesus' death on the cross is only fully grasped after understanding why he had to die.

AILING AGNOSTICISM

I was old enough to vote, and I still didn't know "the question." I also did not realize that I actually did have a worldview after all. Ronald Nash defines a worldview in his book *Worldviews in Conflict: Choosing Christianity in the World of Ideas*: "A worldview, then, is a conceptual scheme by which we consciously or unconsciously place or fit everything we believe and by which we interpret and judge reality."[2]

My operating assumption was that unlike the other 95% of the world's population who believe in a higher power, I was an unbiased spectator when it came to a framework with which to understand the world. Back then, a Gallup poll stated that 96% of Americans said "yes" when asked if they believed in God or a universal spirit while 3% said "no." There was 1% who had no opinion.[3] Back when I biked the brick-paved paths of Carolina's upper campus, I would have represented the 1%. If bound, gagged, and forced to submit an opinion, I would have begrudgingly written with rope-tied hands that I was an agnostic.

There are two kinds of agnostics. The *ordinary* agnostic says they do not know anything for sure. The *ornery* agnostic says they cannot know anything for sure. Are these claims a good way to remain open-minded? Dr. Norman Geisler and Dr. Frank Turek answer this question in their book *I Don't Have Enough Faith to be an Atheist*:

> There's a big difference between being open-minded and being empty-minded. In light of the evidence, we think agnosticism is a decision to be empty-minded. After all, isn't the reason we should be open-minded so that we can recognize truth when we see it? Yes. So what are we to do when there's enough evidence to point us to the truth? For example, what should we do when we see evidence beyond a reasonable doubt that George Washington was the first president of the United States? Should we remain "open-minded" as to who the first president was? No, that would be empty-minded. Some questions are closed.[4]

The agnostic presumptuously claims we absolutely cannot know of God's existence; however, the only way to know this for certain would be to have absolute knowledge of everything. This kind of agnosticism is not only self-defeating, but it also turns man into God. Only an omniscient mind could know everything there is to know.[5] Since nobody has absolute knowledge of everything, honest adherents must bail out* of this position before they go down in flames of irrelevancy. Ordinary agnostics at least have a chance at pulling out of their death spiral.

THE ILLUSION OF NEUTRALITY

This brings up an important question for parents. Are you doing a service to your child by letting them answer spiritual questions on their own? If you answer a child's question with "I don't know" and leave it at that, then you are actually saying "I don't care." We must do better. The influences of pluralism, post-modernism, and subjectivism have convinced some parents that allowing Johnny to decide for himself represents freedom, open-mindedness, and potential for meaningful spiritual growth. When combined with a parent's own negative experience with religion, this seems like a reasonable option.

However, if you have strong convictions, then you would never suggest that your child reject something you know to be true. It is your responsibility to teach your children what is true. Would you let your child decide for themselves whether or not it is true that failing to look both ways before crossing the street can get you killed? The undeniable nature of that truth and the gravity of the consequences ensure you teach it to your children. You would never risk their safety by failing to give them that instruction.

---

* Eject or egress from an aircraft in flight.

Neither would you let your child be exposed to a highly contagious virus. Deadly viruses do not discriminate; they spread at alarming rates, yet ideas are far more contagious and harder to contain. As children leave home, they are bombarded with alternative perceptions of reality espoused by professors, authors, actors, musicians, politicians, and peers. What will become of these children who try to withstand the academic assault of ideas without the shield of faith and the belt of truth? They will be like leaves blowing in the wind: never able to gain a stable perspective on the world around them. They will be casualties—cultural captives in a worldly prison.

THE DECISION NOT TO DECIDE WHICH WORLDVIEW TO TEACH YOUR CHILDREN CREATES ONLY THE ILLUSION OF NEUTRALITY.

Maybe you hope your child will grow and mature while searching for answers. Maybe you hope they will return from their spiritual journey into your waiting arms, nodding as if to say, "You were right all along. We really are all on different paths leading to the same destination." Happy would be the parent whose prodigal returned unscathed by worldviews at war. In the military, hope is not a course of action. The stakes are always too high. Marines never hope for anything. They begin planning, arrange reconnaissance, make reconnaissance, complete the plan, issue the order, and supervise. Hope is not part of the equation.

The decision not to decide which worldview to teach your children creates only the illusion of neutrality. The reality is that you have chosen apathy. Your children will establish a worldview. It will either develop from the outpouring of your love or from an establishment that loves them not.

ATHEISM, ACTUALLY

When adults teach children to find their own truth, what they are actually saying is "go find the answers on your own." The children then sigh with a quizzical shrug and turn to the only people willing to give answers: their peers. Dr. Gordon Neufeld, a clinical psychologist specializing in child development, explains in his book *Hold On to Your Kids: Why Parents Need to Matter More Than Peers:* "The chief and most damaging of the competing attachments that undermine parenting authority and parental love is the increasing bonding of our children with their peers. . . For the first time in history young people are turning for instruction, modeling, and guidance not to mothers, fathers, teachers, and other responsible adults but to people whom nature never intended to place in a parenting role—their own peers."[6] Your children will eventually form ideas about spiritual things. If not by you, then by the skeptical professor, the guy with the Darwin-fish decal, or the girl with the lotus tattoo.

Later on, Karry helped me realize I did have a worldview all along. Claiming agnostic beliefs was an easy way to avoid conflict. If you never think about God, then you have no reason to be adamant about his nonexistence. Agnosticism feels like a natural choice. It seems to display humility in admitting you do not know the answer, open-mindedness (if a seeker is actually willing to accept truth when they discover it), and diplomacy as a level-headed moderator between irritated atheists and frustrated Christians.

I realized my worldview was not based on agnosticism. I had not put forth the effort to determine whether or not God exists. Instead, I based my beliefs on what I assumed was the answer without ever asking the question. I had to conclude, however reluctantly, that my worldview was based on atheism.

I don't know why that troubled me at the time but it did. The atheists I knew seemed like nice people. How could I operate without God when so many others needed him so desperately? I wished I was like the other 95% who believed in God, but I wasn't. I had no religious experiences, no chills up the spine, no bright lights, no visions—no faith. Atheism sounded like a dirty word and I was ashamed to be a member of the club. I knew something was missing, but life could not go on hold. I had a career to begin, and a girl to marry.

---

[1] Shirley Maclaine, *Sage-ing While Age-ing* (New York: Atria, 2007), 2.

[2] Ronald Nash, *Worldviews in Conflict* (Grand Rapids: Zondervan, 1992), Kindle ed., 16.

[3] Frank Newport, "More Than 9 in 10 Americans Continue to Believe in God," last modified April 14, 2013, http://www.gallup.com/poll/147887/Americans-Continue-Believe-God.aspx.

[4] Norman L. Geisler and Frank Turek, *I Don't Have Enough Faith to Be an Atheist* (Wheaton: Crossway, 2004), 32.

[5] Norman L Geisler, *Baker Encyclopedia of Apologetics* (Grand Rapids: Baker Academic, 1999), 14.

[6] Gordon Neufeld, *Hold On to Your Kids: Why Parents Need to Matter More Than Peers* (New York: Ballantine, 2005), Kindle ed., loc. 220.

CHAPTER 5
BLOODY BOOTS

Quantico, Virginia
July 2000

"We are survival machines—robot vehicles blindly programmed to preserve the selfish molecules known as genes."[1]

—RICHARD DAWKINS

"It is the very act of self-sacrifice that demonstrates that there is something more noble than mere survival."[2]

—RAVI ZACHARIAS

CITATION: . . . *Corporal Dunham and his team stopped the vehicles to search them for weapons. As they approached the vehicles, an insurgent leaped out and attacked Corporal Dunham. Corporal Dunham wrestled the insurgent to the ground and in the ensuing struggle saw the insurgent release a grenade. . . . Aware of the imminent danger and without hesitation, Corporal Dunham covered the grenade with his helmet and body, bearing the brunt of the explosion and shielding his Marines from the blast. In an ultimate and selfless act of bravery in which he was mortally wounded, he saved the lives of at least two fellow Marines.*

A SPIRIT OF SELF-SACRIFICE lives in the hearts of our nation's heroes. Corporal Jason Dunham embodied that spirit—the spirit of a savior. Authors write about it. Directors project it

HONOR, COURAGE, AND COMMITMENT ARE THE MARINE CORPS VALUES INGRAINED INTO EVERY RIFLEMAN.

on a widescreen. He could have run; he could have tried to kick it, throw it, or turn away, but he didn't—he ripped off his Kevlar helmet and jumped with it onto the grenade. For his actions in Iraq on April 14, 2004, Corporal Dunham received the Medal of Honor—our nation's highest award for wartime acts of valor.

Honor, courage, and commitment are the Marine Corps values ingrained into every rifleman. Some seek adventure, and others want to serve. Many are branches in a family tree rooted in a legacy of military service. All will become leaders of men and women in harm's way. The Marine Corps has the power to transform. Marines are experts at stripping away individuality and rebuilding each person with a new identity as part of a team. Recruits will graduate with leadership traits ingrained into the camouflage fabric of their being. Using the mnemonic J-J-DID-TIE-BUCKLE, they recite from memory: judgment, justice, decisiveness, initiative, dependability, tact, integrity, endurance, bearing, unselfishness, courage, knowledge, leadership, and enthusiasm. They undergo rigorous exercises to develop each trait and build esprit de corps within the unit. The final products are Marine Corps riflemen ready to go wherever and whenever they are called.

It is called military service for a reason. In exchange for defending our freedom, service members must give up some of their own—freedom of expression (via dress codes and personal grooming standards), freedom of behavior (via the special rules, codes, and policies), freedom of movement (via duty assignments and liberty rules), and freedom of early termination (via government contracts). Professional performance and personal circumstances are carefully monitored to ensure a safe environment at work and at home. To our fighting men and women, this is a small price to pay to serve a grateful nation.

After receiving my NROTC scholarship, my new goal was to become a Marine. Not everyone is cut out for the elite branch of the armed forces whose members bark at the call of "leatherneck," "jarhead," and "devil dog." Few desire to become Marines, and the Marines don't want just anyone. With slogans such as "first to fight," "the few, the proud, the Marines," and "we didn't promise you a rose garden," they have always been looking for "a few good men."

Marine Corps standards of conduct test the character of every prospective Marine. Jesus says, "Many are called, but few are chosen," (Matt. 22:14) and, "Not everyone who says to me, 'Lord, Lord,' will enter the kingdom of heaven, but only the one who does the will of my Father who is in heaven" (NKJV, Matt. 7:21). Bible commentator Warren Weirsbe explains that obedience to His will is the test of true faith in Christ.[3] God commands us to be holy and strive for moral purity as we seek His will. But some discouraged Christians fail to realize we cannot live up to God's perfect standard. Our sin makes this impossible.

The Marine Corps physical and ethical standards are also high, but they are not unattainable. A candidate who falls short will not receive the coveted Eagle, Globe and Anchor (EGA) to wear as a symbol of their membership in the iconic band of brothers. They must first survive the weeding out process, and there is no better gardener than a Sergeant of Marines. My character was cultivated in the summer of 2000 at OCS, just prior to my senior year of college. My father told me it was designed to force every person to ask themselves, "How bad do I really want this?"

He was right.

OFFICER CANDIDATE SCHOOL

Day one began in a parking lot where a Sergeant Instructor assembled the new officer candidates. He instructed us to dump out our sea-bags for a contraband inspection. Prohibited items included weapons, electronics, non-prescription medications, and alcohol. *Alcohol?* I began to sweat. I packed alcohol wipes to clean the marker off my maps. I called myself out, not knowing whether to be more embarrassed about having contraband, or lacking the common sense to know that it was not contraband.

Every day was similar. Wake up early, PT (physical training), eat breakfast at the chow hall, attend classes, eat more chow, conduct field exercises, go to more classes, receive leadership training, eat chow, clean weapons, clean the squad bay, go to bed and repeat. Developing routines would serve me well; they were crucial to succeeding in flight school, strengthening my faith, and being a parent. Nearly every minute was spent under the instruction of two intense Sergeant Instructors and one Platoon Sergeant. Their job was to mold officer candidates into Marines they would be proud to serve, but for six weeks, we could not stand them.

"Freeze, candidate, FREEZE!" the sergeant bellowed, veins and eyes bulging.

At their command we froze like statues, no matter how awkward the position while they issued instructions or corrected a deficiency. Inspections during the summer were miserable. We stood at attention in the sweltering squad bay for what seemed an eternity. Arm sweat slid past my hand, down the barrel of my immaculately cleaned M-16 and pooled onto the spit-shined floor. I fixed my thousand-yard stare directly through the forehead of the candidate across from me and tried to empty my mind while keeping perfectly still.

A sergeant verbally ripped into another candidate beyond my peripheral vision. Getting chewed out is a horrible feeling, but it can be quite funny when it is happening to someone else. In the moments of pain that accompany the stress of remaining at the position-of-attention for extended periods, a bit of humor goes a long way. A quivering lip on my opposing candidate broke my gaze, and then he cracked a smile. My bearing faltered. He snickered as a spasmodic tirade of chastisement laced with "dag-gums" and "ya-undastan'-dats?" descended upon a candidate for the improper execution of his weapon inspection. I gradually lost the ability to suppress the internal crescendo. Fearful of receiving my own face full of a barking Marine, I chopped off the impending guffaw with a quick nasal grunt.

Inspections during my NROTC days provided plenty of opportunity to test my bearing. Laughter in the face of instruction, though, is the ultimate form of disrespect; I needed a technique to kill the giggles. My trick was to physically bite my tongue. An effective solution and undetectable by upper-classmen, inflicting pain was the only way to effectively squash the instinct to laugh out loud.

Just before losing it in the squad bay, I chomped down hard until my body stopped trembling. The din of reproof and the thought of laughter was supplanted by the taste of iron. I relaxed my face, took a breath and waited for my turn. When the formation was finally dismissed, I looked down at the front sight post of my rifle: it was speckled with rust. Whether you are biting your tongue during an inspection, or holding it from speaking evil, you must control it. Otherwise, you may be next in line to receive the enemy's wrath.

BLOODY BOOTS

There were two occasions during OCS where I was tested by my father's question. How bad do I really want this? The first involved an unexpected hump and the wrong pair of boots.

A "hump" is a long hike, also known as a forced march. The platoon advances in a column of twos at an uncomfortably fast pace carrying fully loaded packs. The humps were usually planned in advance and covered distances between six and twelve miles. Foot care is critical during a hump, and having a broken-in pair of boots is crucial.

I learned this the hard way during a hike through Duke Forest my freshman year. When I received my initial boot issue, they did not have my size, so I was given a pair two sizes larger instead. I figured they would have to do. Besides, there was plenty of room in the toes.

Within two minutes of stepping off, I noticed chafing on my heels. We picked up the pace. The next 40 minutes were agonizing. We stopped for a boot check to inspect our feet for hot spots (places where rubbing might cause future problems). I carefully removed my boots and sweat-soaked socks. My heels stung furiously. I peeled back the black cotton which was drenched with not sweat, but blood from quarter-sized open blisters on both heels. Oozing, red circles stared at me in accusation; I wondered how I could possibly continue.

The Navy Nurse-option midshipman inspected my feet and told me I would not. They threw me in the safety vehicle, a van that follows the group with water and emergency medical supplies, where I got to explain why I wore boots two sizes too big for a hump.

MOMENT OF TRUTH

Candidates bring lots of boots to OCS. Light-weight boots are good for long runs and obstacle courses while heavier, all-leather boots are spit-shined to a high gloss for inspections. I brought a third pair of heavy-duty Danners I bought in the summer of '99 during Mountain Warfare training for extra ankle support. Durable construction and stiff composure made it virtually impossible to roll an ankle.

Mountain terrain is rough and Marines cannot scout for the enemy if they are staring at their footing. I had a history of sprained ankles during our runs at Carolina; I could not take chances getting injured and rolling back to the next OCS class.

I wore my Danners at OCS for field exercises when fast humps were not expected. Danners are ideal for cold winter nights on mountain faces, but they are dreadfully hot in the summer.

One day, we made an unexpected hump. It was over 90 degrees Fahrenheit and extremely humid. *Again I've got the wrong boots!*

"Reach up grab HOLD!" This was the call for everyone in the column to grab the pack in front of them—an easy task except when the accordion effect spreads out the column, requiring an even faster pace to catch up. Distance grew behind each candidate, and the chain reaction continued.

"A-T and T!" was another call for us to reach out and touch someone. "Get it down right now," was barked with falling inflection, the permission to drop our arms. We continued along the Quantico trails going who-knows-where to do who-knows-what. I pounded water and refilled my canteens at every opportunity; it was a fast hump. My legs fatigued and I grew short of breath. The "silver bullet"—the term for a bulb thermometer used to check a candidate's body temperature if he falls out of a hump—loomed in the back of my mind as I struggled to keep a tight interval. It is not checked orally.

QUITTING MEANS LETTING YOUR BUDDIES DOWN, AND THAT IS NOT WHAT MARINES DO.

I wanted to quit, but found the strength to continue. Quitting means letting your buddies down, and that is not what Marines do. Hot, sweaty, and tired, I grew concerned as my head throbbed against the suspension band of my Kevlar helmet. I felt my pulse against my temples and a tingling sensation rolled across my scalp in waves, followed by a chill. *This might be serious. Maybe I should say something. Keep going. It can't be long. How bad do I really want this?* Not long after my brain started frying, we arrived back at the squad bay. We were done.

I thought about my dad and was happy I stuck it through. Until then, I never doubted my future as a Marine. However, during that hump the combination of mental stress and physical exertion made me wonder if I really had what it took.

Every Christian will have to ask a similar question: "How truly do I believe this?" The path is narrow and the journey is difficult. Your patience will be rubbed raw and your boots will be bloodied by spiritual warfare. Your feet will ache from walking up hills of conflict. Your brain will throb from worldly derision and doubt. You will wonder if you have what it takes to stay on the path and finish the hump. You will be tempted to quit. In those moments, remember the words of the Apostle Paul: "God is faithful; he will not let you be tempted beyond what you can bear. But when you are tempted, he will also provide a way out so that you can stand up under it" (1 Cor. 10:13).

SLEEPWALKING

The second test of my endurance happened toward the end of the course. Our increased fitness was offset by increasing fatigue. The night hump started around 2:00 a.m. with everyone operating on minimal sleep. We traversed the rocky hillsides with little moonlight to aid our vision. I felt like a sleepwalking zombie jerking one stiff foot in front of the other. My half-dead mind wandered. *All I want right now is a vanilla ice-cream cone. Oh, to have that sweet taste against my parched tongue. To be seduced by that smooth, silky confection. To twirl it and slurp the drips rolling down the sugary cone. Ice-cream...ice-cream...iiiiice-creeeeeam...*

"REACH UP GRAB HOLD!" I was jolted awake and reached up to grab the pack in front like one of Pavlov's dogs. What happened? Did I fall asleep? How long was I out? We stumbled through the night, reaching up, dropping down, speeding up, slowing down, yawning and heaving, drinking and spitting, all the while wondering, "Is this really for me?" These tests pushed me to the edge of my abilities. I peered into the valley of the shadow of doubt and wondered if I would end up in its doldrums with others who forsook their dream of becoming a Marine in a moment of weakness.

After humps and leadership challenges, helicopter inserts and mock attacks, and carrying ammo crates down the final stretch of the "washboard" trail, I stood at attention and received the coveted jet-black Eagle, Globe and Anchor. The weeding was done, and the gardener was gone. After my senior year at UNC, I was commissioned as a United States Marine.

The thrill of completing a six-week test is amazing. I have heard it said the best feeling in the world is the relief of pain. Completing OCS was one of the best feelings in the world. We hardened our bodies and strengthened our minds.

A better feeling will be to finish the Christian race and enter a Kingdom void of pain and tears. During your walk, you must harden your faith and strengthen your spirit. Only then will you experience the best feeling in all of creation: relationship with the Creator. We owed our success at OCS to the non-commissioned officers (NCOs) who trained us. With the pain still fresh in our minds, we were happy to say farewell, but I saw one of them again sooner than expected.

PUGIL STICKS
One of the sergeants became the assistant Marine Officer Instructor at North Carolina State University the following year. The UNC midshipmen conducted freshmen indoctrination training together with midshipmen from NC

State. Only a few months after OCS, I was reunited with my old Sergeant Instructor when we traveled to Norfolk, Virginia and taught the midshipmen how to walk, talk, and wear their uniforms. The midshipmen toured a Navy ship, slept in submarine quarters, ran an obstacle course, and practiced close combat by fighting pugil stick matches.

Pugil sticks have large pads at both ends. They are held with both hands and used to simulate the motions of close combat with a rifle. Geared up with pads and a helmet, contenders battled inside a ring to knock their opponent to the ground. One point is awarded for each knockdown, and three points wins the match. Fans of the '90's television show "American Gladiators" will be familiar—picture Nitro perched on his pedestal with nostrils flaring and waiting to pound on the next mismatched amateur.

I watched the freshmen wail away at each other and then looked at the sergeant. I thought about OCS. I remembered the drills, the freezing like statues, the A-T and T, the butt chewings—the pain. I had an idea. I walked over and sat next to him.

"Sergeant, one of the midshipmen has a request for you," I said. He turned and looked at me while searching for the hidden meaning.

"Oh yeah?" he continued after a slight pause, "What is it?"

"They have challenged you to a pugil stick match."

His eyes brightened, and he cracked a smile—the first one I had seen. He was about five feet 6 inches and completely ripped. The thought of pounding on a helpless freshman must have been appealing. No one in his right mind would challenge a muscle-head like him. The sergeant would enjoy giving the thrashing.

"Oh yeah?" he responded. His next words were crucial. If he denied the invitation, then he might be able to save face with a reasonable excuse. However, if he asked who the challenger was, then he was committed to the fight lest he be accused of declining after sizing up the competition.

"Who is it?" he asked eagerly.

"It's me, sergeant."

I had him. His expression broke and he knew he was taken. I thought about my six weeks under his control during OCS; pugil sticks could not have been more perfect. I second-guessed myself once he turned to face me in his green skivvy shirt. His arms were bigger than I thought. He also looked meaner than I remembered. Too late now. We grabbed our sticks, put in our mouthpieces, and toed the line. He chomped on his mouthpiece and stared me down. I stared back. Few candidates would get this kind of opportunity. The referee counted down to the starting whistle.

"3 . . . 2 . . ."

POP!

My head snapped back as he jabbed me in the face before the count of "1." I could not believe his cheap shot! He sneered with satisfaction through his wireframe facemask. Now I was mad. The referee gave him a warning and we reset for the second round of three. I unleashed a tornado of blows—all offense and no defense— and advanced with each strike. LEFT, RIGHT . . . RIGHT, LEFT, LEFT, RIGHT! Each blow sent my opponent stumbling further back. After the final combination of jabs, he fell onto his back. I straddled him and unleashed my best war cry while the midshipmen cheered. The score was one to one.

The final round was more evenly matched. It went for a minute or two and ended at the whistle with the referee calling a tie. In the end, we had fun and gained respect for each other.

You might perceive other worldviews as hostile and threatening. You might want to challenge others to step into a ring and put on some pads. However, if you hope to find an audience for your message of hope, then you cannot pick up a pugil stick and start pounding. You must display a life of love and service to everyone you wish to reach.

I learned many valuable lessons from my Marine Corps training. I experienced bloody boots because I focused only on the toes, and not on the heels. Some worldviews focus only on the possibilities ahead and fail to address the damage they may leave behind. As a human statue in a squad bay full of Sergeant Instructors, I learned that when your life unravels, sometimes it's best to freeze and let a veteran help correct your shortcomings. And while sleepwalking through the Quantico woods at 2:00 a.m., I learned that sometimes we must be jolted awake in order to begin asking important questions.

Maybe this book is a jolt. Are you sleepwalking through life? Do you know what you believe? Are you prepared to handle suffering? Are you able to help others in their time of need? Saying "my thoughts and prayers are with you" is always a kind gesture. But sometimes people need something more. Will you have anything to offer?

---

[1] Richard Dawkins, *The Selfish Gene* (Oxford: Oxford University Press, 1989), xxi.

[2] Ravi Zacharias and Dr. Vince Vitale, *Why Suffering? Finding Meaning and Comfort When Life Doesn't Make Sense* (New York: Hachette Book Group, 2014), loc. 1788.

[3] Warren W. Wiersbe, *The Bible Exposition Commentary* (Wheaton: Victor Books, 1996), electronic ed., Mt 7:21.

CHAPTER 6
THE MARINES

Quantico, Virginia
September 2001

"Gimme some. PT.* Good for you. Good for me."

-MILITARY CADENCE

*"Physical training is of some value, but godliness has value
for all things, holding promise for both the present life and
the life to come" (1 Tim. 4:8).*

-THE APOSTLE PAUL

TBS IS SIX MONTHS OF training designed to turn every second
lieutenant into a rifle platoon commander. "Every Marine a
rifleman" is the Marine Corps ethos. Whether a part of
force-reconnaissance or the S-1 shop (administration), every
Marine is trained to pick up a rifle and join the fight.

I joined "frozen" Fox Company which began training in
early September of 2001. Married Marines were allowed to
live off-base and were referred to as "brown baggers" since
they commuted to the base, presumably with a brown bag to
carry their lunch. Karry took a nursing job, and we adopted
two kittens and a puppy before our next move.

---

* *Physical Training.*

The routine is similar to OCS except longer, with less harassment, and with training sometimes as fun as it was exhausting. Who else gets dropped into landing zones by helicopters, throws live grenades, conducts urban assaults with lasers and high velocity pellet rounds, and advances against targets with their roommate spraying live rounds from an M-240 Golf automatic machine gun just meters away? That kind of trust is built during training so Marines can maneuver confidently during battle.

I met new people and even ran into some old friends. One of the second lieutenants in my platoon was a classmate from my high school in Iwakuni. Some Marines enlisted before going back to school and receiving their commission. Mike Silva was one of those Marines. We were in the same squad and his room was a few doors down from mine. Merely acquaintances when we left TBS, our paths crossed again later in a significant way.

Performance at TBS partially determines your Marine Occupational Specialty (MOS). MOS categories include infantry, combat engineer, logistics, adjutant, etc. . . . Marines with aviation contracts are slightly different. Our MOS, Naval Aviator, was already assigned which eased some of the pressure. The second lieutenants of Fox Company became experts at navigating through thick woods with a compass and map, reading the terrain, and counting paces while carefully navigating around obstacles and through waist-high streams. Some lieutenants with aviation contracts wore goggles to prevent getting poked in the eyes by sharp branches. I just opted to watch where I was going; it is hard to see the compass when your eyes are covered.

IT IS HARD TO SEE THE TRUTH WHEN YOUR MIND IS COVERED BY A VEIL OF ASSUMPTIONS.

Similarly, it is hard to see the truth when your mind is covered by a veil of assumptions. If you are a seeker, then ask yourself why you believe what you currently believe. Is it because of tradition? Culture? Pragmatism? Are you assuming the things you believe are true? If not, then how have you come to your conclusions? Do not navigate through the forests of philosophy with your mind covered. Remove the assumptions so you can think clearly. Once you plot a course to discover truth, you will be on the right track.

LITTLE PROBLEM, BIG MOUTH

One secret to staying on the right path is maintaining situational awareness (SA). The term is used frequently by the military, but it has application for everyone. Allow me to share a story about low SA and its consequences.

One of the first qualifications was for marksmanship. Range week consisted of an early morning formation, a 3-mile hump to the shooting range, shooting practice, and a 3-mile hump back to the barracks. Rifle qualification was the first opportunity to earn a silver badge to wear on the dress blue uniform. The categories of awards from best to worst include expert, sharpshooter, and marksman. The marksman badge resembles a target consisting of two concentric circles inside of a square and resembles a "pizza box." If an officer under-performed at both the rifle and pistol range on qualification day, then he could end up with double pizza boxes. When you are aiming for a worldview, missing the target can be much more costly. You might end up wearing badges of shame, dishonor, and regret.

I was nervous because my wisdom teeth were scheduled to be pulled the week prior to range week. I arrived for the appointment, rode the recliner back, and stared at a light before feeling my gums run through with a never-ending needle of Novocain. I tried to relax, but found myself gripping the chair like a cat avoiding a bath. *Just relax. Everything will be fine. You are full of Novocain. You won't feel a thing.* He gripped the dental forceps and wiggled my tooth.

ZING!

"Ahh!" I shrieked a sort of gurgle-yelp through his fingers and their instruments of torture. He pulled his hands away. The traffic on the super-pain-highway between my tooth and brain stopped, and I opened my eyes.

"Maybe we'll give that Novocain a little more time to take effect," he said. *Good idea. I'll have time to plan my escape.* He came back strong in Round Two. He worked the tooth back and forth with a firm grip and then pulled again. Pressure . . . pressure . . . ZING!

"Ahhh." The dentist was getting frustrated. He gave me even more Novocain. I was drained and we had barely started. I was all that stood between him and his weekend. Now we had to wait longer. Finally, I was numb enough to proceed and the yanking resumed. The tooth was not cooperating. He tried one of the other wisdom teeth. No luck. I pictured him heaving with both hands, boot firmly braced on my chin and aided by his assistant locked in a bear-hug hold.

"I'll have to break them up," he said. That's when I lost my resolve. I lay like a forlorn animal at the mercy of a periodontal predator. The high-pitched whine of a diamond-coated bur advanced upon my doomed enamel, and gritty fragments flew as he bore into my crumbling teeth. The rest is a blur. All I know is that I left that chair four teeth lighter.

I moped down to the pharmacy to pick up my prescription; it was packed, with few places to sit. Karry saved me a seat and was flanked by a middle-age gentleman in street clothes. I recounted my tale of woe through numb lips and a slobbery tongue. I told her about the pain about how the doctor did not give me enough Novocain, how he appeared frustrated, and that I was probably the only thing between him and an afternoon tee time. I told how he yanked and yanked but failed to extract the teeth and how it took forever for him to drill them out. I ended by describing the procedure as the most horrible experience I had ever had.

The guy beside me leaned over and gave me advice about the prescription I was about to pick up.

"You seem to know a lot about wisdom teeth," I said. "Are you a doctor?" He turned his head and looked me in the eye.

"I was your doctor. You don't recognize me because I was wearing my scrubs and mask." Never have I wanted to become more invisible. Check, please! Extract foot from mouth. Stop talking. This kind of embarrassment was rivaled only by eating lunch with the UNC men's basketball head-coach and his wife, and not knowing it.

("So, do you work for the university?"

"Yeah, I coach men's basketball."

"Oh, I see. Say, look at the time . . .")

My low SA in the pharmacy led to major embarrassment.

QUALIFICATION DAY

I enjoyed shooting the M-16. I was good at it. When I lived in China Lake, Dad signed me up for a shooting class. Every day for two weeks, I rode my bike to the shooting range where the group met. We used a .22 caliber rifle and shot paper targets at a range of 50 feet. I learned how to steady my aim using a sling and natural bone support as well as how to breathe slowly, deliberately pausing after each slight squeeze of the trigger. They were the same concepts I learned in the Marines to become an expert rifleman.

Range week at TBS finally arrived. I settled into the prone position, sling wrapped tight, cheek nested next to the rear sight, and unbraced every muscle. I closed my eyes and took in a full breath. Then I exhaled, drew in half a breath, and paused. I opened my eyes and focused on the front sight post in relation to the small black dot 500 yards away. *Aim is slightly left. I need to move my aim point to the right.*

When shooting a stationary target at long ranges; using muscles to hold adjustments is extremely unstable. A small correction would require a slight shift of my entire body. I pivoted at the hips, reset my feet, settled back into the sling, rested my cheek against the buttstock and went completely limp. Eyes closed, I went through the breathing routine and opened my eyes to check my sights. *Right on target.* Azimuth was solved. My diaphragm was the only muscle affecting the sight post, and with each breath in and out, the aim point moved up and down.

Breath, freeze, squeeze. I constricted my finger around the trigger.

Breathe, freeze, squeeze. I squeezed a little more.

Breath, freeze, sq- BANG!

The shot should come as a surprise. If you know when it is coming, you are probably squeezing too quickly which pulls the shot off target. My goal was to shoot a perfect score on qualification day, and I came close during the pre-qualification round. I dropped a few shots on qualification day; however, this was good enough to earn the title of expert.

> YOU CAN ONLY HIT THE TARGET WITH A STEADY AIM. THE QUESTION IS, "WHAT TARGET SHOULD YOU BE AIMING FOR?"

So often we shoot for a perfect score in life only to be let down time and time again. We are not perfect, and we can never be perfect, but if you aim for the right target, then you can earn a badge reserved for those who love God and are called according to his purposes: the badge of salvation. You can only hit the target with a steady aim. The question is, "What target should you be aiming for?"

SURVIVING THE CHAMBER

Although TBS is not a weeding out process, it still relies on the concept of training how you fight, and that means pushing your body to its limits. It snowed during the first days of our offensive/defensive (O-D) week while we patrolled through the woods. Our packs were stuffed with MREs (Meals-Ready-to-Eat), cold weather gear, bivouac supplies, and a gas mask to protect us from gas attacks.

CS gas, or tear gas, was first synthesized in 1928 and named after two US chemists, R.B. Corson and R. W. Stoughton.[1] It is part of a family of riot-control gasses originally used to rout enemy troops from caves and bunkers and was used in bombing raids prior to infantry assaults.[2] It is described as an "intensely irritating solid that causes profuse weeping and other effects typical of a lachrymator."[3] A lachrymator causes tears to flow and irritates other parts of the body on contact; especially the skin, throat, and nasal passages.[4]

Michael M. Phillips, the author who chronicles Medal of Honor recipient Corporal Dunham's heroism in Iraq, identifies an essential of Marine Corps "theology" in which "glory derives from suffering."[5] CS gas was used during Military Operations Urban Terrain training, and it was important to know what to expect in case you were exposed. CS canisters were also used during field exercises to simulate a chemical attack. Better to first suffer in training than in combat. Therefore, every second lieutenant at TBS experienced the "gas chamber" to learn how to properly don and clear their gas mask and experience the effects of CS.

The small, gray building consisted of an entry way and one main room. In the center of the room was a small table with a receptacle to place the CS tablets. A group of Marines were led in single file and encircled the room with gas masks securely fastened. An instructor heated the CS tablets and fanned the gas rising from the table. The sun beamed through a thick window onto sparkling particulates. It resembled a cloud of fiberglass, and I was about to suck it deep into my lungs.

The training began once the room was engulfed in gas. Instructors inspected each Marine's mask seal and taught how to clear the mask by forcefully exhaling. To build confidence, everyone bent at the waist and shook their heads. Next came jumping jacks. Each exercise gave us more confidence in the mask's ability to filter out poisonous gas. Then each person removed, donned, and cleared their mask. This exposed the face which caused some burning in the eyes and nose, but the lungs remained free of irritants. Mission: complete. Confidence bolstered.

There was one final exercise, and Marines knew it as the trail of tears. A right-face put us in single file again, and they gave the command to take off our masks. We grabbed the blouse of the person in front of us and circled the room's perimeter. The exercise demonstrated that while the effects of CS gas are not pleasant, they are also not lethal. I held my breath as long as possible, knowing that each second I delayed the inevitable breath, the larger the first inhalation would be. Adrenaline and nerves depleted my oxygen quickly. I had to breathe. *Here we go…*

I expected to draw in a large gulp of air, but my breath was involuntarily cut short after the first taste of CS. Following what felt like a fatal drag, I coughed, sneezed, dry-heaved, hiccupped, and contracted from muscle spasms as snot shot out of my nose and tears expelled from my tightly clenched eyes.

"From the halls of Montezuma!" An instructor called out, reciting the Marine Corps Hymn through his gas mask for motivation. I doubled over and kicked my knees up toward my chest and coughed uncontrollably.

"To the shores of Tripoli!" I lost control of my body, and my first instinct was to panic. I clung to the blouse in front of me wondering if I was strong enough to make it through the test.

"We will fight our country's battles!" The room erupted with coughing and heaving. Another instructor sensed my distress and grasped my shoulder. He shouted words of encouragement: "C'mon, you can make it. Just a few more seconds. Don't quit. Ooh-rah!"

"In the air, on land, and sea!" I reluctantly breathed in the gas and somehow prevented a full-blown freak-out.

"First to fight for rights and freedom!" I dismissed the thought of bolting for the door and knew I could stick it out.

"And to keep our honor clean!" I regained control of my body. I tried to relax and waited for the end.

"We are proud to claim the title of United States Marine!"

Finally, the teary train of Marines was led out of the building to recover. Rows of the uninitiated peered at the red-faced gas chamber veterans wondering how their own bodies would react when it was their turn. I remembered the chamber at the pop of every CS canister in woods followed by "GAS! GAS! GAS!" In the field, we always had our gas masks at the ready.

> YOU WILL WANT A TESTED WORLDVIEW AT-THE-READY WHEN LIFE POPS A CANISTER OF TRAGEDY AND THROWS IT AT YOUR FEET.

Do you know how you will respond when you are given a drag of human suffering? Will you lose control and panic when the intense agony of loss saturates your body? Will you run for the door of the church chamber? Do you have a worldview to filter out false teachings and poisonous thoughts? You will want a tested worldview at-the-ready when life pops a canister of tragedy and throws it at your feet. After learning the value of keeping poison out of my body, I learned the importance of keeping nourishment in.

NOURISHING BODY AND SOUL

Chow is continuous in the field. That means you are responsible for keeping yourself nourished with the food you have packed. But as our platoon dug in to a defensive position, I got behind on my chow plan, and my energy dwindled.

Tired and hungry, sitting in a wet, spade-shoveled foxhole, I battled physical exhaustion and mental impairment in the early morning hours preceding an imminent attack. The battle could come at any time, and the psychological effect of waiting was taking its toll. My mind began to slowly unravel. Everyone was tired.

We had spent the previous night searching for a lost Marine after coming up one man short during a head count. In typical Marine fashion, we got on line and began a methodical search of the woods. Starting with the bivouac area, we expanded our search outward while calling his name and sweeping the frost-covered ground with flashlights.

Hours passed with no luck. We even popped flares to light up the woods and help him find the way back. Eventually the lost Marine wandered up to our platoon commander on a road bordering the forest and asked what the commotion was about. Apparently our initial sweep of the bivouac site was not so thorough. Just off the left flank, concealed in defilade and covered with leaves, our lost Marine lay nestled warmly in his sleeping bag.

Sometimes we search for what is lying right under our nose. Unfortunately, many children raised in a Christian home are not equipped to respond to the intellectual criticism awaiting them outside the fortress walls. The result is a child who rejects the Christian worldview in search of a seemingly more defensible faith. Those children also wander in the woods looking for what is right under their nose.

Back in my foxhole I became angry. I waited, rifle ready, butt water-logged, and feet numbed inside damp socks. I started losing it. Thoughts became words. I whispered profanities and chastised the would-be attackers for not engaging us sooner so we could get some rest!

I knew I was cracking, but I couldn't stop it. I was "going internal"—the one thing you must defend against when under physical duress. Instead of diverting my attention to things outside myself, I was stuck in a dangerous bout of introspection at the worst possible time. My buddy realized what was happening and told me to rack out,* sacrificing his own precious hours of sleep. I accepted, and a few hours later, I awoke a changed man. Without food, water, and rest, the body cannot function the way it was designed to function.

The soul also gives an indication when missing a basic need: the feeling of un-fulfillment experienced by those who have not recognized an infinite God. In his classical work *Pensées*, Blaise Pascal calls this the "infinite abyss [that] can only be filled by an infinite and immutable object, that is to say, only by God himself."[6] (Brackets mine.)

The other grass always looks greener. The luster of new-and-exciting is lost to the old-and-boring. As our bodies were designed to be nourished by bread and water, our souls were designed to be nourished with the bread of life and the living water of Jesus Christ. When he is missing, our souls become malnourished.

This hunger drives us to seek something that can satiate our appetite. But attempts to fill this infinite void with anything else will fail. No amount of money, power, respect, family time, or philanthropy will make us feel complete. Look at Isaiah, chapter 26, verse 9: "My soul yearns for you in the night; in the morning my spirit longs for you."

This is why preachers say Jesus is the only thing that satisfies. When a soul accepts the love and grace of Jesus, they receive all the benefits of a soul satiated by its intended source of nourishment. Once both body and soul have been properly addressed, we can function as God intended: in relationship with him and in proper relation to others.

---

* Get some sleep.

In the third sentence of *Confessions*, Augustine writes: "Thou awakest us to delight in Thy praise; For Thou madest us for Thyself, and our heart is restless, until it repose in Thee."[7] I learned the importance of nourishing my body in a small foxhole in the Quantico woods. It was years later before I began a quest to nourish my soul.

Right now, it was time to earn my wings.

---

[1] Benjamin C. Garret and John Hart, *The A to Z of Nuclear, Biological, and Chemical Warfare* (Lanham: Scarecrow Press, 2007), 60.

[2] C.L Taylor and L.B Taylor Jr., *Chemical and Biological Warfare* (New York: Franklin Watts, 1985), 71.

[3] Garret, *The A to Z of Nuclear, Biological and Chemical Warfare*, 60.

[4] Ibid, p. 127.

[5] Michael M. Phillips, *The Gift of Valor* (New York: Broadway Books, 2005), 144.

[6] Blaise Pascal, *Pascal's Pensées* (New York: E. P. Dutton & Co., Inc., 1958), Kindle ed., loc. 1697.

[7] Augustine, *The Confessions of Saint Augustine*, trans. Edward Bouverie Pusey (401 AD), Kindle ed., loc. 36.

CHAPTER 7

WINGS OF GOLD

Pensacola, Florida
June 2002

*"The wax dissolved; and as Icarus flapped his naked arms,
deprived of the wings which had caught the air that was
buoying them upwards, 'Father!' he shouted, again and
again."*[1]

—OVID

*"The reason birds can fly and we can't is simply because
they have perfect faith, for to have faith is to have wings."*[2]

—J. M. BARRIE

Which activities would you enjoy the most?

A)   Have a picnic
B)   Read a good book
C)   Rebuild an engine block
D)   Visit the dolphin exhibit at the local zoo

How would you best describe yourself?

A)   Timid
B)   Bubbly
C)   Daring
D)   Apathetic

THESE QUESTIONS MIGHT BE FOUND on the Biographical Inventory (BI) portion of the Aviation Selection Test Battery—a standardized test for predicting performance and attrition through the beginning phases of Naval Aviation training.

It was possible to ace certain sections but fail the test overall if you chose poorly during the BI questions. As I took the test, I became the most fearless, daring, and mechanically inclined prospective Naval Aviator since A. A. Cunningham, the first Marine Corps aviator.

I passed (barely). The reward was a guaranteed slot in the aviation community. After passing a physical examination and completing TBS, Karry and I moved to Pensacola where I began flight training.

ONE-WAY DECISION GATES

The first step was a program called Introductory Flight Screening (IFS) where students fly a light civil aircraft, such as a Cessna 172 or Piper Tomahawk, prior to Navy flight training. If a student successfully completes IFS, he will be less likely to drop-on-request (DOR) during the rest of flight school. DOR means "I quit."

I attended IFS at Pensacola Regional Airport and flew the Piper Tomahawk. Classes supplemented one-on-one sessions with a flight instructor to learn about checklist procedures, operating limitations, and basic maneuvers. Before long, I was "cleared solo" and exploring the skies of Escambia County, basking in the freedom of flight and the excitement of soaring above the earth at 70 knots.* The first solo fight was a confidence booster and a significant

---

* Nautical miles per hour.

milestone. One of the final flights in the program was a cross-country.

I planned my trip to Monroe County Airport in L.A. (Lower Alabama). The term cross-country is misleading; in aviation lingo, a cross-country is simply a flight that lands at a destination other than the home airport. Takeoff and the flight en-route were uneventful. With the airport in sight, I made the appropriate calls on the common traffic advisory frequency, extended the flaps, set up for a left downwind entry, and slowed to my final approach speed of 62 knots. With careful timing, I pulled power and lifted the nose to flare.[*]

I parked and went inside the general aviation facility to check the weather for my return trip. The plan was to delay only long enough to refuel and scarf down some food. I called the local flight service station from the cockpit radio and filed a visual-flight-rules flight plan back to Pensacola Regional airport.

After takeoff, I scanned the horizon to find cumulonimbus clouds building to the south. Walls of rain seemed suspended in mid-air and smudged the horizon into the sky. Lightning in the distance increased my concern. I faced my first real-time aviation-related judgment call. If I continued to Pensacola, then I would have to deal with the rain—something I had no experience flying through or navigating around. If I turned back, then I would be staying overnight in Monroe County. I checked my fuel and calculated the distance to Pensacola to see if I would encounter any one-way decision gates along the way.

A one-way decision gate is a term pilots use for actions which cannot be undone once completed. An example is crossing the "point of no return" along a route after which

---

[*] Decrease the rate of descent prior to touchdown during an aircraft landing.

you no longer have enough gas to turn around and fly back to your previous destination. Another example is shutting down an engine which cannot be restarted later. You must be careful before you go through a one-way decision gate.

I looked south again and saw more lightning; I banked left and made a radio call with my intent to land back at Monroe. After landing, I accepted a ride to a local motel and called Karry to tell her I'd be spending the night. I spoke with the lobby attendant in the morning.

"Can you please give me the number to a taxi service?" I asked.

"A what?" was the reply.

"A cab. I'd like to call a taxicab to take me to the airport," I continued.

"Son, we don't have taxis here," she informed me.

"Does the airport provide a shuttle service?" A silly question, but all I could muster at the time.

"No, we don't have anything like that, but it is only about a mile down the road. You can easily walk it," she assured me. I grabbed my headset and started down the road for the airport. Clear weather made for an uneventful return flight, and I wondered if my decision to turn back the day before was too conservative. I probably had plenty of gas to fly around the scattered showers, but I was uncomfortable deviating from the original route.

"WHAT KIND OF PILOT MESSES WITH THE WEATHER?" HE ASKED, AND THEN ANSWERED, "A DEAD ONE."

Later in my career, my dad shared a saying that reminded me of that day: "What kind of pilot messes with the weather?" he asked, and then answered, "A dead one"—a poignant reminder of the power of nature hidden by opaque clouds and invisible wind.

HELO-DUNKER

With IFS complete, I began the Navy's flight training program. The first phase was Aviation Preflight Indoctrination (API) at Naval Air Station (NAS) Pensacola. Students learn about aerodynamics, aircraft systems and engines, aviation weather, air navigation, flight rules and regulations, and aerospace physiology.

They also complete water survival training which can be fun for strong swimmers. We had to swim in full flight gear (including helmet and boots), release harness fittings while being dragged across a pool by a cable and straps, simulate helicopter hoist operations, and demonstrate life raft procedures. The training also included a one-mile swim while wearing a flight suit. That is thirty-two lengths of a 50-meter pool without interruption. An energy-conserving breast-stroke was the preferred method, and there were no breaks allowed.

During underwater egress training, we escaped from the helo-dunker after capsizing in a deep, indoor pool. This device was connected to a crane and simulated a helicopter fuselage complete with doors, windows, and an open back section for emergency escape. Once we were strapped into our seats, the device was slowly lowered down into the pool. Water rushed in through the windows and rose steadily up towards the roof. Then the entire fuselage rotated 180 degrees leaving us upside-down and underwater.

Our bodies were designed to function right-side-up with the inner ear controlling our sense of balance. Sudden and violent accelerations are extremely disorienting, and adding water and darkness complicates determining which way is out and which way is up. In order to survive the helo-dunker, you must find points of reference along the fuselage to find your way.

Once inverted, we were cleared to unbuckle our lap belts, find the nearest window, and swim to the surface. Then we did it blindfolded. Multiple SCUBA equipped instructors monitored the drills and were ready with regulators in case something went wrong. Later on, I realized that life without a coherent worldview is like riding the helo-dunker, but without instruction, points of reference, or safety instructors to prevent drowning.

PRIMARY FLIGHT TRAINING

After API, I began primary flight training at NAS Whiting Field in Milton, Florida where I joined VT-6 and learned to fly the T-34 "Turbo-Mentor." The aircraft is powered by a turboprop engine with inverted flight capabilities and can pull 4.5 Gs and reach 280 knots. Emergency procedures (EPs) had to be memorized and executed immediately when required.

One practice maneuver involved recovering the aircraft from a spin. If a spin becomes unrecoverable, then the only option is to bail out and parachute back to earth. Bailing out of the T-34 involved notifying the other crewmember, opening the canopy, disconnecting cords, releasing the restraining harness, diving toward the trailing edge of either wing from a crouched position, and deploying the parachute. As the pilot dives toward the edge of the wing, the airflow normally ensures that the pilot will clear the aircraft structure.

When my dad was a flight instructor in VT-6 twenty-one years earlier, a fellow instructor had to bail out of an uncontrollable spin. After jumping over the side, he found himself sitting on the wing as the aircraft plummeted toward the earth. After a moment of disbelief, he scrambled toward the edge of the wing and pulled himself over the side to clear the aircraft.

A parachute's purpose is to save your life when you are plummeting toward certain death. It is a backup system for getting safely back to earth when the primary system (landing the aircraft) fails. When your life unravels at the seams, do you have a rip cord to pull? What will keep you from accelerating into an abyss of despair? The Apostle Paul tells us in Romans 13:14 to "put on the Lord Jesus Christ." When you put him on, there is no fall from which you cannot safely recover.

One of the perils of flying at low altitude in the Florida panhandle is the threat of colliding into a turkey vulture. These scavenger birds can have wingspans up to 6 feet and weigh up to five pounds. We heard stories of a bird strike that penetrated the canopy glass and injured the instructor, forcing the student to land the crippled aircraft.

One day, I walked by an aircraft that took a bird to the canopy. The glass was smashed in several places and covered with blood, feathers, and chunks of turkey flesh. Years later, I struck a bird on landing rollout at MCAS Iwakuni while it was lifting off from the runway. A bird strike is always a threat, and you never know when it is coming.

NO ONE IS MORE QUALIFIED TO PILOT YOUR VESSEL THAN THE ENGINEER WHO DESIGNED IT.

So it is with trials in life. When you are struck and become injured, do not give the controls to an unproven student; let God take control of your life. No one is more qualified to pilot your vessel than the engineer who designed it.

THE COST OF INACTION
Sometimes the hardest trials are suffered by the ones you love most. The Pensacola beaches were something to dream about, but we were about to experience a nightmare. On July 4, 2002, Karry and I drove to the beach to see the fireworks. We paused next to a restaurant to choose a good viewing location, and as we scoped out the scene, a tiny projectile screamed flatly through the air with a high whistle and pop. Concerned about shooting bottle rockets in a crowded location, I traced the thin smoke-trail horizontally back to its point of origin: a group of young men with beers in hand.

How could they be so stupid? Another mini bottle rocket shot across the crowd, only feet above the ground, and crashed next to a small family sitting 50 feet in front of us. *Did that just hit a little girl?* The parents got up and inspected their child; I couldn't tell whether or not anyone was hit. The father looked around, and for a moment, he fixed his gaze in my direction. *Is he looking at me? I can't believe those idiots just hit that girl with a bottle rocket!* I had to make a decision. Do I try to talk sense into the drunken buffoons? Do I force them to give up their bottle rockets? Do I call the police? Movement in my peripheral vision broke my gaze at the family. A quick hiss preceded a dampened thump as a bottle rocket passed inches in front of my face and slammed into Karry's left eye. Upon impact, she released my hand, spun to the left, and dropped to the ground.

Suddenly I was in a war zone, and my buddy just went down. I had flashbacks from *Saving Private Ryan* while I looked at Karry lying on the sand, crying out and covering her eye. I could not survey the damage behind her cupped hand—she refused to pull it away. Enraged, I stormed over to the offenders.

"You just hit a little girl and shot my wife in the eye!" I screamed.

I didn't know what else to do. I wanted to berate them more. I felt like teaching them a lesson. I really wanted them to beg for forgiveness. Maybe they would cry at the thought of destroying someone's sight from such recklessness. All they could muster was confused looks, aggressive posturing, and slurred mutterings of denial. I didn't have time for anything else. I gave them a quick tongue lashing and returned to help Karry.

We passed by a police officer on the way to our car who provided us an escort to the nearest emergency room. Karry's vision was blurry. She looked in the sunshade mirror; blood was coming from a gash on her eyelid. She had managed to close her eye before impact avoiding a direct collision with her cornea.

The doctor on call washed and examined her eye. Aside from the small cut on her eyelid, he didn't see any damage to the eye itself. He recommended we follow up with an ophthalmologist as soon as possible. Since Murphy's Law dictates that all injuries occur on weekends and holidays, we would have to wait.

By the time she saw an ophthalmologist, the blurriness had not improved. He placed a handheld magnifying instrument close to her eye and leaned forward to peer inside. He looked back up almost immediately.

"She has a retinal detachment," he said.

"Is that serious?" I asked.

"She'll be okay, but she's going to need surgery."

Eye surgery? It was worse than we thought. We mulled over when the surgery could be scheduled.

"No, no," he said, "she needs to have surgery today. I'm calling a surgeon now to begin preparations."

My heart sank. If only I had acted after seeing the first rocket streak over the crowd; I could have prevented it; I failed. I was too uncomfortable to have a confrontation. Their reckless action endangered others, and I did nothing. Because I failed to see the importance of acting on a moral duty, Karry was in jeopardy of losing her sight permanently.

She had surgery that night. A scleral buckle was implanted around her eye to help keep the retina intact. It will be there for life. I don't sit back anymore when foolish people endanger others. Those men on the beach were physically reckless and my wife paid the price. If you are spiritually reckless, your family will pay the price.

FLYING WITHOUT INSTRUMENTS

I continued training in the T-34 and entered the Basic Instrument phase—one of the more difficult phases in primary flight training—and learned how to navigate via instruments during instrument meteorological conditions (IMC). These conditions occur when there is no visible horizon or ground reference to help the pilot maintain proper flight attitude and orientation.

IMC is opposed to visual meteorological conditions (VMC), where there is good visibility and a distinguished horizon. When flying in IMC, a pilot must transition to instruments by going "heads-down" and begin a methodical scan of the instruments inside the cockpit. A vertical gyro system provides the pilot with indications of aircraft pitch and roll. The tactical air navigation system (TACAN) uses ground-based transmitters to determine aircraft position.

Degraded conditions were simulated by putting up "the bag," a white tarp which fastened to the inside of the canopy to block the outside view. While the instructor's portion of the canopy remained unobstructed, the student perspired under the bag and coped with the stress of navigating a plane at 200 knots by looking at spinning arrows, changing numbers, and fluttering needles. I was so consumed with learning procedures that even sleep was exhausting. I dreamt about descent rates, let-down points, and lead radials. Poor sleep was common before a check ride, where demonstrating proficiency in a skill set determined whether you passed the flight or "downed" it.

Living with an insufficient worldview is like flying under the bag. While it is easy to move forward, it is difficult to stay pointing in the right direction. If you don't know how to fly using instruments, or you read them incorrectly, you will veer off course.

However, there is something you can do about it—you can take down the bag. By developing a truth-based worldview which corresponds to human experience, you can

YOU DON'T HAVE TO BE STRUCK BLIND BEFORE YOU CHANGE THE DIRECTION OF YOUR LIFE.

unmask the canopy to reveal a glorious horizon. When you can see the horizon, you can always find which way is up, and with a bit of good weather, the sun will help you find true north. The Son covered the eyes of the Apostle Paul to help him find the way, but you don't have to be struck blind before you change the direction of your life.

At the end of Primary, I selected jets and moved to Kingsville, Texas. During Advanced flight training in the T-45A "Goshawk," aviators learn how to handle a jet engine versus a turbo-prop. The T-45 has more power, more procedures to memorize, and everything happens faster. It was also the first aircraft in flight school to have an ejection seat at the time. Once pilots learn the fundamentals of flying a jet, they learn how to employ it as a weapons system. The training is difficult, and unfortunately not every flight goes as planned.

DOWNER

I downed (failed) a flight during an air-to-ground check ride. It is not uncommon for pilots to down at least one flight in the course of flight training. Repercussions involve extra instruction, formal counseling, and re-flying the syllabus flight. My flight involved dropping practice bombs on a target near El Centro, California.

Frequently students will pass the tactical portion of the flight, but fail the administrative portion (flying to and from the working area), and that is exactly what happened in my case. We flew the T-45 in a circular dive-bombing pattern with four planes rolling-in sequentially to release a single Mk-76* on each pass.

After dropping my last bomb, I was confident I had scored well. All that was left was to get back together and

---

* A small, blue, 25-pound practice bomb that simulates the ballistics and trajectory of a heavyweight general purpose bomb.

return to base. The join-up deconfliction plan involved stacking the planes from high to low, and required each aircraft to see the aircraft above it before climbing higher than their assigned safe altitude.

I have learned one principle that always rings true: whenever something goes wrong, it is because something was different; a checklist is interrupted; a habit pattern is disturbed, often caused by encountering a new situation. In this case, it was being in the "dash-4" formation position that led to my error.

In previous flights, I was always dash-2. This affects the timing of the off-target-rendezvous maneuver to get rejoined. Dash-2 can easily see dash-1, begin his turn, and leave his safe altitude. Dash-4, however, must delay his turn off target since he has three aircraft in front of him to account for instead of one. Turning too soon and failing to see all three preceding aircraft can be deadly if strict altitude contracts are not honored.

Going off the timing of my previous flights, I began my turn early with two aircraft in sight but no sign of the third. I continued to climb, looking for my interval (dash-3) out of the right side of the canopy, expecting to find him at the two o'clock position. Suddenly, as I was transiting through my safe altitude, I snapped my head to the left and picked up dash-3 passing from left to right at 11 o'clock. Already in a climb, I deconflicted above him as we passed with 3,000 feet of separation (extremely closer than we should have been).

After a moment like that, you take a few deep breaths. My lack of SA led to an unexpected close pass. *I think I just blew it. Maybe there's a chance he'll still pass me. Nah, I blew it.* Once we were back on deck, he informed me that I blew it. My bombing scores were great. The rejoin was not. Especially for a check ride.

It's not always what you see that will get you, but what you don't see. Downing a flight is like stumbling into sin. As hard as you try to avoid it, it is going to happen sooner or later. A pilot should not wallow in substandard performance after downing a flight just as we should not wallow in sin after a momentary stumble. I learned from my failure, moved on, and prepared for the final phase of flight training.

It was time to land on an aircraft carrier.

---

[1] Ovid, tr. by David Raeburn, *Metamorphoses: A New Verse Translation* (New York: Penguin Books, 2004), 305.

[2] J.M. Barrie, *The Little White Bird* (Nisyros Publishers, 2013), Kindle ed., loc. 1273.

CHAPTER 8
YOU REALLY
BELIEVE THAT?

Somewhere Off the Florida Coast
March 2004

"Don't think. Feel."[1]

-*BRUCE LEE*

"The unexamined life is not worth living."[2]

-*SOCRATES*

GOING TO THE BOAT* IS one of the most exciting phases of flight training. Soon I would fly a multimillion-dollar aircraft off the coast of California and rendezvous with the USS Nimtz to land on a moving platform 135 feet long and 20 feet wide. A Marine pilot's first carrier landing is always solo. No one wants to be in the back seat when the new guy has a bad day at the boat.

Each pilot spends weeks in preparation for this milestone. Flights are dedicated solely to practicing carrier landings, and the carrier deck is simulated by a small landing zone painted on the runway. Each landing is assisted and graded by a

---

* Slang term for an aircraft carrier.

Landing Signals Officer (LSO), a pilot specially trained in talking pilots down into the wire. He sits in a small shack by the runway next to the optical landing system known as the "meatball."

The meatball uses lights to indicate whether or not the pilot is on the appropriate glide path to land in the touchdown zone. The orange ball appears to move up and down in relation to a fixed point of reference called the datum lights. When the ball is lined up with the horizontal datum lights, the pilot is on glide slope. If the ball rises above the datum lights, the aircraft is high. The ball turns red if the aircraft gets low, and the LSO can initiate emergency wave off lights if the pilot doesn't make a timely correction. At the boat, the price of being too high is landing past all four wires and boltering;[*] the price of being too low is crashing into the back of the ship.

As the pilot rolls out of the final approach turn into the groove,[†] he must make immediate corrections to power and AOA[‡] in order to stay on glide slope and hook the cable on touchdown. During the final approach, his eyes dart back and forth between the landing point and the meatball enabling him to detect minute movements of the ball and apply corrections. He must also maintain lineup with the centerline and listen to instructions from the LSO over the radio.

"Lined up right . . . power . . . you're high, step it down," the LSO instructs.

The left hand becomes a robotic extension of the flying machine, quickly making three-part corrections with the throttle and accounting for the characteristic delay in aircraft

---

[*] Executing a touch and go back into the landing pattern.

[†] Final portion of a landing approach.

[‡] Angle of attack: the angle between the relative wind and the chord of the wing.

response of jet engines. The eyes continue their darting scan all the way to touchdown where the aircraft slams—almost crashes— onto the deck while the pilot selects full afterburner. If he catches a wire, the jet will go from over 130 nautical miles per hour (kts) to 0 kts in under two seconds. If he bolters, selecting full power ensures a minimum takeoff rolling distance (a requirement for carrier operations).

Four cables are strung across the carrier deck. The optimal wire to engage is the 3-wire. Another good cable to catch is the 2-wire. Catching the 4-wire means you were close to boltering, but that is a recoverable error. The 1-wire is not good. It means you were low. And the worst is known as a "taxi 1-wire." That means you touched down even earlier and then rolled into the 1-wire. Any earlier and you crash into the stern of the boat.

You might be having a similar experience in your life, that of being on track, only to find yourself sinking slightly below glide path. A correction puts you back on course, but soon you sink lower. Your target is in sight—a healthy marriage, a reputable business, financial freedom—but if you don't make a correction immediately, you're going to crash. You cannot accept being low. You must get on glide path.

THE INCREDIBLE FLYING APPLE

One year after qualifying in the T-45, I went to back to qualify in the F/A-18 Hornet during both day and night carrier operations. I crossed the California coast and cruised over the Pacific scanning the horizon for the USS *Nimitz*. Before takeoff, I shoved a water bottle and a green apple into my helmet bag and stuffed it beside the ejection seat.

After reporting a sweet lock with the ship's TACAN[*] and spotting the carrier in the distance, I banked right and lined up for the overhead break.[†] The carrier was surrounded by ships—quite an audience. In reality, seamen conducted drills inside cramped quarters surrounded by noisy, grey bulkheads and cranky Senior Chiefs.

But fighter pilots suffer from airborne-induced myopia; seeing only themselves, their mission, and the Marine on the ground clearly. Over the carrier deck at 600 feet, I rolled up on a wing and pulled back on the stick and felt 5 Gs bleed my energy to setup for the downwind leg.

Carrier landings are one of the most difficult procedures in Naval Aviation. The final approach turn is a descending maneuver thru 180 degrees and must be executed precisely to get the pilot on glide slope, on speed[‡] at ¾ of a mile. If conducted properly, the pilot will pick up the meatball through his last 30-45 degrees of turn. I took a deep breath and wiggled my fingers and toes, hoping to avoid a bolter on the first attempt.

I COMPLETED THE LANDING CHECKLIST AND SET UP FOR THE FINAL APPROACH.

The tiny aircraft on the carrier deck looked like Matchbox toys. I completed the landing checklist and set up for the final approach.

"Shooter-21, three-quarters of a mile, call the ball." The LSO began the litany he had done hundreds of times before.

---

[*] TACAN: Tactical Air Navigation System. A "sweet lock" means my system was providing proper direction and distance to the aircraft carrier.

[†] 180 degree maneuver over an intended landing area.

[‡] The appropriate landing speed and angle of attack for landing an aircraft.

I rolled out, and the golden glow of the ball slowly rose into view from beneath the datums.[*]

"Shooter-21, Hornet ball, 6.3," I keyed the mic and responded. The last number represents 6,300 pounds of fuel remaining. Fuel quantity determines when a pilot must cease carrier landing attempts and divert to the nearest land base. This predetermined fuel state is referred to as "bingo" and is carefully adjusted for weather and distance from divert airfields. Fuel states in the pattern are continuously monitored. I rolled out in the groove and began the rhythmic scan we had practiced, except now the landing area was surrounded by ocean.

"Come left," the LSO commanded to ensure proper alignment.

After a slight correction, I was lined up on course. Shoulder harness: locked. Catching the wire was supposedly violent, and I didn't want my upper body slamming into the forward displays. The ball was still slightly low; I added power. *Never lead a low ball.* I remembered one of the mantras of carrier landing corrections. When fixing a low ball, the cardinal sin is to pull power too soon creating a ball that rises, yet never reaches, the datums. In other words, after the correction, you're still low. I added more power to get above glide slope and then made a few choppy power corrections to shave off extra altitude in the final seconds. Pulling too much power could result in violating another cardinal rule: never trade a high ball for a low, especially in close.

"Power . . ." he spoke calmly and slowly, indicating only a slight correction was needed. As the ship grew larger, the sailors and aircraft on the flight deck came into focus. Lineup was good as I crossed the ship's stern. One more power correction sent the ball slowly rising toward the top of the

---

[*] The datums are a horizontal row of lights providing the point of reference from which glide slope deviations are measured.

lens. I slammed into the deck and shoved the throttle full forward to light the afterburner. My body slid forward before the shoulder harness arrested its movement. I kept my left hand pinned against the throttle while my head and right arm were thrust forward of my pinned torso with the violent stop.

My helmet bag shot forward and something flew out towards my feet. Slightly off centerline, the jet wiggled left and right before the hook-point settled toward the center of the cable. Like a pit bull pulling against its owner's leash, 32,000 pounds of thrust pulled the ship by its cable until I complied with the signal to throttle back. I raised the hook and followed the signals directing me to the catapult. There was approximately one moment to relish what I had just accomplished, and then it was back to work.

I went through my takeoff checklist and searched the area around my right foot. If a loose item remained in the jet, I would have to shut down, have the jet searched, and re-schedule the flight. I felt something round and grabbed it. My green apple! I threw it in the main pocket and ensured all zippers, Velcro, and buttons were secure.

I checked my fuel and used hand signals to adjust the weight-board that was used to confirm the catapult power settings. The launch bar in front of the nose wheel was connected to the shuttle and the barrier behind the catapult rose into position. I ran up the power and wiped out the controls, ensuring the flight control system was operating properly before launch. I crisply saluted, pushed my helmet back against the headrest, and grabbed the towel rack. A few seconds later, the steam-driven slingshot released its energy.

The catapult pinned me against the seat, inducing momentary apnea as I accelerated toward the boundary of water and steel. In a final jolt, the rumble of the aircraft ceased as the jet cleared the ship's bow, and flight control computers engaged to dampen out turbulence. I grabbed the stick once clear of the carrier and flew the jet back into the landing pattern. Then I grasped the oversized hook handle jutting out from the front right console and pushed it down causing the arresting hook to drop into position for the next trap.[*] The cycle continued until I completed the required number of daytime arrestments.

BINGO ON THE BALL

The next challenge was to do it at night. If you can manage not to get blown off the ship while navigating the crowded and dangerous flight deck while trying to find your jet, you've won half the battle. The landing pattern is different at night and allows for a straight-in approach with the aid of the automated carrier landing system. Similar to a civilian instrument landing system, the equipment provides course and glide slope information to get you to the ball at ¾ of a mile. With the use of coupled autopilot and auto-throttles, the F/A-18 is capable of landing itself on the carrier without pilot input if needed.

Beyond the greenish glow of the cockpit lighting was complete darkness. The sea joined the sky—the horizon cloaked by a moonless night. Looming in solitude was a single light marking the meatball's position. The surrounding ship was invisible, no more matchbox planes, no more flight deck crew—just a small amber light amidst the gloom. I boltered several times after sending the ball up and off the lens by adding too much power.

It was after midnight, and I was the only Hornet left in the pattern; I only needed one more night trap to complete my qualification. "Bingo, Bingo," came through the headset from the aural warning system. I checked my fuel and reset my bingo number for the established divert. If she squawked

---

[*] Slang for an arrested landing.

at me again, I would be heading back to shore for the night. I only had one more chance to catch a wire.

There I was, bingo on the ball, at night, alone and unafraid. Well, alone. I knew what was at stake.

I glanced down at my kneeboard and thought about checking my divert numbers. I reached halfway down and stopped. *No. You're not going to divert. You're going to trap.* I put my hand back on the throttle and breathed deeply through my oxygen mask. Floating cities and divert procedures would have to be compartmentalized for the next 60 seconds while I focused my attention on lineup, power, AOA, and the ball.

I called the ball at ¾ of a mile and started down on glide slope. I couldn't bolter again, but bracketing low is the last thing you ever want to do at the boat. How much time do you have to fix a low ball at night? The rest of your (short) life.

I had a slightly high ball and worked to chip it down. I pumped the throttles in short spurts being careful not to bring them back too far for too long. The ball crept down towards the datums and sunk one ball low. *Easy . . . not too much.* I jabbed a short burst of power to arrest the downward trend. Up the ball

I WAS LANDING A FIGHTER JET ON AN AIRCRAFT CARRIER, BUT I DIDN'T KNOW HOW TO MAKE SENSE OF THE WORLD.

went. *Get it back . . . don't lose it now.* I cut power in small chops lasting fractions of a second. I was over the ramp. Lineup was good. One second to touch down. I glanced one last time to the left to see the ball heading for the top of the lens . . .

Landing on the boat at night was difficult. It was stressful. There were so many places to land a jet more easily. Why must I continue down the difficult path?

Approach on the glidepath. For wide is the corridor and broad is the path that leads to destruction, and many enter through it. But small is the landing zone and narrow the path that leads to the 3-wire, and only a few find it.

I had earned the coveted Eagle, Globe, and Anchor, and after completing flight school, I earned wings of gold. But I was also searching for something else that could never be earned. I was landing a fighter jet on an aircraft carrier, but I didn't know how to make sense of the world. I was seeking wisdom, purpose and some way to know what is true. I was seeking God. I had become a seeker.

YOU REALLY BELIEVE THAT?

Little did I know, God was seeking me. God works in mysterious ways to bring people to Christ, and in my case, he used a single question from my wife.

"What do you think happens when we die?" Karry asked.

It was 10 years since our first kiss on the seawall in Iwakuni, and we would celebrate our fourth wedding anniversary in June. This was one of our first serious conversations about death. When she asked this question one night in our one-bedroom San Diego condo, I was politely dismissive.

"I don't know. Nothing? Blackness?"

Sitting upright in bed, I set down what I was reading to ponder her question. It might have been a copy of Scientific American. I liked the precision and discovery of science—the rationality of it all. An exchange like this would normally be brief and inconsequential. But something was different that night. Her approach combining concern and patience was by the Book.

"YOU REALLY BELIEVE THAT?" SHE GENTLY RESPONDED.

"You really believe that?" she gently responded.

Her eyes longed for a husband who would take her Christian faith seriously. I sensed disappointment—even a bit of pity—as she shifted back onto her pillow. She was raised in a Christian family, but I didn't grow up going to church. With those four words, she made me feel something unusual. It was a feeling she would never intentionally arouse but resulted from my unpreparedness to answer her simple question. I felt…stupid.

I could not tell her what I believed because I had never given it any serious consideration. I thought religion was the opiate of the masses and the cause of most world conflicts. I figured religion was for little old ladies with hymnals and people too dumb to realize Darwin killed God. Virgins don't have babies, and dead people stay dead.

That night, I realized that I had no justification for my presuppositions other than "someone once said" or "that's what I was taught in school." Surely, our country's public school system must afford equal time to all possible models for understanding the creation of the universe and the appearance of first life, right? If this God stuff is not even allowed to be taught in public school, doesn't that mean it is heinously flawed and ridiculously naive? That is how I thought back then.

For some reason, instead of the obligatory thirty seconds normally given to these seemingly unanswerable questions, I pondered the fate of my soul. Up to that point, my views were passively atheistic and naturalistic, and the word "soul" would have meant some unknowable thing religious people talk about. I thought of our first-born son, then 15-months-old, and his baby sister who was due in the summer. What would I teach them when they ask what happens after death? "Blackness" was an unsatisfying answer resulting from twenty-six years of spiritual apathy.

I came to a disconcerting realization: I was unprepared to give my children meaningful answers to life's important questions. This was not my first misgiving of being a father unqualified for the job. There was already a gnawing notion that although I was already a dad, I lacked something fathers should have. The unidentified shortcoming haunted me, as if a Ghost of Future Failure was walking along side, waiting for the tragedy I could neither avoid nor endure. *Maybe I haven't read enough books.* I was a good reader but lacked a passion for literature.

My intuition was eventually validated, but the missing ingredient was not the quantity of reading; it was the subject. The day I began asking questions about spiritual things marked the end of an era of apathy, cowardice, and fear.

You really believe that? A single question changed my life forever. It stopped my rising tide of fighter-pilot machismo in its tracks, and I realized that professional trophies cannot shine in a home darkened by the spiritual ineptitude of their champion. I didn't lack an education. I didn't lack drive or courage. I was willing to face danger despite the unsettling fear that comes from a worldview whose only guarantee is death. What I lacked, I could not receive from ordinary books or the ordinary people who wrote them.

I lacked wisdom. And to get it, I would have to find God. Strike that; He would have to find me.

---

[1] Bruce Lee, *Enter the Dragon*, directed by Robert Clouse (1973; Burbank, CA: Warner Home Video, 1986), VHS.

[2] Socrates. Quoted in Plato, tr. by Harold North Fowler, *Plato in Twelve Volumes, Vol. 1* (Cambridge: Harvard University Press, 1966), Apology 38a.

CHAPTER 9

READ, FLY, REPEAT

San Diego, California
May 2005

*"Faith is the great cop-out, the great excuse to evade the
need to think and evaluate evidence. Faith is belief in spite
of, even perhaps because of, the lack of evidence."*[1]

—*RICHARD DAWKINS*

*"Now faith is the substance of things hoped for, the
evidence of things not seen" (Heb. 11:1).*

—*AUTHOR OF HEBREWS*

"LET'S GO TO CHURCH," KARRY said.

"Okay," I responded. We had occasionally attended
church together in Iwakuni. Although I knew I would be
uncomfortable, just as I always was when surrounded by
religious people, I also knew they had something I didn't. It
may have been faith, or security, or wisdom. But was their
faith blind? Was their security falsely perceived? Could I be
mistaking wisdom for ignorance? One thing was certain: I
did not understand, or relate to Christians. Since I had been
married to a Christian for going on three years, I figured that
area deserved some attention.

Whether the fascination with things eternal was justified
or concocted, I needed to know whether it was reasonable to
believe in objective morality, a supernatural creator of the

universe, miracles, the incarnation, and the resurrection. There had to be more to life than you're born, life's tough, and then you die. Some say we need to believe in God to keep from going insane—that belief in a Creator is a cosmic security blanket and tolerated to prevent pandemonium. However, to borrow a term often used by author and Christian apologist Ravi Zacharias, even atheists fail to communicate their ideas without "smuggling in" an objective morality used as a guide for human decisions.

Centuries ago, men were the spiritual leaders of the household. Men of courage were strong in their convictions and fought battles for God and country. They went to their deaths rather than recant what they knew to be true. It shaped how they viewed the world and related to others. Under God's authority, they defended their countrymen's inalienable rights to life, liberty, and the pursuit of happiness.

Times have changed. Today, Christianity is mocked in the media, dismissed by university professors, and challenged by litigious secularists. Men who devote their lives to Christ are likened to Ned Flanders (the stereotypical Christian on the popular animated series *The Simpsons*) and dismissed as soft, emotional, goody-two-shoes pansies. One who follows and enforces the rules might be called a whistle-blower, a traitor, or even (gasp!) un-cool.

Toward the end of the film *Legends of the Fall*, the character played by Aidan Quinn laments to his younger brother played by Brad Pitt, "I followed all of the rules, man's and God's. And you, you followed none of them. And they all loved you more."[2] We are sent the same message today. If you want to be cool, do the in-thing. Get on the bandwagon. Live in the now. Follow the world, and the world will love

WHY DO I NEED JESUS TO HEAL ME IF IT CAN BE DONE WITH HERBS, PILLS, MASSAGE, MEDITATION, NEEDLES, HYPNOSIS, AROMAS, INTENTIONS, OR ENERGY?

you more. The question Quinn's character should have asked himself is: from whom should he desire love, man, or God?

Don't people believe in God only because their mommy told them to when they were little? Isn't God outdated? Hasn't he been replaced by oneness with the earth, a global awakening of consciousness, and the quest for enlightenment? Why do I need Jesus to heal me if it can be done with herbs, pills, massage, meditation, needles, hypnosis, aromas, intentions, or energy? More important, what is broken and in need of healing? My list of questions was growing, and I needed answers.

In the meantime, I continued training.

READ, FLY, REPEAT

Mastery of any skill set requires repetition; natural ability will carry a person only so far. Hornet training is conducted in the Fleet Replacement Squadron. That is where I spent a year learning how to employ the F/A-18 as a weapons platform. It's also where I was first introduced to sacred fighter pilot literature known as tactical manuals. If a new guy is not flying, he should be studying. Hundreds of pages over several manuals explain the finer art of employing ordnance and fighting air-to-air battles.

Basic Fighter Maneuvering (BFM) is one of the more difficult skills to master. No matter how many times you read and re-read the chapters, you cannot fully grasp the proper execution until you have flown the flights. That is where sight pictures described in the manuals become real, and concepts can be confirmed through application. BFM is a battle where every second counts. Multiple errors compound over time to yield an advantage. If your opponent is winning, you are losing. No amount of wishful thinking or denial of reality can change that fact. If the bogey's on your six, you had better shake him.

Fighter pilots read the manuals, fly the missions, and re-read the manuals. With each successive study, concepts and relationships become more clear. They improve their maneuvers with each flight, bolstering confidence in certain techniques and revealing weaknesses in others. Then it's back to the books. The best fighter pilots move beyond simply knowing the material—they live the tactics.

The Bible is the tactics manual for life. Other manuals have hit the shelves over the last 2,000 years: the Vedas, the Sutras, the Koran, the Book of Mormon, the Four Books and Five Classics, Isis Unveiled, the Tao Te Ching, Dianetics—the list goes on. The problem is that when different manuals make exclusive truth claims (and they do), they cannot all be true. Even religions that claim neutrality and champion the idea of universal acceptance are exclusive because they exclude the exclusivists!

Unfortunately, the secularization, pluralization, and privatization of America has run so deep that people will do or say anything to avoid being branded the most shameful label our culture has to offer: intolerant. Slapped with this major infraction, there is no shortage of lawyers willing to make you pay for supporting the death penalty, natural marriage, or anti-abortion legislation.

Public expressions of religious faith have become taboo in America. Let me re-phrase that: Christianity has become taboo while worldviews that espouse enlightenment, oneness, and "tolerance" are celebrated. Television coverage on faith-based issues is intentionally polarizing and unbalanced. The general public knows that there is a debate about abortion. The media mostly addresses the issue in the context of women's rights, while pro-life advocates focus on religious freedom without ever fully explaining why they believe abortion is murder. Bring up the idea of a Creator God who has created each person with intrinsic value, inseparable from its relative size or level of development, and prepare for scoffs reserved for antiquated and irrelevant zealots.

The slogan at the top of the ACLU website says, "Because freedom can't protect itself." Neither can the unborn. The belief that freedom is better than bondage reveals an assumption of moral values. Objective morality requires the existence of a perfect and transcendent being who can and will enforce it. Ascribing value to worldviews that deny such a being's existence is an oft-unrecognized exercise in irrationality. All people deserve equal value, not their religions.

OBJECTIVE MORALITY REQUIRES THE EXISTENCE OF A PERFECT AND TRANSCENDENT BEING WHO CAN AND WILL ENFORCE IT.

The Bible contains all the principles you need to live a fulfilling, meaningful life. Like a pilot's tactical manuals, it cannot be read once and then set aside. Its principles should be tested against reason, logic, and human experience. The Psalmist writes in chapter 103, verses 1-6:

> Praise the LORD, my soul; all my inmost being, praise his holy name. Praise the LORD, my soul, and forget not all his benefits—who forgives all your sins and heals all your diseases, who redeems your life from the pit and crowns you with love and compassion, who satisfies your desires with good things so that your youth is renewed like the eagle's. The LORD works righteousness and justice for all the oppressed.

This sentiment is echoed in Psalm 37:4, "Take delight in the Lord, and he will give you the desires of your heart." If the Lord satisfies our desires with good things, then our desires must have been good.

What if you desire bad things? The Psalmist is telling us that God changes our desires when we put our faith in him. Doing good things is not a requirement for salvation, but anyone who is truly saved will begin desiring good things. However, we must do more than read about God's transforming power; we must live out our faith. Paul ministers to us in Romans 13:12: "So let us put aside the deeds of darkness and put on the armor of light. Let us behave decently, as in the daytime, not in carousing and drunkenness, not in sexual immorality and debauchery, not in dissension and jealousy. Rather, clothe yourselves with the Lord Jesus Christ, and do not think about how to gratify the desires of the flesh."

Other translations say to "put on the Lord Jesus." It is inadequate to read about him and say, "Hmph. Sounds like a nice guy. He seems to have some good advice." We are supposed to try him out, put him on and see if he can deliver on his message of hope. Only then can you see if he has changed the desires of your heart. There is no substitute for experience, and experience requires repetition. Study tactics, fly by the book, and repeat. Read, fly, repeat. Read the Bible, live by the Book, and repeat. Read, live, repeat. Failure to do either can give the enemy the upper hand.

A STEP OF FAITH

Sunday became an exciting day. While learning to fly the Hornet in San Diego, Karry and I joined a church with services at a local elementary school auditorium. I was interested in what kind of message the pastor would deliver each week.

I enjoyed listening to the worship team. They were full of energy and played a mix of upbeat and slow arrangements—each creating a reverent atmosphere for worship. The congregation clapped their hands and swayed to the movement of Christ moving through them.

There were still awkward moments, specifically prayer, communion, and the altar call. You can never know if prayer works unless you have prayed, and you can never believe in

God unless you have been open to believing. Communion symbolizes Jesus' body which was broken and his blood that was shed when he died on the cross. It is a sacrament to be performed by followers of Jesus. As merely an investigator of Jesus, I did not take communion when offered.

At the close of one service the pastor offered a free book by Lee Strobel called *The Case for Faith* for anyone interested in learning more about Jesus and Christianity. That was me! I devoured it over a few nights. The book took some of the most common stumbling blocks to faith and addressed them via interviews with scholars in various fields. The book contained every reservation I felt toward Christianity, and I resonated with each response given by this award-winning former atheist and legal editor of the Chicago Tribune.

FAITH REVEALED

At work, I was learning about a different kind of faith. When you think about it, flying a multimillion-dollar jet aircraft is like something out of a Wile E. Coyote cartoon. You are strapped to a giant rocket, the fuse is lit and a controlled explosion sends you hurling through the sky. The disastrous launch of the space shuttle *Challenger* in 1986 is a sobering reminder of the miniscule margin of error surrounding the design and operation of complex machines. Failure of an O-ring seal combined with a higher than normal wind shear doomed the crew shortly after liftoff. The space shuttle *Columbia* was damaged by a piece of insulation foam during liftoff in 2003 and never made it back to earth intact. One ring and a piece of foam claimed the lives of fourteen of our nation's heroes. These are perhaps the most memorable examples to the public, but mechanical failures are not uncommon in the field of aviation.

Most of the time, mechanical issues are minor and affect non-critical flight systems. Marines work in specialized fields and keep rigorous maintenance practices to ensure that jets stay in good working order. Every procedure and inspection process is explained in a publication, and the Marines are expected to follow the checklists religiously.

Major problems in flight are solved by executing emergency procedures and keeping a cool head. Nevertheless, materials fail and humans make mistakes. Sometimes maintenance problems are caused by misunderstanding a procedure or using the wrong part. Components can be wired improperly, installed backwards, damaged during installation, forgotten, left unfastened, exposed to chafing, or deteriorated.

Fortunately, most of my issues in the jet have been minor, and this gets to the heart of the message: despite the risks, despite the thousands of components on the jet that could fail, despite the abundance of human interaction and susceptibilities to error, I have never thought twice about strapping on the jet and flying a mission. I would be even more confident if I could confirm all the maintenance done on the aircraft, but that is both impossible and impractical.

I have faith in the Marines who work on the jets; they have faith in my ability to fly them—together, we complete the mission. Marines are expected to maintain the highest standards of discipline, professionalism, and integrity. Every lance corporal turning a wrench knows he is part of a team. Without his help, jets will not fly, and without his attention to detail, pilots will not succeed. He does his best because that's what Marines do. They do not settle for average. Marines work day, night, and through the weekends to make sure the job is done right. That's why I have faith in the Marines who maintain the fleet.

This was a revelation. I never thought of myself as a man of faith, yet I was beginning to see how much faith I had in

> I NEVER THOUGHT OF MYSELF AS A MAN OF FAITH, YET I WAS BEGINNING TO SEE HOW MUCH FAITH I HAD IN EVERYDAY THINGS.

everyday things. I need faith to drive to work every day. I have faith I will receive a paycheck for my work because legal checks and balances ensure compensation and deter unfair business practices. And I must trust architects because I don't worry about roofs collapsing on my head. In order to remain sane, I must trust these events will not occur despite a lack of proof.

I have faith in the Marines, but even Marines fall short. Many moral infractions are minor, infrequent, and regretted. However, like the rest of the world, some are living a lifestyle of hedonism, relativism, and deceit. For a detailed description of life in a fighter squadron, read Jonathan Dowty's *Christian Fighter Pilot is not an Oxymoron*. He tells his story from the vantage point of an Air Force F-16 pilot, and while the details of the culture are different, the principles are similar. It is a life of excitement, hard work, long hours, and rewarding experiences.

Fighter pilot culture is rich in history, honorable in purpose, and filled with heroes rightfully revered by generations of Americans. It can also be a life full of challenges for those seeking to live in accordance with Biblical principles.

My first challenge as a fighter pilot was to see if I had what it took to succeed in combat. One of my son's favorite verses is "there is a time for everything" (Eccles. 3:1). In July of 2006, I deployed with my squadron to Iraq.

It was time to go to war.

---

[1] Richard Dawkins, "Lecture from 'The Nullifidian' (Dec 94)," The Richard Dawkins Foundation for Research and Science, last modified March 2, 2009, http://old.richarddawkins.net/articles/89.

[2] *Legends of the Fall*, directed by Edward Zwick (1994; Culver City, CA: Columbia TriStar Home Video, 2001), DVD.

Chapter 10

WILL SEND THE
HORNET

Al Asad Air Base, Iraq
November 2006

"He who desires peace, let him prepare for war."[1]

— VEGETIUS

"In peace I will lie down and sleep, for you alone, Lord,
make me dwell in safety" (Psalm 4:8).

—DAVID

MY ALARM BUZZED AT 6:00 P.M. I rolled out of the bottom bunk and stood on the sand-filled carpet I purchased months earlier. The window air conditioning unit was on full blast to keep the small unit cool, and the scent of Downy blew from fabric softener sheets I placed inside the filter. I thought about caffeine and glanced at my burnt-out coffee pot.

The "cans" were our living spaces and ran on 220-volt electricity. Plugging in American devices required an adapter and step-down converter to reduce the voltage. I grazed my face with an electric shaver in front of a small mirror hung on the wall, letting the stubble float down into and around the small wastebasket beneath.

I grabbed my toiletry kit and towel and headed for the showers in the adjacent trailer. The sun dipped below the horizon, and I shielded my eyes from sandy wind as I walked in my silkies, skivvies, and flip-flops to the shower area. Something was wrong with the water pressure. *Great. Another water bottle shower.* I unscrewed the cap to the first bottle and stepped into the stall wondering what the night's flight would bring. I poured the cold water over my head and quickly scrubbed my body to create warmth.

I threw on my tan flight suit and holstered my standard issue 9mm Beretta. Our squadron spaces were just across the road, and it was dark by the time I arrived. Since I was on the night page, most of my flights would begin and end in complete darkness. It also meant I had to sleep during the day. We kept our unnatural circadian rhythm in its groove with blacked-out windows and careful measures to avoid seeing the sun. It was somewhat vampire-esque— appropriate for a squadron known as the "Bats."

A Lesson Relearned

We had been flying there for three months and covered much of the flight brief with "standard." The pilots and WSOs in the flight talked about coordination with the supported ground units as well as how to tactically employ our weapons. The arsenal mostly consisted of laser guided bombs, air-to-ground missiles, and the 20mm cannon.

My WSO and I suited up in our flight equipment and headed out to the jets. After chatting with our plane captain, we climbed up the ladder, strapped in, and ran the checklists. Everything that happened inside the cockpit was part of a strict routine. *Straps secure. Leg restraints—attached. Helmet bag—stowed. Maps—accessible and stowed. Gloves—on. Cockpit* *sweep—complete. Switches—check.* Kneeboards—secure. Mechanical pencil—ready (3 clicks of lead). Notepad—prepped. Canopy rails—clear. Area—clear. Pre-start checklist—complete. Ready for engine start.* With the engines fired up we completed our checks with the plane captain and taxied our section[†] out to the runway. *Controls—check. Radar—check. Screens—set. Navigation system—tight. Trim—set. Seat—armed. Takeoff clearance—received. Ready to go.*

We taxied on to the runway along with my wingman, ran up the engines, and checked the flight controls. *Engines look good. Controls are good. Wingman looks good.* I gave the signal, released the brakes and threw the throttles into full afterburner. Thirty-six thousand pounds of thrust pushed me back against the seat as we accelerated down the runway. The jet climbed away from the runway and the last glimmer of cultural lighting provided by the airfield disappeared. I flipped down the night vision goggles (NVGs) and let my eyes adjust to the grainy, green circle.

My wingman approached from behind and maneuvered his jet for the join up. A quick glance under the goggles toward my 5 o'clock position revealed a flashing strobe light. *He's right where he should be.* We completed our en route checklists and tested our flares. It was a quick flight to Ramadi—one of the main areas we supported in Al Anbar province over Iraq.

Enemy activity was sporadic. Although major force-on-force engagements were not as heavy as during Operation Phantom Fury in Fallujah in 2004, indistinguishable combatants, improvised explosive devices (IEDs), and mortar attacks were an everyday threat to the Marines. They routinely patrolled the streets on foot and sent convoys between various forward operating bases. We loitered

---

[*] Checklist item completed.

[†] Group of two aircraft.

overhead in case they ran into trouble. We established radio communication with the Marines. There was some activity in the area.

"I need you to proceed overhead and get your sensors into this area, standby for grid," the forward air controller's (FAC)* voice crackled over the radio. My wingman was first on the scene and prepared to go kinetic. We put our targeting pods on the grid and my wingman continued the radio dialogue.

"I'm tracking a vehicle surrounded by a large crowd of people." "YOU ARE CLEARED TO TAKE OUT THAT VEHICLE," HE CAME BACK.

"Roger that. That vehicle is dragging a body through the street. We've got positive identification and you are cleared to take out that vehicle," he came back.

I listened carefully and kept my sensor in the target area to record the action. I stared at the small screen on the aircraft console to determine what was happening. The vehicle pulled away from the crowd. Sure enough, there was an object dragging behind it, though it was difficult to make out what it was. Someone ran up to the object and kicked it as it was grated over a dirt road. I figured you probably wouldn't run up and kick a dead dog, or goat, or sheep; that kind of hatred is usually reserved for humans—a sobering reminder of the fallen state of our world.

The vehicle jettisoned the body and headed south out of the city. I thought of the four American contractors who were dragged through the streets after being burned and hung from the "Blackwater Bridge" in 2004, prompting offensive operations to re-take the city of Fallujah. The car

---

* Personnel qualified to provide airborne terminal attack control for the employment of fires, especially in close proximity to friendly units.

continued down the road out of the city where the buildings and houses were more spaced out. Then it came to a stop.

"The car just stopped next to another vehicle," my wingman reported.

"Copy that. You are cleared to take out that vehicle with twenty mike-mike," the FAC replied.

That was slang for the 20mm Vulcan canon mounted in the nose of the aircraft. The semi-armor-piercing-high-explosive-incendiary rounds were lethal when precisely employed. I monitored the situation and looked outside to watch for any small arms fire or other surface-to-air threats, though the chances of getting engaged by a man portable air defense system, known as MANPADS, were small. I watched as dash-2 set up his attack geometry for a strafing run. He rolled into a dive and carefully aimed the gunsight onto the car. Just as he rolled out wings level, the car pulled away from the other vehicle and continued down the street.

"I'm gonna lead him!" his WSO exclaimed from the back seat. The WSO was responsible for target acquisition and maintaining a good weapons delivery solution. Now they had to hit a moving target—no easy task.

I watched from above, waiting for fire to erupt from his nose as his flashing strobe light descended into the darkness. He let out a long burst of bullets and quickly pulled off target. The string of bullets hit short and then walked up the road slicing directly through the moving car. The vehicle exploded into a fiery wreck and the heat signature washed out the infrared targeting pod screen. I glanced under the goggles to see a rolling inferno in the darkness. Back on the targeting pod, we watched as the damaged car rolled to a stop. The doors flew open and four men fled in different directions. They disappeared into the countryside and never reappeared.

The FAC wanted the other car that pulled up next to it disabled as well, and its occupants had already fled. My wingman gave me the shot. I selected the gun, checked my delivery parameters, and acquired the target. We lined up on a good axis and began our dive. I started the methodical instrument scan and symbology crosscheck that would continue until I squeezed the trigger and pulled off target.

"Arm it up!" my WSO called from the back.

Whew! I had committed a rookie mistake. In all the commotion between monitoring the first burning car, listening to the radios, setting up attack geometry, and rolling in, I skipped one of the most important parts of the employment checklist: moving the armament switch to ARM. I was re-learning a lesson from a different desert half a world away, when in the excitement of an emergency situation I forgot to disarm the kill switch on my dirt bike. Without this backup from my WSO, I would have pulled the trigger to the sound of silence and frustration. Low SA almost led to a failed attack.

Embarrassed, but with no time for heavy sighing, I armed it up and continued the dive. The designation kept drifting to the right and my WSO labored to keep our sensor on the target. I squeezed the trigger and sent supersonic bullets ripping through the air. Quick glances at the targeting pod screen showed where the bullets hit—they impacted slightly right of the target. We missed.

Desired results not achieved.

I envisioned the intelligence summary of my failed attempt to hit the car and remembered an oft-repeated truism: the first pass is the one that counts; you may not get a second shot.

RE-ATTACK

In Raid on the Sun: Inside Israel's Secret Campaign that Denied Saddam the Bomb, author Rodger Claire describes the attack in 1981 on Osirak, a nuclear reactor in Iraq. The Israeli pilots trained for months and practiced every day for the dangerous and difficult mission. The attack was a success and the reactor was destroyed. But at the moment of truth, as one of the less proficient pilots approached his weapons solution and pickled (released) his bombs, he knew something wasn't right. He was ". . . far too good a combat pilot not to know. He had missed. His bombs had not hit the target. He had failed. The realization came to him like a knife to the gut."

"Can you hit this target?" my wingman asked over the radio.

Blood pulsed faster through my veins. Employing the gun at night was challenging and scary. There's nothing relaxing about diving steeply towards the ground in the pitch black and trying to hit a point target with an area weapon. Poor gun employment technique can spray a diluted pattern of bullets over a large area whereas skillful employment can lay down a dense pattern with precision in a tight grouping.

"I can hit it," I said.

"You can, or you will?"

"I will hit the target!" I emphasized, slightly irritated, but now more committed to success. We had exposed ourselves to possible low altitude threats and with nothing to show for it. We couldn't miss again.

We lined up again and re-ran the employment checklist, ensuring that we were armed up this time. Down the chute we went with the sensor on the target and gun symbology in place. I fired again and listened to the Gatling gun rattle off 6,000 rounds per minute for what seemed like an eternity. I pulled back on the stick and the Gs came on. In three quarters of a second, my body weight increased to 1,000 pounds. Under heavy eyelids, my eyes darted right to watch the screen for impact. Dirt kicked up around the car and sparks shot out from its metal frame. Bullets shattered the back windshield and the car shook from the impact of several other rounds finding their target.

I breathed a sigh of relief. The car was disabled. But the victory was not in the destroyed car—it was in the successful attack. A fighter pilot's measure of success comes from whether or not he has the knowledge, skill, and discipline to do what is required of him.

> THE PILOT'S BIGGEST FEAR IS LETTING THE INFANTRYMAN DOWN.

As the grunt charges with fixed bayonet over land, the fighter pilot flies like an arrow over the battlefield.

The infantryman's biggest failure is letting his buddies down; the pilot's biggest fear is letting the infantryman down. The time for reflection on the nature of peace, war, and defense is long past and far removed. All that matters is a successful attack.

CASUALTIES

On another night mission, we responded to a group of military-aged males (MAMs) being tracked by a nearby ground unit. They were positively identified emplacing IEDs along a road to ambush coalition troops. We achieved positive identification and followed them through the city.

I already personally witnessed two IEDs explode while flying overhead. The first explosion occurred at dusk about 10 miles away from the area we were orbiting. The massive explosion caught my eye and I changed course to investigate. We set up an orbit and found a 5-ton truck engulfed in flames.

We tracked a group nearby as they approached a building where more people emerged before heading to the next building. The group became a crowd which continued to grow. The gathering was either going to be the biggest bucket brigade in history or the incitement of a mob. I thought of the scene in *Blackhawk Down* where the Somalis burned tires and used cell phones to alert the people to rise up against the injured Americans. The radios were busy with a steady stream of frenzied chaos as they mobilized a quick reaction force (QRF).

By then it was dark and the crowd advanced toward the wreckage. There was no way for us to tell exactly where our friendly forces were, and we were almost out of gas. I decided the bucket brigade was wishful thinking and set up for a low fly-by.

We descended from our perch and zoomed down, avoiding the ground with the aid of our NVGs. I popped out flares as we performed our sneak pass directly above the mob and sent them scattering back into the neighborhoods. We hoped we bought them more time for the QRF to arrive. I later learned three Marines perished in that IED attack.

Soon, an attack of my own would force me to probe further into what it means to be alive and the significance of death.

---

[1] Publius Flavius Vegetius Renatus, tr. N.P. Milner, *Vegetius: Epitome of Military Science*, 2*nd* *Revised Ed.* (Liverpool: Liverpool University Press, 1993), 63.

CHAPTER 11

MORE THAN ATOMS

Al Asad Air Base, Iraq
February 2007

"... *[Man's] origin, his growth, his hopes and fears, his loves and his beliefs, are but the outcome of accidental collocations of atoms ...*"[1]

—BERTRAND RUSSELL

"*A human being is a collection of atoms in the same way that Shakespeare's plays are collections of words, or Beethoven's symphonies are collections of notes.*"[2]

—DINESH D'SOUZA

A FEW MISSIONS LATER, MY WSO tracked IED emplacers with our targeting pod. The four MAMs were casually walking down the city roads, unaware they were caught burying deadly explosives under the road and being monitored from above. We surveyed the surrounding area and looked for attack geometry that would minimize collateral damage.

Minimizing damage to the civilian populace was always a high concern. Some weapons were prohibited in certain areas and some attacks had to be aborted due to a sudden change in circumstances. One pilot was seconds away from firing on enemy insurgents when a group of unidentified individuals wandered into the scene. With only an instant to make a decision, he pulled off target without firing. I watched his video of the attack, wondering if I would have aborted.

The roads were lined by one and two-story structures closely spaced together. The men continued walking down the street as my wingman rolled in for a gun attack. I watched as the first bullets hit in the general area, but snaked off the road and up and around the buildings next to it. I winced as bullets impacted walls and roofs and hoped no one inside was injured. It was not the precision we had hoped for. The men, of course, began to run. Two of them split up and headed east while the other two stayed together.

We continued to track the pair and were approved to use another precision weapon. The two men tired from running and began a slow walk. They came to an open intersection next to a house and sat down on the dirt road. We launched a weapon. I fired the laser to mark the target and wondered if they could feel the energy as it pulsed on their bodies and the surrounding dirt. We watched in anticipation, hoping the weapon would not go stupid and veer off course. With ten seconds to impact I only hoped I wasn't screwing anything up. I double checked to make sure the laser was firing. Suddenly, both of their heads quickly turned to the south, as if they detected a strange noise or disturbance in the air. One second later, the missile exploded where they lay.

ONE INSTANT THEY WERE THERE, AND THE NEXT . . . GONE.

And then they were gone. One instant they were there, and the next . . . gone. We scanned the surrounding area. There was nothing left but a charred road. They had not escaped. There would be no running to a hospital. The heat and pressure from the exploding warhead had indiscriminately torn their atoms apart.

I felt relieved that the attack was successful. In peacetime, I reflect on questions of good and evil, justice and mercy, life and death, etc. . . . When a life is taken, whether by accident or intention, we should give pause and consider the circumstance, meaning, and eternal significance involved. We should think about the difference between killing, murder, capital punishment, and all out war. I carry the burden of recognizing these distinctions and wish for perfect justice and mercy in every case. We should be students of history and study man's propensity to wage war. We should strive to find the best ways to create a lasting peace. We should love our fellow man, and we should pray for our enemies.

However, in the midst of an attack there is little time for reflection. Military personnel must act under the tension of man's responsibility and God's sovereignty. I am confident that if we put our faith in him and study his word, it will become easier to seek and accept responsibility in accordance with his will.

One minute, the insurgents were alive. The next minute, they were dead. I wonder what the naturalist would make of the insurgents' new physical arrangement. If human beings are simply an accidental collocation of atoms that is dancing to its DNA,[*] what happens to our humanness when our DNA is spread to the winds? If what the naturalist believes is true—that we are not special, that we just happen to be— then we are no more special when our atoms are co-located than when they are not. On naturalism, being human has no intrinsic value. There would be no difference between killing and murder because the concept of innocence and guilt are dissolved by the universal acid of relativism.

IF THEISM IS TRUE . . . THEN WE ARE VERY SPECIAL INDEED.

On the other hand, if theism is true—if we have been intentionally designed with purpose and have intrinsic value from our identity as one of God's beloved children—then we are very special indeed. A God of justice and love will

---

[*] Deoxyribonucleic Acid; the "building blocks" of human life.

allow for free will and enact justice upon its misuse. Guilt and innocence are real concepts based on a morality measured from an absolute standard of moral perfection found only in the God of theism.

Things were becoming clear. My worldview was taking shape, and it was rising from a foundation based on Jesus Christ, not for need or want, but from the undeniable conclusions resulting from my decision to follow the truth wherever it led.

But my questions did not end, and my doubts remained. What are we to make of people who never get the chance to hear about Jesus? Is there a difference between murder and killing? What does it mean to be spiritually dead? I needed more answers, and I could not rest until I found them.

A MATTER OF TIME

It's natural to wonder, "What about those who have never heard about Jesus or the Gospel?" Romans 1:19-20 reveals that everyone has a chance to recognize God and acknowledge him: "What may be known about God is plain to them, because God has made it plain to them. For since the creation of the world God's invisible qualities—his eternal power and divine nature—have been clearly seen, being understood from what has been made, so that people are without excuse." This is known as general revelation and can be observed by every person via both internal and external phenomena. It is the reason why some people look up at the night sky with its sextillions of stars or marvel at the information evident in a molecule of DNA and conclude there must be a Designer of the universe and everything in it.

I had a conversation about this topic with one of my peers. We discussed the fairness of people dying before they accept Christ. One comment stood out: "They had their chance." On its face, this sounds callous and unloving, but

God places every person on this earth exactly where they are supposed to be. He knows who will accept his word and who will reject it. God places those who will accept the Gospel in a position to hear it. Similarly, those he knows will reject his Word may be placed where they never hear it. It is a legitimate question, but it is far from unanswerable. Unfortunately, confused and hyper-sensitive casualties of philosophical pluralism promote superficial platitudes at the expense of the most important idea worth spreading: the fact that truth is objective, knowable, and found in the person of Jesus Christ.

It is helpful to realize that God does not exist in time the way we do, for time itself had a beginning along with matter and space in the moment the universe came to be. Time also has an end. God exists in an unfathomable realm outside of time and space, yet by some mystery he can enter into time and interact with his creation. From his vantage point, he can "see" the entirety of the universe; the future as seen from our vantage point is already completed from his. Our existence (including the space time of the universe) is like a book with a beginning and an end. God wrote the book and it is a finished work; he knows the whole story. We are simply the characters bringing life to its pages, and sometimes his pages are ripped out before our story ends.

A DATE WITH DEATH

Who determines the appropriate time, age, and method of death? Why is it assumed that dying in your bed at the age of 80 is the only right way to die? What if most of those 80 years were filled with misery, injustice, and pain? Who decides a life should end a bit sooner? Even atheists know human life is special, although their worldview

EVEN ATHEISTS KNOW HUMAN LIFE IS SPECIAL, ALTHOUGH THEIR WORLDVIEW IMPLICATES OTHERWISE.

implicates otherwise. Only an all-knowing God with the authority to take the life which he has given can determine the time of death that will provide the greatest good, the least suffering, the most mercy, and the highest justice.

Can a Christian serve in the military where they may have to kill the enemy when one of the commandments says "Thou shalt not kill?" The word used in the original Hebrew text is *ratsach* and can refer to killing or murder. While some Bibles, such as the King James Version and the American Standard Version, translate Exodus 20:13 "Thou shalt not kill," most of today's top Bibles, including the *New King James Version, English Standard Version, New International Version, Holman Christian Standard Bible, New American Standard Bible, New Revised Standard Version, New Living Translation*, and *The Message,* all use the word "murder."

J. I. Packer, Christian theologian and Board of Governors' Professor of Theology at Regent College in Vancouver, British Columbia comments, "The word signifies malicious and unlawful killing, so 'murder' is more accurate. Judicial execution (e.g., for murder) and killing in war are not in view."[3] I have come to the same conclusion.

There are instances in the Bible where God sanctions killing. Capital punishment is addressed in the Book of Exodus, and killing in wartime is justified in the Book of Deuteronomy. Skeptics will point out that those are both books in the Old Testament. Surely the Jesus of the New Testament would never approve of killing another human being, would he? Romans, chapter 13 suggests an endorsement of capital punishment in the context of the government's authority to enact justice on evildoers. Regarding war, J. S. Feinberg, author of *Ethics for a Brave New World* expounds upon problems with understanding Jesus' teaching as staunchly pacifist:

A fundamental problem with pacifist interpretations of Jesus' teachings is the failure to distinguish between private and public duties, personal duties, and duties of a state. As a private individual I may turn the other cheek when unjustly attacked. However, my responsibilities are quite different when I stand in the position of a guardian of a third party as a civil magistrate or parent. Because I am responsible for their lives and welfare, I must resist, even with force, unjust aggression against them. Moreover, loving my neighbor or enemy does not mean I must stand idly by as my child is kidnapped and murdered. I am to use whatever force is necessary to protect his or her life and safety.[4]

It is easy to be a pacifist when you are on the sidelines. It's more difficult when your life is threatened—it must be unimaginable with a son or daughter in the hands of the enemy. If you wonder about the moral baggage service members must carry; or if you are a service member confused about the legitimacy of orders your President asks you to execute; you may rest knowing God in his wisdom has allowed us to act in order to prevent evil and promote the greater good, and sometimes that includes government sanctioned killing.

DEATH OF A DIFFERENT KIND

What happened to the four men than fled from the first car my wingman strafed? We may never know. What I do know is when you drag a human body through the street, you are guilty and deserve judgment. At the same time, I began to realize the sinful nature inside those men was the same sinful nature inside of me. Our sins were different, but the price we pay is the same, "For the wages of sin is death, but the gift of God is eternal life in Christ Jesus our Lord" (Rom. 6:23).

Their death was physical. Mine was spiritual. After spending time in the Word and with the Church, I was getting the impression that my condition was much, much worse.

Luke gives us a sobering reminder: "Do not be afraid of those who kill the body and after that can do no more. But I will show you whom you should fear: Fear him who, after your body has been killed, has authority to throw you into hell" (Luke 12:4-5).

Their story was over. My story will end, too. The character of Kazim, protector of the Holy Grail in *Indiana Jones and the Last Crusade* said something to Dr. Jones in the face of death we should all reflect upon: "My soul's prepared. How's yours?"[5]

A leader with an unexamined worldview will lack both the confidence to assert his beliefs and the authority to defend them. He will avoid absolutes and fear hypocrisy. He will lack consistency and avoid transparency, a quality which can only reveal an embarrassing lack of substance. He will demure from the hard stance because he's not sure it's the right stance, and his lack of conviction will yield an inappropriate desire for popularity, hurting himself, his organization, and his mission.

To become a better leader, a better spouse, and a better parent, you must first discover what is true. Then you must learn how to detect what is false. The world is full of lies: all religions are basically the same, Christians are anti-education, humans are just animals, sex is not sacred, and drunkenness is harmless. Your worldview will inform your judgments on these notions and more. Right and wrong exist, and the world, while sometimes grey, still has poles of black and white.

Be not deceived.

---

[1] Bertrand Russell, "A Free Man's Worship," Philosophical Society.com. accessed April 11, 2013, http://www.philosophicalsociety.com/Archives/A%20Free%20Man's%20Worship.htm.

[2] Dinesh D'Souza, *What's So Great About Christianity* (Washington, DC: Regnery Publishing Inc., 2007), Kindle ed., loc. 3763.

[3] J. I. Packer, *Growing in Christ* (Wheaton: Crossway Books, 1996), 258–259.

[4] J. S. Feinberg, P. D Feinberg, and A. Huxley, *Ethics for a Brave New World* (Wheaton: Crossway Books, 1996), 356.

[5] *Indiana Jones and the Last Crusade*, directed by Steven Spielberg (1989; Hollywood, CA: Paramount Home Video, 2003), DVD.

PART II

BE NOT
DECEIVED

CHAPTER 12

GOOD-TO-GO

San Antonio, Texas
June 2001

"Man is naturally good."[1]

—JEAN-JACQUES ROUSSEAU

"There is no one who does good, not even one" (Rom.
3:12).

—THE APOSTLE PAUL

YOUR UNDERSTANDING OF MAN'S humanity and God's divinity
will have a major impact on your worldview development.
How can people made in the image of a perfect God become
so perfectly wretched? When investigating Christianity, it is
important you understand some traditional qualities
attributed to the God of the Bible in order to make an
informed opinion about his existence.

To do this we must seek to know God through his
revelation. In order to arrive at a true knowledge of God, we
must pray without ceasing, study Scripture, and learn from
the saints who have devoted their lives to revealing his glory.

THE NATURE OF GOD

Christians believe God is good and the source of all things,
but you may still have questions about believing in an
invisible god. If you have ever asked, "How could a loving

God [insert action here]," this section is for you. Before going all-in on a worldview, it is important to understand the attributes of your deity. Norman Geisler's four-volume work *Systematic Theology* is an excellent resource for this topic. This section will reference Volume II which deals with God and Creation. According to orthodox teaching, God is simple, necessary, immutable (unchanging), infinite (limitless), omniscient (all-knowing), and perfect. This is not an exhaustive list, but it will suffice to illustrate God's worthship, and therefore, justification for Christian worship.

GOD'S SIMPLICITY

Think about the competing ideas about God in the spiritual market place:

Your pastor says there is one God (monotheism).

Your yoga instructor says everything is God (pantheism).

Your life coach says the world is part of God (panentheism).

Your shaman friend tells you there are many gods (polytheism).

Your favorite author says there is no God (atheism).

Your neighbor says God exists but does not interact with the natural world (deism).

Your therapist claims God is in you (autotheism).

Discerning truth with such a variety of claims is difficult. But God used Peter to give us a clear warning:

But there were also false prophets among the people, just as there will be false teachers among you. They will secretly introduce destructive heresies, even denying the sovereign Lord who bought them—bringing swift destruction on themselves. Many will follow their depraved conduct and will bring the way of truth into disrepute. In their greed these teachers will exploit you with fabricated stories. Their condemnation has long been hanging over them, and their destruction has not been sleeping (2 Pet. 2:1-3).

Wouldn't it be simpler—if God was simple?

When you think of God, you might think of the most mysterious, incomprehensible, and unfathomably complex being in existence. Mysterious? Yes. Incomprehensible? Frequently. However, a bit of logic will show us that for everything else God is, he is also a simple being. The word simple means to be without parts. God's simplicity follows from his Pure Actuality. God is complete and pure actualization. That means he lacks any kind of potentiality. There is no area where God needs work, and there is nothing he lacks. Everything God could be, he already is.

If he lacks potentiality, then he lacks the potential to be divided. This also follows from his immutability (unchangeability). If he cannot change, he cannot be divided. Since "simple" means without parts, and God cannot be divided into parts, he must be a simple being. When we understand God as a simple being, we avoid illogical assumptions about his nature. God's simplicity rules out polytheism, pantheism, and panentheism.

GOD'S NECESSITY

"This is the way it has to be." That line might come at the end of a romantic comedy, but in the context of God's existence, it is quite profound:

Question: when does something have to be a certain way?

Answer: when it is impossible to be any other way.

Norman Geisler explains: "A necessary Being is one whose non-existence is impossible."[2] God's necessity follows from several other attributes. If God exists and he is unchangeable, then he must always have existed and cannot cease to exist. Entering into or out of being

IF OUR UNDERSTANDING OF GOD'S NATURE IS CORRECT, THEN HE CANNOT *NOT* EXIST.

would constitute a change. This also follows from the fact that God is an uncaused being. Beings that are caused are called contingent; they can either exist or not exist, contingent on the condition from which their causality is based.

If God is an uncaused being and he exists, he must exist necessarily. Finally, God's necessity follows from his pure actuality. If God fails to have the potential to not exist, then he must necessarily exist. If our understanding of God's nature is correct, then he cannot *not* exist.[3] God's necessity rules out atheism.

GOD'S IMMUTABILITY

How are people different from God? People change, but God does not. While God's immutability may not be absolute as Greek philosophy implies, his immutability is certain in at least six areas: in his life, character, truth, ways, purpose, and his Son.[4] Dr. William Lane Craig expounds upon this on his *Reasonable Faith* website article on the "Doctrine of God: Part 10."

In order for something to change, it must have the potential to change. Since God lacks potentiality, he cannot change. This also follows from his simplicity, necessity, and perfection. People change their minds, and they change their hearts. God's "heart" never changes. Knowing God is immutable should allow you to confidently put your trust in him. His love is an unchanging love, an unfailing love.

GOD'S INFINITY

"My dad's the strongest."

"No, my dad's the strongest."

"My dad's the strongest times ten!"

"My dad's the strongest times ten-thousand."

"My dad's the strongest times infinity!"

We learn about infinity at an early age. Infinity is the ultimate argument winner (until you get to infinity plus one). God's infinity means he is without limits. People, however, are severely limited in the physical realm. We breathe only gas, our muscles lift limited amounts of weight, and our body lives for a finite period.

In the non-physical realm we can begin to see infinity working in our lives. A father of six has limited time with his children, but his love for them is immeasurable. When we gaze at the stars, it is easy to imagine the infinite heavens above where our tables await. Dr. Geisler explains, "Infinity is what describes each of God's attributes including his power, knowledge, justice, and love. This is why the Bible uses the heavens to help us grasp the infinite height of God's love."[5] When you understand that God does not have any limitations, you can avoid wild goose chases about what God can and cannot do.

GOD'S OMNISCIENCE

Nobody likes a know-it-all, but with God we should make an exception. If it is possible for a being to know everything, and a being exists who does know everything, then that would be the only being worth worshiping. God has knowledge of the past, present, and future. This follows from

God's infinity since a god without limits cannot have limited knowledge.

God knows who will believe and who will not, who will fall away from the faith and who will return, and who will stare death in the face before accepting his gift of life. No one can fully comprehend the complexity of the universe God designed. When you want to learn how to use a computer program, you do not seek help from the end-users trying to figure it out as they go. You go to the source—the omniscient programmer—for answers.

GOD'S OMNIPOTENCE

To say that God is omnipotent is to say that God can do whatever it is possible to do. When we describe God as Almighty, we are referring to his unlimited power. God's omnipotence follows from his infinity, Pure Actuality, and simplicity. God does not have power, he is power. Therefore, power is not something he could lack. He is power, simply, actually, and without limits.[6]

When you have a problem at work, to whom do you turn? You probably have a structured staff with a hierarchy. In the military, it is called a chain of command. Problems are vetted through the supervisor at the next level up. If the supervisor cannot fix your problem, then your grievance is forwarded further up the chain. Up it continues until reaching someone with the authority, knowledge, and power to solve it.

You would probably rather avoid the bureaucracy and address the Chief Executive Officer (CEO) directly. Why bother with a chain of command when you know the CEO can solve your problem immediately?

That system would work wonderfully for you, but your CEO would become swamped with extra duties. It is not the most effective use of their time and it gives them additional responsibilities. God is like the CEO of the universe. He has ultimate authority, knowledge, and power, except he never gets swamped; he has all the time in the world (literally); and his ability to handle additional responsibilities is limitless.

A common tactic to challenge God's omnipotence is to ask a question involving a logical impossibility such as "can God create a stone so heavy he can't lift it?" This example results from a misunderstanding of omnipotence which deals with the realm of what is *actually* possible. Logical impossibilities are exempt. People arguing against God's omnipotence on illogical grounds are not right; they are not even wrong. They are confused.

GOD'S PERFECTION

There is only one way to describe a being with the power to speak the universe into existence, the knowledge to create the best of all possible worlds, the wisdom to ensure ultimate justice prevails, the mercy to exhibit unconditional love, and the grandeur of a limitless nature: perfect.

The word "perfect" is frequently understood to mean without blemish or imperfections. While that is true of God, he also embodies another kind of perfection. The Bible often uses the word "perfect" to mean "complete." What could be more complete than a being who exists with no beginning and no end? Incompleteness requires time. However, God existed before he created time. Anything God could be, he already was, currently is, and will forever be. He is perfect in every sense of the word.

It is one thing to think about what it means to be complete. It is another thing to feel complete. Before I learned about God's perfection, I was interested in another being. I didn't know much when I got married (not much has changed), but once we both said, "I do," I knew we were complete. Marriage helps us learn to love another person more than ourselves. It teaches us how to think of someone else first, to compromise, and to deny the natural selfishness which suffocates relationships. The Bible compares the relationship between Christ and the church to a bridegroom and his bride. Christ is the bridegroom and he loves the church with unfailing devotion. The church (body) is his bride, and we are to shower him with adoration and submit to his authority. This is the relationship prescribed for us through his special revelation.

ONLY WHEN WE RECOGNIZE OUR OWN BROKENNESS WILL WE SEE THE NEED FOR A SAVIOR.

Yet something keeps us from attaining this perfect ideal. We cannot function the way God intended for us to function. While our actions convey purity, our thoughts remain defiled by sin. Only when we recognize our own brokenness will we see the need for a savior; and only a savior who is eternal, righteous, and good can adequately address questions about origins, meaning, morality, and destiny.

The Apostle Paul comments on our nature in Romans 3:10-12: "There is no one righteous, not even one; there is no one who understands; there is no one who seeks God. All have turned away, they have together become worthless; there is no one who does good, not even one." He continues about our inability to stay good in Romans 7:15-24:

> I do not understand what I do. For what I want to do I do not do, but what I hate I do. And if I do what I do not want to do, I agree that the law is good. As it is, it is no longer I myself who do it, but it is sin living in me. For I know that good itself does not dwell in me, that is, in my sinful nature. For I have the desire to do what is good, but I cannot carry it out. For I do not do the good I want to do, but the evil I do not want to do—this I keep on doing. Now if I do what I do not want to do, it is no longer I who do it, but it is sin living in me that does it. So I find this law at work: Although I want to do good, evil is right

there with me. For in my inner being I delight in God's law; but I see another law at work in me, waging war against the law of my mind and making me a prisoner of the law of sin at work within me. What a wretched man I am! Who will rescue me from this body that is subject to death?

American pastor and author John MacArthur further testifies to man's brokenness and warns of a diluted Gospel message:

I am convinced that the popular evangelistic message of our age actually lures people into this deception. It promises a wonderful, comfortable plan for everyone's life. It obliterates the offense of the cross (cf. 1 Cor. 1:23; Gal. 5:11). Though it presents Christ as the way, the truth, and the life, it says nothing of the small gate or the narrow way. Its subject is the love of God, but there is no mention of God's wrath. It sees people as deprived, not depraved. It is full of love and understanding, but there is no mention of a holy God who hates sin. There is no summons to repentance, no warning of judgment, no call for brokenness, no expectation of a contrite heart, and no reason for deep sorrow over sin. It is a message of easy salvation, a call for a hasty decision, often accompanied by false promises of health, happiness, and material blessing. This is not the gospel according to Jesus.[7]

In *The End of Reason: A Response to the New Atheists*, Dr. Ravi Zacharias comments: "Though the sacred is offered to us, the will is arrogant and refuses to submit to God's authority. No one of us is any different from or better than any other; some just mask their true nature better."[8]

One way to handle a problem is to identify it, understand it, and work to remedy it. Another way is to ignore the problem by redefining it as illusory or non-problematic. The latter is used rampantly in New Age circles and by high priests of the "New Spirituality." Dr. Zacharias continues:

> Everyone knows that Karl Marx said that religion is the opiate of the people. But very few go on to finish what he said next; that it is the sigh of the oppressed and the illusory sun that revolves around man as long as man doesn't revolve around himself. The New Spirituality has solved that dilemma. We have found a religion that has helped us to revolve around ourselves, and once we have believed that the spiritual imagination needs no boundaries because we are gods, everything else becomes plausible and nothing needs justification.[9]

Believing we are good because we are not as bad as other people—or worse, believing we are divine—will lead to a worldview void of coherence, consistency, and correspondence to human experience.

BEFORE THE FALL

Although we desire to be good, we are capable of great evil. How often do you wish to be content but find yourself coveting your neighbor's things? You want to be positive but harbor hatred toward others. You vow for the hundredth time to keep your thoughts pure only to fail at the first glimpse of temptation. This is the sentiment Paul explained in Romans 7 (I want to do "X," but instead I do "Y"). While the first humans entered into a good creation, the rest of us were born into something less.

The Bible is clear: humans were a part of his perfect creation deemed "very good" on the sixth day. Adam and Eve thrived in the garden without shame. Adam heard the voice of the Lord and walked with him in righteousness. Eve was the perfect helpmate—a match made in heaven. They tended to the garden without fear, guilt, or insecurity.

However, they had one perfect gift from God which, if misused, could ruin everything: free will.

The reality of free will is debated philosophically, but it is hard to deny experientially. Could your decision to continue reading this book or throw it out the window really be the end of a thoughtless chain reaction beginning with the Big Bang? A world without free will is a world without responsibility—hardly an accurate depiction of our society where the rule of law demands consequences for human action.

The gift of free will allows us to choose whether or not to obey God's commands. Until Adam and Eve received the knowledge of good and evil, their decisions were free but without moral consideration. They could choose wrongly, but they literally could do no evil. The first sin became a sin nature—a flawed inheritance received by us all. In the Christian worldview, man was originally created good. We brought the burden of sin upon ourselves. In the Garden, it was one strike and you're out. With sin came shame and the promise of death. Fortunately, it was not "game-over" in the mind of God. He had a plan for redemption.

WHAT ABOUT THE CLAIMS THAT CHRISTIANITY IS NOT ONLY RIDICULOUS, BUT HARMFUL?

The Christian worldview acknowledges man's desires to be good in spite of his tendencies to be selfish. Selfishness has been described as the root of all sin. Charles Spurgeon said, "Beware of no man more than of yourself; we carry our worst enemies within us." There is only one being who is good: Almighty God.

But what about the claims that Christianity is not only ridiculous, but harmful? Is religion the cause of all major wars? Are Christians anti-education? Is science the enemy of faith? Sometimes myths, like children, need to be put to bed.

It's bedtime.

[1] Jean-Jacques Rousseau, tr. by Ian Johnston, *Discourse on the Sciences and the Arts* (Arlington: Richer Resources Publications, 2014), Kindle ed., loc. 1786.

[2] Norman Geisler, *Systematic Theology*, vol. 2, *God Creation* (Minneapolis: Bethany House, 2003), 64.

[3] Ibid., 65.

[4] William Lane Craig, "Doctrine of God (part 10)," Reasonablefaith.com, accessed October 19, 2013, http://www.reasonablefaith.org/defenders-2-podcast/transcript/s3-10.

[5] Geisler and Turek, *I Don't Have Enough Faith to Be an Atheist*, loc. 2006.

[6] Ibid., 158-161.

[7] John F. MacArthur, *The Gospel According to Jesus* (Grand Rapids: Zondervan, 2008), 186.

[8] Ravi Zacharias, *The End of Reason: A Response to the New Atheists* (Grand Rapids, Michigan: Zondervan, 2008), 58-59.

[9] Ravi Zacharias, *Why Jesus? Rediscovering His Truth in an Age of Mass Marketed Spirituality* (New York: Faith Words, 2012), 10.

CHAPTER 13
SPLASHING MYTHS

Marine Corps Air Station Miramar, California
May 2006

*"Because there is a law like gravity, the universe can and
will create itself from nothing."[1]*

—STEPHEN HAWKING

*"In the beginning God created the heavens and the earth"
(Gen. 1:1).*

—MOSES

I WAS LOW ON MISSILES and we already lost one fighter. We managed to hold back the first wave of enemy aircraft, but air intercept control (AIC) was already calling out more groups. There was no time to mourn for Dash-4; he made a tactical error and paid the price. Marine aviation is not unsafe, but it is unforgiving. We'd have to finish the mission as a three-ship.

Our mission was to defend the carrier strike group (CSG), and I was in charge of the division. We found another group on our radar and received positive confirmation it was hostile—mostly likely a pair of MiGs.[*] Each pilot pulled the

---

[*] Aircraft designed by the Russian Aircraft Corporation MiG (Mikoyan and Gurevich).

trigger, igniting the launch-motors of our AMRAAMs (Advanced Medium Range Air-to-Air Missile) and sending them off the rails toward the enemy fighters. I followed the smoke trail of my missile until it disappeared from view. In a few moments, we would potentially be engaged with multiple fighters, where the struggle for an advantage becomes less a numbers game, and more the reward of mastering the art and skill of aerial combat.

I looked out to where I expected to see a small dot gradually expanding—the visual signature of an aircraft at long range. In that vicinity, an orange flash birthed a black smoke cloud which hung in mid air.

"Splash-one!" I called over the radio. Several more fireballs followed, accompanied by splash calls from my wingmen indicating our air-to-air targets had been destroyed. The enemy was dead, and the blood was on our hands. But the CSG was protected. We completed our mission.

We received no air medals for our action that day. It was all part of routine simulator training aboard Marine Corps Air Station Miramar.

ASKING QUESTIONS

The night Karry asked me about death found my heart in fertile soil. I was fortunate never to have a hatred or contempt for God; I just never bothered to give it any thought. After deciding it deserved some serious contemplation, I started going to church. I read Lee Strobel's *The Case for Faith* and felt an immediate connection with this former atheist and legal affairs editor of the Chicago Tribune who investigates the claims of Christianity. Here are a few assumptions that were challenged as I conducted my own investigation:

> Don't you have to check your brain at the door to believe in God?

Aren't religions like Christianity anti-science?

Doesn't religion cause most major wars and conflicts?

Didn't Darwin kill God?

Isn't the existence of a loving God improbable given the amount of evil and suffering in the world?

Isn't all that God and Jesus stuff kind of feminine?

Miracles? Come on . . .

SCIENCE: A FRIEND OF GOD

The idea that Darwin has called "splash-one!" at a merge with God (i.e. God is dead) was popularized by Nietzsche in his work *Thus Spake Zarathustra*. Those who have taken the theory of evolution as the ultimate meta-narrative believe scientific theories will eventually fill our gaps in understanding—gaps that the masses fill with God. This has resulted in a sentiment that science and religion are strange bedfellows. Nothing could be further from the truth.

Christians understand God as the creator of everything including the natural world, the laws of physics that govern it, and the field of science which studies it. If this is true, Christians have nothing to fear from scientific discovery, for it will inevitably confirm what he has already revealed to us. This is captured in the Roman Catholic Catechism:

Though faith is above reason, there can never be any real discrepancy between faith and reason. Since the same God who reveals mysteries and infuses faith has bestowed the light of reason on the human mind, God cannot deny himself, nor can truth ever contradict truth. Consequently, methodical research in all branches of knowledge, provided it is carried out in a truly scientific manner and does not override moral laws, can never conflict with the faith, because the things of the world and the things of faith derive from the same God. The humble and persevering investigator of the secrets of nature is being led, as it were, by the hand of God in spite of himself, for it is God, the conserver of all things, who made them what they are.[2]

So far the track record is good. Scripture tells us the universe had a beginning. Genesis 1 says "In the beginning, God created the heavens and the earth." This means the universe is not eternal; it had a beginning. Previously, the idea of an eternal universe was popular in scientific and academic communities. Many were content to believe that the universe always *was* and had no need to find a cause for its existence. But by the late 20th century, scientists made revealing discoveries which pointed undeniably to a beginning. One widely accepted theory is known as the "Big Bang." Norman Geisler and Frank Turek display several lines of evidence that point to this conclusion in *I Don't Have Enough Faith to Be an Atheist.*

The Second Law of Thermodynamics says that systems always progress from a state of order to disorder and the usable energy decreases. If the universe was eternal, enough time should have already passed for the usable energy to be fully depleted, which is not the case. The confirmation that the universe is expanding (and accelerating) allows scientists to theoretically trace the expansion backwards to a point so dense and infinitely small that it is mathematically nothing. Logically prior to this point, matter, space, and time do not exist. The discovery of cosmic background radiation (light and heat from the initial explosion) in 1965 confirmed earlier predictions of the Big Bang theory, as did the discovery of temperature variation "ripples" in 1992 by NASA's Cosmic Background Explorer satellite. Finally, Einstein's theory of General relativity said that "time, space, and matter were co-relative and demanded an absolute beginning."[3]

For the last forty years, the Big Bang theory has been widely accepted as a powerful explanation for scientific discoveries in cosmology. But evidence that the universe had a

ANYTHING WITH A BEGINNING REQUIRES A BEGIN-ER.

beginning (and is not past eternal) makes some scientists squeamish. Anything with a beginning requires a begin-er. The ancient philosophers recognized this fact and engaged in much discourse on postulating a First Cause for the universe. According to theists, God is the uncaused cause and the only agent capable of such an act of creation.

Christianity teaches the universe was created *ex nihilo,* or "out of nothing," from the spoken Word of God. Secularists often claim that the universe was created "out of nothing, from nothing." However, it's hard to disagree with Fräulein Maria's lyrical counter-argument: "Nothing comes from nothing, nothing ever could . . ."

Stephen Hawking and Leonard Mlodinow attempt to support creation "from nothing" in their book *The Grand Design.* They conclude, "Because there is a law like gravity, the *universe can and will create itself from nothing.* . . . Spontaneous creation is the reason there is something rather than nothing, why the universe exists, why we exist. It is not necessary to invoke God to light the blue touch paper and set the universe going."[4] (Italics mine.) Hawking and Mlodinow posit the existence of a quantum vacuum prior to creation. However, as Dr. William Lane Craig explains, "The quantum vacuum . . . [from which spontaneous creation supposedly arises] is not nothing."[5] (Brackets mine.) The quantum vacuum is something: it is a quantum vacuum. The field of quantum theory has become the great equalizer of pseudo-science, providing interpretations of reality to suit every personal fantasy.

In the second chapter of Genesis, the Bible says "the LORD God formed a man from the dust of the ground and breathed into his nostrils the breath of life, and the man became a living being." Advances in technology and microbiology have shown that at the molecular level man and the earth are made of the same stuff consisting of elements, molecules, particles, and atoms.

Werner Gitt is a former engineering professor at Germany's national institute for natural and engineering sciences and offers intriguing insight from Genesis 2 in his book *In the Beginning Was Information*: "Man does not consist of matter only, but he received a vital non-material component, a spirit, through God's breath. . . . He became a living being through the union of the material and the nonmaterial parts."[6] Science can identify the "dust," but identifying and explaining the spirit lay outside its strictly physical domain.

The post-Enlightenment retreat by some Christians from the academic battlefield was unwarranted. Unfounded fears that science and education threatened God's existence harmed Christianity's reputation as a rational worldview. Today in the tug-of-war between Biblical Christianity and secular atheism, Christian pastors, philosophers, and theologians are pulling the flag back towards center with increasing momentum.

Antony Flew was one of Britain's most famous atheists whose influence spanned over five decades. His paper "Theology and Falsification" is described as "the most widely reprinted philosophical publication of the last century."[7] In 2007, he changed his mind:

As I see it, five phenomena are evident in our immediate experience that can only be explained in terms of the existence of God. These are, first, the rationality implicit in all our experience of the physical world; second, life, the capacity to act autonomously; third, consciousness, the ability to be aware; fourth, conceptual thought, the power of articulating and understanding meaningful symbols such as are embedded in language; and, fifth, the human self, the "center" of consciousness, thought, and action.[8]

Only a precommitment to naturalism demands a rejection of God. Science by definition describes the natural world, but it does not follow that the natural world is all there is. It is simply the only thing science has to work with.

RELIGION MEANS WAR, OR DOES IT?

Is religion the cause of most wars? I certainly thought so as I lay in bed wondering whether or not to begin exploring this particular religion called Christianity. Those making a case against religion are quick to point to the Crusades, the Middle East, and conflict in Northern Ireland to support their claim. But religion is not the root cause for why these violent clashes occur. Christian apologist and author of *What's So Great About Christianity* Dinesh D'Souza explains the Crusades as a response to Islamic imperialism:

Muhammad's armies conquered Jerusalem and the entire Middle East. They then pushed south into Africa, east into Asia, and north into Europe. They conquered parts of Italy and most of Spain, overran the Balkans, and were preparing for a final incursion that would bring all of Europe, then known as Christendom, under the rule of Islam. . . . In the eleventh century the Christians attempted to recover the heartland of Christianity and defend it against militant Islam. These efforts are now called the Crusades . . . [and] can be seen as a belated, clumsy, and unsuccessful effort to defeat Islamic imperialism.[9] (Brackets mine.)

As D'Souza has commented in various podcast debates, Muslims and Christians were not fighting over whether Muhammad was a greater prophet than Jesus. The conflict arose from the physical expansion and conquest of invading armies. "In

THE MOST HEINOUS ATROCITIES COMMITTED IN THE 20TH CENTURY WERE COMMITTED IN THE NAME OF ATHEISM.

the same vein, the Protestants and Catholics in Northern Ireland aren't fighting about transubstantiation or some point of religious doctrine. They are fighting over issues of autonomy and over which group gets to rule the country,"[10] writes D'Souza. Regarding the clashes in Iraq and the Balkans, he notes that these are ethnic rivalries engaged in a power struggle.

On the contrary, the most heinous atrocities committed in the 20th century (the bloodiest century in the history of man) were committed in the name of atheism. D'Souza points out that though Hitler used Christian rhetoric to manipulate his public image, he was an atheist convinced that social Darwinism was the path to a superior race of man. With no God to whom he must answer, he killed ten million people in pursuit of this Nietzschean ideal. Stalin killed around twenty million people in Communist Russia after rejecting his religious upbringing, and Buddhist-turned-atheist Mao Zedong killed over seventy million of his own people in China.[11] The underlying causes of sectarian violence are often rooted in power struggles, ethnic rivalries, and political division.

The accusation that religion is the cause of most wars is oversimplified and uninformed.

THE PROBLEM OF EVIL

Those attempting to disprove the existence of God often raise the problem of evil and suffering. Watching children suffer at the hands of selfish adults invokes a strong emotional response. When thousands perish in natural disasters, it's natural to wonder how a loving God could allow such tragedies. No one can diminish the pain of losing a loved one, but if you can understand why God might allow these events to occur, then you might not so quickly reject the other One you have loved.

Augustine and Thomas Aquinas both addressed the problem of evil. They explained evil as the result of God's perfect creatures freely choosing wrong acts. Free choice is a good attribute given to us by God. God did not create evil, but he allowed for the possibility of evil as a result of free choice.[12] God's creation remained perfect and without stain until the first man wrongly used his freedom by disobeying God's commands.

Evil can be defined as bad character or conduct. This reveals two things. First, "All questions about evil and suffering," Dr. Zacharias notes, "are raised *by* a person or *about* a person."[13] The implication is that good and evil cannot arise from a non-personal god or "god-source" or "All-That-Is" as pantheists believe. Second, evil is not a thing in itself; rather, it is dependent on the existence of good. Dr. Geisler likens evil to a wound. A wound is an injury to the body; therefore, it cannot exist without a body. Evil can only exist in contrast to what is known to be good. If evil really exists, then good must exist as something apart from evil. This argument disputes moral relativism

GOD DID NOT CREATE EVIL, ALTHOUGH HE ALLOWED FOR ITS POTENTIAL.

and defangs any claims that good and evil are identical or illusory.

The main point is that God did not create evil, although he allowed for its potential as an unfortunate byproduct of a maximally perfect attribute called free choice. It is human beings who actualized the potentiality of evil. G.K. Chesterton has described evil as "an invasion or yet more truly a rebellion,"[14] two acts that come not from God but from man's rejection of him.

Today secular humanism has actualized the potentiality of conflating good and evil. The results are given by Francis Schaeffer in *How Should We Then Live?*: "Modern humanistic man in both his secular and his religious forms has come to the same awful place. Both have no final way to say what is right and what is wrong, and no final way to say why one should choose non-cruelty instead of cruelty."[15]

HUME-OR ME

If you've taken Philosophy 101, you are sure to have heard of David Hume. The 18th century Scottish philosopher's *An Enquiry Concerning Human Understanding* remains the bunker from which naturalists grab ammunition for the assault against miracles. "Miracles? Are you kidding? Haven't you read David Hume? Slam dunk. Case closed."

Hume defined a miracle as "a transgression of a law of nature by a particular volition of the Deity, or by the interposition of some invisible agent."[16] He argues that violations of the laws of nature would be so rare that it is always more reasonable to assume you are either being deceived by your senses, or the person giving the miraculous account is lying.

Lee Strobel addresses Hume's arguments during an interview with Dr. William Lane Craig in *The Case for Faith*. Dr. Craig defines a miracle as "an event which is not producible by the natural causes that are operative at the time and place that the event occurs."[17] He points out that arguments against miracles based on probability don't hold much weight. He uses a lottery analogy to point out that when a particular combination of numbered balls with an infinitesimally low probability of materializing is announced as the winning combination, we have no problem believing in that number combination.

Hume would say that since the odds of those numbers arriving in sequence are so unbelievably low, it is more reasonable that you are hallucinating those numbers, or that those numbers did not actually arrive in that sequence. You can extend this example to many scenarios. Hume makes it irrational to believe in anything with a low probability of happening.

"You just got hit by lightning!"

"Nah . . . it must be your imagination."

"Dude, you're smoking!"

"Whatever, man (cough). You must be lying to me. The chances of me getting struck by lightning this year are one in one million. Now help me find my other shoe."

This flies in the face of human experience. Dr. Frank Turek concludes that miracles "are not only possible; miracles are actual because the greatest miracle of all—the creation of the universe out of nothing—has already occurred."[18] Hume said a miracle was a transgression of a law of nature. Craig says it is an event that's not possible from natural causes operating at the time and place in question. Before the beginning of the universe (the singularity, the Big Bang, etc. . .), there was no *time*; there was no *place*. At the moment of creation, nature (and thus natural laws) did not exist. Therefore, the event of creation could not be produced by natural causes. This makes the creation of the universe a miracle by definition.

Perhaps the biggest miracle still occurring today is the explosive growth of Christianity. Believing that Jesus is the son of God and that he was raised from the dead is very unnatural. The notion that *natural* resurrection is possible, but has only happened to one person in the history of humanity, is ludicrous. If only natural causes were at work in the hearts and minds of seekers for the last 2,000 years, Christianity should have died shortly after Jesus.

But from the time of the early church fathers to modernity, people have believed in Jesus Christ and put their faith in him. Christians continue to preach the gospel

THE *SUPERNATURAL* RESURRECTION OF JESUS IS PERFECTLY RATIONAL.

throughout the world, and the Holy Spirit moves where two or more are gathered. The *supernatural* resurrection of Jesus is perfectly rational and the best explanation for events for which we do have knowledge. Establishing your stance on miracles deserves more than a default to the secular bias.

The world is full of misinformation and myths. Ignorance, not religion, is the enemy of truth, and you cannot shoot down a myth without preparation. But with training, you can properly identify a myth and engage it to destruction. After the flash, when the black cloud hangs where the lie once was, relax. If only under your breath, call out "splash-one!" You've made the world a better place.

I found plenty of adequate answers to debunk the myths surrounding Christianity. What remained were the myths about its followers, the Christians themselves. What are we to make of the unthinking Christian, the gullible Christian, the Christian merely fulfilling psychological needs? Simple: we make the Christian caricature. Rather, he is spoken into existence by his creators, filled with straw on the sixth day, and then burned to the ground every day thereafter.

It's time to help destroy the Christian caricature.

---

[1] Stephen Hawking and Leonard Mlodinow, *The Grand Design* (New York: Bantam Books, 2010), Kindle ed., loc. 1819.
[2] *Catechism of the Catholic Church*, Part One: The Profession of Faith, Sec. 1, Chap. 3, Article 1:III, 159, accessed December 19, 2014,

http://www.vatican.va/archive/ccc_css/archive/catechism/p1s1c3a1.
htm

[3] Norman L. Geisler and Frank Turek, *I Don't Have Enough Faith to Be an Atheist* (Wheaton: Crossway, 2004), loc. 1486.

[4] Stephen Hawking and Leonard Mlodinow, *The Grand Design* (New York: Bantam, 2010), Kindle ed., chap. 8.

[5] William Lane Craig, "Hawking's Curious Objections to Divine Creation," *Q&A with William Lane Craig #22*, Reasonable Faith, accessed April 24, 2013, http://www.reasonablefaith.org/hawkings-curious-objections-to-divine-creation.

[6] Werner Gitt, *In the Beginning Was Information* (Green Forrest: Master Books, 2005), Kindle ed., chap. 14.

[7] Antony Flew and Roy Abraham Varghese, *There Is a God* (New York: Harper Collins Inc., 2007) Kindle ed., preface, loc. 60-69.

[8] Ibid., 161.

[9] Dinesh D'Souza, *What's So Great About Christianity* (Washington D.C.: Regnery Publishing Inc., 2007), 205-206.

[10] Ibid., 210.

[11] Ibid., 214.

[12] Norman L. Geisler, *Baker Encyclopedia of Christian Apologetics* (Grand Rapids: Baker, 2009), 219.

[13] Ravi Zacharias, *Has Christianity Failed You?* (Grand Rapids: Zondervan, 2010), Kindle ed., chap. 4, loc. 1511.

[14] Gilbert K. Chesterton, *The Everlasting Man* (Radford: Wilder Publications, 2008), Kindle ed., loc. 3795.

[15] Francis A. Schaeffer, *How Should We Then Live? (L'Abri 50th Anniversary Edition): The Rise and Decline of Western Thought and Culture* (Wheaton: Crossway, 2005), Kindle ed., 178, chap. 9, loc. 1529.

[16] David Hume, *An Enquiry Concerning Human Understanding* (Public Domain, 1902), Kindle ed., loc. 2162-2163.

[17] Lee Strobel, *The Case for Faith: A Journalist Investigates the Toughest Objections to Christianity* (Grand Rapids: Zondervan, 2000), Kindle ed., loc. 1011-1012.

[18] Geisler and Turek, *I Don't Have Enough Faith to Be an Atheist*, loc. 3691.

CHAPTER 14

THE CHRISTIAN CARICATURE

Somewhere Off the California Coast
February 2005

"Faith can be very very dangerous, and deliberately to implant it into the vulnerable mind of an innocent child is a grievous wrong."[1]

—*RICHARD DAWKINS*

"Let the little children come to me, and do not hinder them, for the kingdom of heaven belongs to such as these" (Matt. 19:14).

—*JESUS*

BUT SMALL IS THE LANDING *zone and narrow the path that leads to the 3-wire, and only a few find it.*

It was my last shot at getting aboard the boat and I was about to blow it. One-quarter mile from the stern of the carrier (about three seconds from touchdown), the ball started rising toward the top of the lens. If I missed the cables with a bolter, I would have to divert to shore and complete my qualification the following night.

I quickly chopped the throttle back and then forward, increased my sink rate, and froze the meatball to stay on glide path. My muscles tensed the closer I got to the landing zone.

With one second to touchdown, the ball rose again. There was no time for power chops. I was about to bolter. The jet slammed onto the deck as I shoved the throttles forward to full afterburner.

Please catch a wire!

A fraction of a second later, the tailhook caught the cable strung out across the deck. The nose yawed slightly back and forth as the hookpoint slid toward the center of the cable and the jet lurched to a stop. I throttled back and glanced out over the water. I was awestruck by the magnitude of the moment: the movement of the carrier as it steamed through the moonlit ocean waves, this twenty-five-year-old pilot landing a Hornet on an aircraft carrier at night, plane captains conducting an orchestra of taxiing jets and folding wings, scurrying sailors and Marines over the din of whining turbines ripping the air. Few people will get such an opportunity.

SOMETHING MISSING

On that carrier, I realized my failures could not only cost my own life, but the lives of others as well. Until that point, life still felt like an extension of childhood. Although I had been married for four years, and had two children, my life was still self-centered.

It was not until that moment that I felt like a grown man. But even then, something was missing. I was bothered by a lingering thought that I was still inadequately prepared to be a father. Earlier, I thought I hadn't read enough books. It turns out my problem wasn't quantity, it was content. A canon of sixty-six books would eventually solve the mystery of my parental angst.

Every person has a different conversion experience. Chuck Colson, known as Richard Nixon's "hatchet man" during the Watergate scandal, opened his heart to Jesus after reflecting on a conversation with a Christian friend. US Navy

Seal and author Chad Williams had a dramatic experience during a church service and can tell you the day and moment that he was saved. The apostle Paul was literally struck blind on the road to Damascus and would from that moment on see the world with new eyes.

My conversion was not like any of these. It was a slow process. There was no smoking gun that allowed me to flip the belief switch to the "Christian" position. The decision to follow Christ came slowly as I studied his Word and read authors with talents for excising unfounded objections.

THE GREAT INFLUENCE

I noticed three things as I studied Christianity. First, there are more self-professed Christians in the world than I thought. Second, you would never know it unless they told you. And third, many Christians won't tell you. The recent surges in the campaign of secularists to eradicate displays of religious liberty from the public square has made it almost a crime to display a Christian faith.

SCIENCE CANNOT WEIGH IN ON THE SUPERNATURAL.

Some authors with naturalist assumptions have turned a love affair with the wonders science can explain into an obsession with the things it cannot. Although something supernatural may be responsible for science, science cannot weigh in on the supernatural. The finite natural world is a wonderful playground for the scientist. It's also wonderfully small when measured against an eternal, non-physical realm.

My first assumption about Christianity, or any religion for that matter, was the only way people could believe those things was if they suspended rational thought and took everything on blind faith (emphasis on the word blind). My religious biases were shaped mostly by movies and television. In the 80s and 90s, you could still catch re-runs of *Leave It to*

Beaver, *The Andy Griffith Show*, and *The Brady Bunch*, all of which seemed to promote incontrovertible values in an unambiguous way. These shows represent the idealism of their producers and a desire to show how people *should* think and act. But other shows portrayed different ideas about life, family, and religion.

Married with Children (which I was not allowed to watch) featured Al Bundy, a character who "disliked fat women, his neighbor, his job, and the prospect of having sex with his wife. He loved nudie magazines, nudie bars, and free beer."[2] His wife was "lazy, always on his case and spent most of her time parked in front of the TV watching talk shows such as Oprah or robbing Al blind to go shopping."[3] His daughter was a promiscuous "dumb blond" and his son, Bud, was named after beer and preoccupied with sex. In contrast to the shows mentioned in the previous paragraph, the Bundy family represented the way many people *actually* think and act.

The Simpsons contributed to Christian stereotypes via the character of Ned Flanders. I have a special place in my heart for this show. In more than a few school pictures you will find Bart's jagged-haired profile adorning my t-shirt (don't blame my mother; she didn't know when it was picture day). The show is funny, intelligent, and operates on multiple levels. William Irwin along with other philosophers conducts a thorough analysis of what draws us to the show and its characters in *The Simpsons and Philosophy: The D'oh! Of Homer*. Raja Halwani writes of Homer: "Homer is a habitual liar . . . [and] lacks sensitivity to the needs of others; he seems to lack both benevolence and justice. . . . He's not inclined towards generosity. . . . It is something of a problem even to claim that Homer has goals and activities, other than drinking, that is."[4]

The character of Lisa is deconstructed in the context of understanding American anti-intellectualism and the "American ambivalence about expertise and rationality" as she is mocked for her intelligence and sophistication.[5] Bart is analyzed as a candidate for the Nietzchean *Übermensch*, though this notion is ultimately rejected for a more simple evaluation as one who "defines himself in opposition to authority."[6]

THE CHRISTIAN CARICATURE

But I want to focus on Ned. He is a Christian described as over-bearing, naïve, and ever-preaching. He "consults religious authorities and scriptures to settle every dilemma he faces, from those concerning morality and ethics to those about fashion and breakfast cereal."[7] His "adherence to divine command theory" and bothersome consultations with the Reverend Lovejoy for mundane decisions prompts responses such as, "Ned, have you thought about one of the other major religions? They're all pretty much the same."[8] He asks God for explanations confessing, "I've done everything the Bible says; even the stuff that contradicts the other stuff!" and his faith is described as "as blind as it is complete."[9] Homer treats Flanders "in indecent ways, ranging from indifference to disdain."[10] Flanders' pesky portrayal easily makes you want to scream "don't have a cow, man!" and his goody-two-shoes, whistling-dixie, hi-diddley-ooskey persona invites mockery on every occasion.

Flanders undermines his reasoning with blind and automatic misapplications of Biblical principles. In these failures, he represents how many real world Christians are, rather than how they should be, and is rightfully portrayed as empty-minded and un-cool. I know one officer who was given the callsign "Flanders" for being devout in his faith. Some pilot cliques refer to Christians as the "God squad," and aircrew who refuse to debase themselves are called "leaf eaters" by some overbearing (and usually senior) "meat eaters."

Popular movies portray Christians as zealous, nut-job whackos. In the 2001 movie *Contact*, it is the religious zealot who sabotages the launch platform with a suicide vest. In *Indiana Jones and the Temple of Doom*, the villain is a member of a religious cult that practices human sacrifice. And the movie poster for Steve Martin's portrayal of a fraudulent Christian "healer" in *Leap of Faith* sported the subtitle: "Real Miracles, sensibly priced."

Show these movies to a kid without worldview guidance and they end up thinking anyone who joins a group that believes in a higher power must be dumb, gullible, or just plain crazy.

I HAD A HARD TIME SEEING HOW ANYONE COULD BE AN INTELLECTUALLY FULFILLED THEIST.

One thing was certain: no one with half a brain could believe in a god that is untraceable, all-powerful, perfect, omniscient, and allows suffering. Based on such grand and seemingly contradictory attributes, I had a hard time seeing how anyone could be an intellectually fulfilled theist.

To the secular ear, nothing rings "anti-intellectual" louder than a Christian's skepticism of evolution. The Christian *caricature* rejects all forms of evolution and embraces Creationism with delusional flamboyance. But the real Christian has good intellectual reasons to question the scope of macro-evolution's explanatory power.

BLIND FAITH IN A POPULAR THEORY

Evolutionary biologist Richard Dawkins speaks of a dissatisfaction with atheism in the *The Blind Watchmaker* resulting from "inadequate explanations for the complexity of life prior to 1859 when Darwin's *Origin of Species* was first published."[11] He states, "Although atheism might have been *logically* tenable before Darwin, Darwin made it possible to be an intellectually fulfilled atheist."[12] But not everyone finds Darwin's theory of evolution so all-encompassing. Dinesh

D'Souza suggests that the design evident in both life and the universe is not an illusion, as Dawkins suggests, but the work of a Designer.

Evolution, whose primary mechanism is death, cannot explain the origins of life. As D'Souza puts it, "Evolution seems right as far as it goes, but it doesn't go very far."[13] Writer, physicist, and Arizona State University professor Paul Davies displays a common precommitment to naturalism as he investigates the origins of life: "Even the simplest bacterium is so immensely complex it strains credulity to imagine such an entity popping into existence wholly as a result of the random shuffling of molecules. Yet clearly *there must exist a pathway of physical processes* that leads from simple chemicals to complex life."[14] (Italics mine.)

Though he is overwhelmed by the complexity of biology (implying possible evidence of design), he forces himself to accept the credulity-straining position that somehow life can arise from non-life. No scientist can truly "follow the evidence wherever it leads" if they ignore the metaphysical path that must be taken to explain the origins of first life and the universe.

Neither can evolution explain the apparent "fine tuning" of the universe. Science has shown us that certain forces in our universe must have their current values in order for the universe to continue its expansion and keep from collapsing. Physicist and atheist Stephen Hawking gives an example using the expansion rate of the universe: "If the rate of expansion one second after the Big Bang had been smaller by even one part in a hundred thousand million million, the universe would have recollapsed before it even reached its present size."[15] These

IF THE NUMBERS WERE DIFFERENT, IT WOULD MEAN MORE THAN NO LIFE—THERE WOULD BE NO UNIVERSE TO BEGIN WITH.

special values define the physical properties of the universe and must be exactly what they are in order for life to exist. This fine tuning to support human life is known as the anthropic principle.

You might suggest that if the numbers had different values, then human beings would have evolved anyway. Here is the problem: if the numbers were different, it would mean more than no life—there would be no universe to begin with. If a universe with different properties had formed, then some other species might have flourished within its bounds. Unfortunately, it is impossible to gain knowledge about other universes with different laws of physics—a limitation which places their conjecture beyond the bounds of science (a method of making predictions based on natural, repeatable events).

Determining how to live a life consistent with beliefs based on truth is one of your most important missions. After examining the issues, you will easily reject claims that Christianity is not only false, but harmful. I once thought you had to check your brain at the door to believe in Christianity. On the contrary, Christians seeking to understand their faith are using its full potential.

So, you can be an intellectually fulfilled Christian. But must you speak softly, close your eyes in church, and become the death of every party? Does spirituality mean weakness? The Christian faith is built upon a man (a God-man). Men were largely responsible for the growth of Christianity over the last 2,000 years. So why do some men view faith as the mark of a eunuch—an irrational choice of self-sterilization—leaving him barren of reason and masculinity?

It was time to explore what was happening to our men of faith.

---

[1] Richard Dawkins, *The God Delusion* (New York: Houghton Mifflin Company, 2006), 308.

[2] Wikipedia, "Al Bundy," accessed August 5, 2012, http://en.wikipedia.org/wiki/Al_Bundy.

[3] Ibid.

[4] William M Irwin, Mark T. Conard, and Aeon J. Skoble, *The Simpsons and Philosophy: The D'oh! Of Homer* (Open Court: Chicago, 2008), Kindle ed., loc. 174.

[5] Ibid., loc. 364.

[6] Ibid., loc. 1016.

[7] Ibid., loc. 629.

[8] Ibid., loc. 746.

[9] Ibid., loc. 755.

[10] Ibid., loc. 251.

[11] Richard Dawkins, *The Blind Watchmaker* (London: Penguin, 1986), 6.

[12] Ibid.

[13] Dinesh D'Souza, *What's So Great About Christianity* (Washington D.C.: Rengery, 2007), loc. 2372.

[14] Paul Davies, "The origin of life I: When and where did it begin?" ASU Cosmos, accessed August 7, 2012, http://cosmos.asu.edu/publications/papers/OriginsOfLife_I.pdf.

[15] Stephen Hawking, *A Brief History of Time* (New York: Bantam Books, 1996), 126.

CHAPTER 15

A FIGHTER'S FAITH

An Undisclosed Location
Winter

"Heaven is not a location but refers to the inner realm of consciousness."[1]

—ECKHART TOLLE

"The LORD looks down from heaven on the sons of men to see if there are any who understand" (Ps. 14:2).

—DAVID

SOME MEN THINK CHURCH IS not for them. After all, Sunday is just such a good day for golf (or watching football). Some churches have a noticeable lack of men. And some men in church look like they're waiting for the results of a prostate exam.

I can relate to these men. I love golf. And it wasn't long ago I stood there with my own waiting-for-the-results look in my eye. *Let me get this straight. I get up early and drive to a place where they tell me what to think, pester me to volunteer, beg for money, and read from a book written two centuries ago? And I miss golf? How am I supposed to be excited about this?*

I am convinced the secret to awakening the spiritual strength of a man's heart is convincing him that God is greater than golf. It is easy for us to say. It is something else entirely to actually believe it. But there is a reason men are having trouble embracing the spiritual side of life: they think they will become less of a man.

Men disinterested in the spiritual side of life see only what a man stands to lose, and none of what he stands to gain by surrendering his life to God.

"Dead man walking!" shouts his inner-voice during an altar call. He watches curiously as his friend—let's call him Jim—moves closer to the execution of his manhood. He sees Jim about to surrender his life, and "surrender" is not an appealing concept to men. No more poker night. No more jokes. No more golf on Sunday. No more...Jim.

WE ALL WORSHIP SOMETHING.

But Jim knows something the other man doesn't. Whether God or the idols he condemns, we all worship something. He is learning that spiritual development is a part of being human. And he is about to discover the power of surrendering to an ally whose might far exceeds his own.

THE END OF MEN?

Young males in America have been subjected to a process of emasculation for decades. Once the spirit of political correctness descended upon America, adults started speaking in strange tongues about how Johnny and Suzie should behave more like each other. In spite of obvious physical differences, girls were told they are no different than boys, and boys were told it is okay to be just like girls. After $10,000 dollars and 5-6 hours under general anesthesia, a boy can even become a girl (anatomically, anyway). Or you can save that money by moving to California where little dudes can now use the little dudettes room if they feel like gender-identifying as girls.

But just because we can, doesn't mean we should. The word "should" belongs to a family of normative terms—words which imply the rightness of an act. In the name of autonomy, with the spirit of ingenuity, by the power of technology, and through the acceptance of plurality, we have forgotten about morality.

Some young males are becoming increasingly disinterested in girls all together. In Japan, these young men are called *soshoku danshi*, or "herbivore men," and have decided that getting the girl is too much work. Likewise, a growing number of young Japanese women have indicated they are "uninterested in or averse to sex."[2]

Emasculation of males has become the spirit of the age in America, accompanied by an overemphasis on feelings, emotions, and the "self." We became a touchy-feely society and children were told that their feelings were the ultimate judge of morality. Teachers disavowed absolutes and severed philosophical moorings, setting them adrift into a sea of incoherency. I'm okay, you're okay, everybody's right, and by the way, Jesus loves you.

Jesus loves me? Must be part of the campaign to turn everybody into mindless, sexless, lovey-doveys. The message in the 90's was focused on the Good News that Jesus loves us and died for our sins. But like so many false converts and backsliders from that era, I didn't hear much about the bad news, that we have all sinned and fallen short. In fact, secular America was teaching the opposite. "You're not a bad boy. There are no bad boys. Let's talk about how you *feel*."

I was feeling confused. I didn't even know whether it was right or wrong to swing back if someone sucker-punched me. In *The Demise of Guys*, Philip Zimbardo explains what it is like to be a guy today:

> Our culture is presenting a confusing and unfulfilling reality full of distorted ideals and truths. Guys are told they can be anything they want to be, but it doesn't feel that way. With modern pressures to constantly perform flawlessly in all areas of life—school, career, socially,

sexually—it's no wonder guys seek validation and refuge in other environments like porn and video games or even gangs, or are relieved when their anxiety or depression is diagnosed and given a label that other dudes also share, like attention-deficit disorder (ADD).[3]

IS GOD FOR GIRLIE MEN?

It was within this milieu that as a young man, I assigned femininity to the Church. If there were strong men with powerful voices calling their flocks to wield the sword of the spirit, I didn't know about them. I had never heard of Billy Graham, Chuck Swindoll, or John MacArthur. I was unfamiliar with church history, tradition, the role of men in the church, the increasing feminization prior to the 19th century, or the more recent "muscular Christianity" movement. I did not attend church regularly until I had children of my own. I had no idea what God or the church were really about.

The word "God" conjured the concept of "faith." In fairy tales, the maiden waits faithfully for a knight to come for her, but the knight is a man of action. The word "church" conjured images of grey haired grandmothers, hymnals in hand, joyfully singing praises in their Sunday best. "Jesus" evoked the image of the innocent lamb in the pasture or the watchful shepherd corralling his sheep. "Heaven" was a fantasy fabricated to ease the frightening prospect of death. "Bible study" sounded like what the kindergarteners do with a big picture book between crafts and snacks. As for the Bible, why should adults study a book full of fairy tales written by men that's full of contradictions?

Today I feel differently about God, faith, and Christianity. What has changed? I discovered that Jesus of Nazareth was a real person, a man who worked with his hands, a man of strength, courage, and conviction who respected and loved his Father and was unashamed to demonstrate it, who performed miracles, was killed on a Roman cross, and rose again three days later. The apostle Paul acknowledged that the truth of Christianity hangs explicitly on the cross, or more specifically, what happened to Jesus after the cross. He told Christians in Corinth, "If Christ has not been raised, our preaching is useless and so is your faith" (1 Cor. 15:14).

STRENGTH IN WEAKNESS

Now I see Jesus as both the lamb *and* the lion. Church is not a building full of old souls clinging to outdated traditions. It is a body of strong, faithful followers—men and women, young and old—committed to living holy lives in an unholy world. Heaven is the final resolution of injustice and upheld by the law of love. God *used* men to write his word, complete with fascinating mysteries and conundrums, but void of contradictions. Bible study is the search for understanding, wisdom, and truth.

Christians acknowledge Jesus as their Lord and Savior and would rather face death than the holy treason of renouncing their faith. In the Book of Daniel, Shadrach, Meshach, and Abed-nego refused to bow down and worship a golden idol fashioned by King Nebuchadnezzar. Knowing they would be thrown into a fiery furnace for their disobedience, they replied, "King Nebuchadnezzar, we do not need to defend ourselves before you in this matter. If we are thrown into the blazing furnace, the God we serve is able to deliver us from it, and he will deliver us from Your Majesty's hand. But even if he does not, we want you to know, Your Majesty, that we will not serve your gods or worship the image of gold you have set up" (Dan. 3:16-18).

THE CHRISTIAN CAN BOLDLY ACT IN THE FACE OF DEATH WITH AN ASSURANCE NOT GUARANTEED BY OTHER WORLDVIEWS.

STRENGTH IN SACRIFICE

The Christian can boldly act in the face of death with an assurance not guaranteed by other worldviews: a promised inheritance of a perfect life hereafter. There is no compelling reason for me to leap from the parapets and charge the enemy foxhole knowing should I perish, I might return as a cockroach or a grub. Karma is a poor motivator for altruism. Neither could I find reason not to abandon my brother and save my own skin if this life is all we get. Posthumous justice for sacrificial heroism has no place in the mind of the Naturalist.

Jesus tells us, "Greater love has no one than this: to lay down one's life for one's friends" (John 15:13). He also assures us, "Our citizenship is in heaven" (Phil. 3:20). Others with different worldviews can be heroic; however, they have no reason to be heroic. Telling myself "everything is going to be okay" in the heat of battle only makes sense if in the end, everything really is going to be okay. Total annihilation is not an "okay" state of affairs. It is a non-state of affairs.

As the title of Eric Metaxas's biography reveals, Dietrich Bonhoeffer was a pastor, martyr, prophet, and spy. He was a theologian and co-conspirator in an assassination plot on Adolf Hitler in 1943. Principles based on Christian morality compelled him to return to Germany in 1939 when he could have remained in the United States. His life ended on the gallows one month before the fall of the Nazi regime, but he finished the race. He lived his life proclaiming the gospel and defending the faith even unto death. On Christianity, he wins. On naturalism, he loses. What evolutionary advantage is there in allowing for your own demise? We are not doing our genes (or memes)[*] any favors by getting ourselves killed.

---

[*] Meme theory itself is a theoretical meme. Therefore, it would be rendered meaningless by its own extinction.

STRENGTH IN RIGHTEOUSNESS

The apostle Paul was no pushover. He was a staunch Jesus-hater and persecutor of his followers. He held the coats of the Jews and priests of Jerusalem who stoned Stephen to death. But his real masculinity came after his conversion to Christianity. Neither toil nor conflict could subdue his zeal for Christ after hearing the Lord's voice on the road to Damascus. Paul addressed the Corinthians:

> I have worked much harder, been in prison more frequently, been flogged more severely, and been exposed to death again and again. Five times I received from the Jews the forty lashes minus one. Three times I was beaten with rods, once I was pelted with stones, three times I was shipwrecked, I spent a night and a day in the open sea, I have been constantly on the move. I have been in danger from rivers, in danger from bandits, in danger from my fellow Jews, in danger from Gentiles; in danger in the city, in danger in the country, in danger at sea; and in danger from false believers. I have labored and toiled and have often gone without sleep; I have known hunger and thirst and have often gone without food; I have been cold and naked. Besides everything else, I face daily the pressure of my concern for all the churches. Who is weak, and I do not feel weak? Who is led into sin, and I do not inwardly burn? (2 Cor. 11:23-29).

PRAYER AND ACTION

You might be thinking, "I pray for them." While prayer is an important and powerful part of our relationship with God, he didn't intend for us to hole up in our comfortable homes and do nothing but pray. We are told to pray without ceasing, but we are also commanded to reach out to the lost. As Paul said in his letter to the Romans, "How can they believe in the one of whom they have not heard? And how can they hear without someone preaching to them?" Preaching is not just the responsibility of the preacher.

In 1 Peter 2:5, the Bible says those who have answered the Lord's calling are part of God's spiritual house and members of a holy priesthood. If you have answered his call, it's time for you to call upon others! Those dead in their sins are in a burning building right now. They are dead men walking. Christians who fail to act may not be convicted in a court of law, but how will they fare when standing before the final Judge? "I was uncomfortable," or "It would have been embarrassing," or "I didn't know I was supposed to," isn't going to fly.

WHAT'S THE MEANING?

"What we do in life echoes in eternity."[4] Those were the words of Maximus to his men before a battle in Ridley Scott's movie *Gladiator*. Actions can only have meaning now if they have meaning in eternity. This is a bold statement which deserves some investigation. Your assessment on whether or not life has meaning could have disastrous consequences (or meaningless consequences, depending on your assessment). The Romans may have worshiped a different God than the first century Disciples, but the concept of eternal consequences for our earthly behavior is almost universally recognized within the world's major religions.

If what we do in life does not echo in eternity, then it doesn't really matter what we do in life. If that's the case, our myopic view of life creates only the illusion of meaning. Helping others, fighting injustice, and expressing love to your beloved feel like meaningful acts, but what meaning will there be to human life when we are extinct? Your great-great-grandfather may have helped to make the world a better place, but if we all perish from an asteroid impact, nuclear war, or overexposure to weight loss infomercials, the concept of "better" will disappear altogether.

This philosophical notion was recognized by theoretical physicist Brian Greene before discussing his theories on the makeup of time and space in *The Fabric of the Cosmos*. Quoting Albert Camus, he addresses the notion that the only truly philosophical problem is suicide. All other fields of study and their associated questions become secondary to answering the most important question: is life even worth living in order to ask questions and seek answers?[5]

Greene answers yes and determines that "an informed appraisal of life absolutely required a full understanding of life's arena— the universe."[6] This statement has two hidden assumptions. The first assumption is the universe is life's only arena. There is no room here for a spiritual realm existing outside of our universe or any possible means of interacting with it. The second assumption is the life we know now will be our only existence. These assumptions cannot be proven true. Neither can they be falsified. They are metaphysical, inductive conclusions. Circular reasoning prevails when such distinctions go unrecognized. Naturalists make assumptions about the universe from their commitment to naturalism, but their naturalism is a result of these assumptions.

GOD IS FOR ALL MEN

Today when I think of a Christian, I don't think of Ned Flanders. I think of King David. He was Jewish and before Jesus' time, but the Father of Abraham and the Father of Christ are one in the same. I see him standing over the body of the giant from Gath. I see him peering down at the smooth stone sunk into the Philistine's forehead who moments earlier mocked the Israelites and defied the armies of the living God.

I think of Joseph, left for dead by his own brothers and appointed to the highest levels of office in Egypt. It was an act of strength, not weakness, when he forgave his brothers for their trespasses. It was strength that enabled him to defend against the seductions of Potiphar's wife.

I think of Pastor Youcef Nadarkhani, an Iranian Christian pastor imprisoned for more than three years and sentenced to death for refusing to renounce his faith. I think of the Roman military commander, Maurice, described by Francis Schaeffer in *How Should We Then Live?* who refused an order to persecute Christians and joined them instead.[7]

I think of how my high school football coach tied moral standards to team membership, and I think of a squadron commander who skillfully excised misconduct like a tumor while leaving his Marines' spirit intact. I think of a Top Gun graduate who held Bible studies in his transient quarters while overseas. I think of business executives with the conviction to remain firm in the face of public scrutiny. I think of our nation's Presidents, most of whom have been Christians (though obviously no less susceptible to sin).

I think of the Apostles who kept their faith in the risen Lord in the face of certain death. According to church tradition, Matthew was cut down by the sword in Ethiopia. Mark breathed his last breath while being dragged through the streets of Alexandria. Luke's neck snapped in a noose strung upon an olive tree in Greece, and Peter was crucified upside down in Rome. James the Greater was beheaded at Jerusalem, and James the Less was thrown from the temple roof and clubbed to death. Philip was "imprisoned, scourged, and crucified."[8] Bartholomew was alive when his skin was peeled from his body. Andrew preached his last sermon from the cross. Thomas was impaled by a lance, and arrows pierced the body of Jude whereupon he gave up his spirit. Matthias was stoned and decapitated while John was boiled alive but managed to escape. He died in Ephesus at the age of 94. Barnabas was stoned to death at Salonica, and the apostle Paul was beheaded in Rome.[9]

I WAS WRONG

Ignorant of theology, philosophy, and history, I wrongly ascribed femininity to the worship of a higher power. I deferred to popular projections from disinterested and arrogant spear throwers. There is nothing girlie about a father's love for his son. There is nothing girlie about a boy's love for his father. These are concepts all men understand. It is fitting that Jesus uses the father-son analogy so frequently for the relationship between God and man. Just as we have an earthly father, we also have a heavenly Father. Our earthly parents helped create our bodies, but God brings everything into being.

God created both man and woman perfectly equal in worth, with equally different roles. God designed men to marvel at woman's femininity just as he designed women to appreciate masculinity in men. When my eldest son was baptized, we didn't give him flowers or a Hallmark card. We gave him a sword—an Excalibur style, silver steel, two-edged broadsword that stood taller than he. Inscribed upon its blade is Ephesians 6:17: "Take the helmet of salvation, and the sword of the spirit which is the word of God."

He has already learned that the word of God is not just a message of hope for the penitent. It is a cutting instrument of truth that divides households, peoples, and nations. It will separate people now and in eternity. Each individual must choose whether to be on the side of humility, temperance, and truth, or the side of pride, indulgence, and denial. Be assured, upon our return, he is waiting to receive each one of us, just as the father embraced the prodigal after his leave of absence.

God recognizes that evil is a real force to be reckoned with. As long as evil lurks like a roaring lion ready to pounce, we will need warriors to secure peace by waging war in defense of the weak. God appeals to the Spirit-led nature of men with a call to arms in Ephesians 6 by describing a soldier preparing for battle:

> Stand firm then, with the belt of truth buckled around your waist, with the breastplate of righteousness in place, and with your feet fitted with the readiness that comes from the gospel of peace. In addition to all this, take up the shield of faith, with which you can extinguish all the flaming arrows of the evil one. Take the helmet of salvation and the sword of the Spirit, which is the word of God.

My worldview was taking form, and I was finally able to think critically. It was time to begin wading into the relevant cultural issues that would affect my children as they faced major life decisions. I quickly learned the river is wide, and the water runs deep.

---

[1] Eckhart Tolle, *A New Earth: Awakening to Your Life's Purpose* (New York: Penguin Group, 2006), 23.

[2] Mark Hanrahan, "Japan Population Decline: Third Of Nation's Youth Have 'No Interest' In Sex," The Huffington Post, January 31, 2012, http://www.huffingtonpost.com/2012/01/30/japan-population-decline-youth-no-sex_n_1242014.html.

[3] Philip G. Zimbardo and Nikita Duncan, *The Demise of Guys: Why Boys Are Struggling and What We Can Do About It* (New York: TED, 2012), Kindle ed., loc. 517.

[4] *Gladiator*, directed by Ridley Scott (2000; Universal City, CA: DreamWorks LLC and Universal Studios, 2000).

[5] Brian Greene, *The Fabric of the Cosmos: Space, Time, and the Texture of Reality* (New York: Random House, Inc., 2004), Kindle ed., loc. 309-310.

[6] Ibid.

[7] Schaeffer, *How Should We Then Live? The Rise and Decline of Western Thought and Culture*, loc. 231.

---

[8] Steven L Cox and Kendell H. Easley, *Holman Christian Standard Bible: Harmony of the Gospels*, Issues in Gospel Harmonization (Nashville: Holman Bible Publishers, 2007), "The Apostles: Four Lists."

[9] Paul Lee Tan, *Encyclopedia of 7,700 Illustrations: Signs of the Times* (Garland: Bible Communications, Inc., 1996), part D, sec. 1147.

CHAPTER 16

A GIFT FROM GOD

Bangkok, Thailand
February 2009

*"There is no holy life. There is no war between good and
evil. There is no sin and no redemption."*[1]

—DEEPAK CHOPRA

*"If we claim to be without sin, we deceive ourselves and the
truth is not in us" (1 John 1:8).*

—THE APOSTLE JOHN

IT WAS FRIDAY NIGHT IN Bangkok, and we were ready to cut
loose after an intense week of flying exercises with the Royal
Thai Air Force. Unfamiliar smells came in waves as we
maneuvered the crowded street to find the next meeting
place. I passed by vendors offering baskets of fried crickets,
grasshoppers, and water beetles. There was commotion up
ahead; something caused the crowd to swell in our direction.
The crowd thinned to reveal a baby elephant prodded along
by a young boy. Solicitations from both flanks stole my
attention.

"Muhtaaazsh . . . Muhtaaazsh?" women called out from
barstools with rising inflection. Scantily clad in shorts and
spaghetti straps, their twangy voices reverberated in my ears.
At first we had difficulty understanding their offer for a
massage. In this district, there was a good chance you could

choose your own ending. Unacknowledged, the calling waned; if I looked in their direction, it continued. More women chimed in if I made eye contact. We were quickly desensitized to the unceasing propositions and pressed on.

We were in the devil's lair running a spiritual gauntlet. Buzzing neon lights captured glazy-eyed tourists and drew them toward music, liquor, and titillating shows. A mother strolled her baby down an alley filled with brothels. Voluptuous signage pulled like a tractor beam and storefront greeters beckoned to break my will. There were two battles raging to avoid sexual immorality: in the body and in the mind. My feet easily turned my body away from the physical dangers, but my mind stubbornly prodded my eyes to linger far longer than they should have. Turning the head away is a simple habit required for developing good character. But we all know that sometimes the simplest things are difficult. They say the first look is natural. The second look is sin. The Bible tells us in Matthew 5:28 you don't need physical contact to be an adulterer, "But I tell you that anyone who looks at a woman lustfully has already committed adultery with her in his heart." Contrary to the slogan assuring you things can "stay in Vegas," what happens in Bangkok, and the deeds impressed upon the wandering heart, stay with you forever.

God often compares sexual immorality with spiritual adultery. Any time we put other idols above God, we become like a harlot. Instead of pursuing a sacred and monogamous relationship with God, we partner with multiple idols offering comforts only later recognized as unholy. You may not be an adulterer in the bedroom, but have you been unfaithful in your own house of worship? Violate the former and you've broken the seventh Commandment; violate the latter and you've broken the first. One will cause your spouse to weep, the other, God—in both instances you have broken a heart.

Advice with no more substance than to "follow your heart" and "do what you feel" sells books and supports the woo economy. But when these philosophies are actually lived out, they ultimately fail. Why do girls love bad boys? Why do boys want to be bad with girls? We know that sexual union is a good gift from God, but why does it entice us in ungodly ways? In order to resolve the tension, it will help to understand both the physical and spiritual elements of sexual desire.

A GIFT FROM GOD

Ravi Zacharias answers the "why" by explaining these feelings as a perversion of God's original framework for the love relationship: "God has given us the gift of the intensity of passion within the context of the sacredness of love. Take away either the passion or the correct context, and you have something less than what God intended it to be."[2]

The Biblical view of sex acknowledges its legitimacy in the context of the marriage relationship between a man and woman. In order to have a discussion with those with opposing views, you must be able to answer the following: "what is the purpose of sex" and "where did it come from?"

SOMETHING IS GOING ON HERE BEYOND THE SATISFACTION OF PHYSICAL DESIRES.

Christians understand sex as a gift from God for marriage. It is not merely a means for procreation. God has infused this gift with meaning and purpose beyond fruitful multiplication. The mystery of two becoming one involves an intimacy unrivaled in the human experience. The bond formed between lovers is strong and everlasting. Something is going on here beyond the satisfaction of physical desires.

Your children can be caught deep in enemy territory in the battle against sexual immorality. To borrow language from the military Code of Conduct, some enthusiastically accept special favors from the enemy, while others continue to resist by all means available. Some examples of prohibited sexual behavior I will focus on include adultery and fornication.

A BIBLICAL VIEW

Let's take a look at what a Biblical perspective can teach us about God's intention for the union between a man and woman. Appropriately, we begin in the Book of Genesis: "A man leaves his father and mother and is united to his wife, and they become one flesh" (Gen. 2:24). This idea is also reinforced in Matthew 19:5 and 1 Corinthians 6:16. Instead, our sinful nature entices us to believe the foolish woman of Proverbs, chapter 9, who calls out to ensnare those who lack judgment: "Stolen water is sweet; food eaten in secret is delicious!" Even with full knowledge of the consequences of illegitimate sex, we continue to believe the lie that stolen waters are sweeter. Instead, we should look to another verse in Proverbs for how God designed us to be satisfied:

> Drink water from your own cistern, running water from your own well. Should your springs overflow in the streets, your streams of water in the public squares? Let them be yours alone, never to be shared with strangers. May your fountain be blessed, and may you rejoice in the wife of your youth (Prov. 5:15-18).

The following verses comment on marriage and adultery: "Marriage should be honored by all, and the marriage bed kept pure, for God will judge the adulterer and all the sexually immoral" (Heb. 13:4). "A man who commits adultery has no sense; whoever does so destroys himself. Blows and disgrace are his lot, and his shame will never be wiped away" (Prov. 6:32-33). "Do you not know that he who unites himself with a prostitute is one with her in body? For it is said, 'The two will become one flesh.' But whoever is united with the Lord is one with him in spirit" (1 Cor. 6:16-17). "You shall not commit adultery" (Exod. 20:14).

Late-night adultery is so harmful that it made a Top Ten list long before David Letterman popularized them on late-night television: it is number seven on God's list of Commandments. Listen to how men are to react to the immoral woman:

> Do not lust in your heart after her beauty or let her captivate you with her eyes, for a prostitute can be had for a loaf of bread, but another man's wife preys on your very life. Can a man scoop fire into his lap without his clothes being burned? Can a man walk on hot coals without his feet being scorched? So is he who sleeps with another man's wife; no one who touches her will go unpunished (Prov. 6:25-29).

Without a moral prohibition on indulging the lustful desires of our sin-filled hearts, we will soon surrender to illicit passions and lewd bits of bandwidth. Despite today's mainstream celebration of hooking up, one night stands, and friends with benefits, we must heed the message given to the people of Ephesus:

> But among you there must not be even a hint of sexual immorality, or of any kind of impurity, or of greed, because these are improper for God's holy people. Nor should there be obscenity, foolish talk or coarse joking, which are out of place, but rather thanksgiving. For of this you can be sure: No immoral, impure or greedy person—such a man is an idolater—has any inheritance in the kingdom of Christ and of God (Eph. 5:3-5).

A GIFT PERVERTED

We live in a world obsessed with pleasure. Legitimate pleasures resonate, reduce stress, and foster a sense of well-being. Illegitimate pleasures are transitory, hollow, and get us into trouble. The illegitimate use of sex and drugs knocks our heroes off their pedestals. Every time we act, we participate in a cycle of desire, gratification, and reflection. If we analyze these stages of behavior and how the cycle becomes tweaked, then we can better understand how we have gone from "the greatest generation" to a culture rife with narcissistic hedonists.

First, our senses create desires. Second, we choose whether or not to gratify those desires. Third, we reflect upon our action. With a legitimate pleasure, you will find satisfaction in all three stages. A pure desire yields enjoyable anticipation. I see my wife. The gratification of a legitimate pleasure creates a climactic and untainted experience of joy. I move toward her and kiss her. And reflection upon a legitimate pleasure will be guilt-free, reinforcing the rightness of the act. I am happy to remain affectionate in a committed, life-long relationship with one woman.

With illegitimate pleasures, satisfaction is missing from one or more of the stages. In the beginning stages of drug use, the user may be satisfied by desire and gratification, but will likely find dissatisfaction in the reflection stage. Once a user is hooked, desperation replaces satisfaction in the desire stage, gratification lessens with each use, and reflection leads to depression.

In the case of illegitimate sex, the pleasure comes only in the desire and gratification stages. You see an attractive man or woman, and you gratify your desires with them. But reflection will always stir up moral discord sooner or later. In the end, your indiscretion haunts you for the rest of your life. The celebration of illegitimate pleasure in our culture is the result of either a refusal to enter the reflection stage, or unabashed denial in its midst.

Maybe you're not an adulterer, but you enjoy a night with the gang at the local strip club, or you regularly indulge in explicit content available on the Internet. Are these fantasies harmless? Is morality divided between our five senses? Is it okay to look, but not touch? To smell, but not taste? Can we ever be condemned for what we allow ourselves to hear? All five senses are entryways to the brain. The brain enables the mind, and the mind informs the heart (although some operate in the reverse, allowing their heart to control their mind).

We are not only to avoid acts of sexual immorality; we are to avoid sexually immoral thoughts as well. It sounds like "mission: impossible." But Jesus' words are clear, and we are to continue fighting the war no matter how many battles we lose. What's the big deal about thoughts and secret desires? James explains in 1 James 1:14: "Each person is tempted when they are dragged away by their own evil desire and enticed. Then, after desire has conceived, it gives birth to sin; and sin, when it is full-grown, gives birth to death."

Some will say it's both silly and unreasonable to worry about your thoughts. The world says it is natural to have these desires—that our sexual appetites are as natural as feelings of hunger or thirst. C.S. Lewis argues that something has gone very

SOMETHING HAS GONE VERY WRONG WITH THIS PARTICULAR APPETITE.

wrong with this particular appetite in *Mere Christianity*. The following excerpt is particularly helpful:

> Chastity is the most unpopular of the Christian virtues. . . . The Christian rule is, 'Either marriage, with complete faithfulness to your partner, or else total abstinence.' . . . either Christianity is wrong or our sexual instinct, as it now is, has gone wrong. . . . I think it is the instinct which has gone wrong. . . . Perversions of the food appetite are

rare. But perversions of the sex instinct are numerous, hard to cure, and frightful. . . . There is nothing to be ashamed of in enjoying your food: there would be everything to be ashamed of if half the world made food the main interest of their lives and spent their time looking at pictures of food and dribbling and smacking their lips. . . . Our warped natures, the devils who tempt us, and all the contemporary propaganda for lust, combine to make us feel that the desires we are resisting are so 'natural', so 'healthy', and so reasonable, that it is almost perverse and abnormal to resist them. Poster after poster, film after film, novel after novel, associate the idea of sexual indulgence with the ideas of health, normality, youth, frankness, and good humor. Now this association is a lie.[3]

Let's compare this with an excerpt from another publication with a different philosophy which . . .

Condones any type of sexual activity which properly satisfies your individual desires—be it heterosexual, homosexual, bisexual, or even asexual, if you choose . . . [and] also sanctions any fetish or deviation which will enhance your sex life. . . . Adherence to the sensible and humanistic new morality of . . . [_____] can—and will— evolve society, a society in which children can grow up healthy and without the devastating moral encumbrances of our existing sick society.[4] (Brackets mine.)

Can you fill in the blank and name that worldview? In the parlance of our times, the above passage could easily be describing as accepting, forward-looking, tolerant, and non-judgmental. When someone lures you with health, satisfaction, and progress, it is easy to take the bait. This passage was taken from the Satanic Bible and smacks of something Uncle Screwtape would have instructed his young demonic nephew.

But we needn't be prodded by a demonic uncle to learn the ropes of sexual sin. Our entire culture grooms men to become career patrons of pornography, and our training begins early.

In my case, the price of admission into a kingdom of emptiness was a B-B gun. But the coin I received in return cost more than a half-broken air rifle. The small novelty, having no value of its own, stole some of mine.

In a glance, my innocence was gone.

---

[1] Deepak Chopra, *Buddha: A Story of Enlightenment* (New York: Harper Collins, 2007), 243.

[2] Ravi Zacharias, *Has Christianity Failed You?* (Grand Rapids: Zondervan, 2010), 92.

[3] C.S. Lewis, *Mere Christianity* (New York: Harper Collins, 1980), Kindle ed., 100.

[4] Anton Szandor LaVey, *The Satanic Bible* (New York: Avon, 1969), 25.

CHAPTER 17
DOWN IN FLAMES

Marine Corps Base Camp Pendleton, California
July 1988

"Remember, it's important to enjoy erotica in moderation."[1]

—*LAURA BERMAN, LCSW, PHD*

"You are a slave to whatever controls you" (NLT, 2 Pet.
2:19).

—*THE APOSTLE PETER*

WHEN I WAS EIGHT YEARS old, I had a BB gun. I don't remember
how I acquired it—most likely through a trade. I only had
the gun a short time; an older boy was interested in my gun
and made me an offer. He pulled out a coin. This was no
ordinary coin. It was bronze and about the size of a quarter.
I was surprised when I looked at the inscription on its face:

Heads, you win.

Embossed was the image of a woman's head and torso,
arm raised above her head and exposed upper half. I spun
the coin around to reveal a racy, round rump underneath
which was inscribed:

Tails, you lose.

I accepted the trade immediately. My friend took the gun
and left, and I stood there looking at my new coin. It was
something exciting, something new. A few minutes later, the

newness faded and I missed my gun. I traded something of value for a worthless trifle of smut.

The coin floated around my room for a number of years and would occasionally resurface to remind me of the disappointment. I have forgotten a lot of things over the years, but I can remember seeing the sides of that coin as if it were yesterday. The memory refuses to leave, like a houseguest whose welcome has worn.

What will you teach your children about sex? What is natural and what is taboo? Where is the line between beauty and profanity? How will you keep them from joining the celebration of illegitimate pleasure? Will you teach them to respect the moral purity of others? How should your daughter respond to aggressive boys? How should your son deal with the immoral woman? What will you teach them about pornography? Is it just a harmless fact of life, or is it an epidemic affecting the brain pathology of children and parents alike?

A few years later, a *moving* image added more poison to my well of long-term memories.

BE CAREFUL LITTLE EYES

I held a consistent morning routine before school. After breakfast, I did a quick set of pull-ups. My dad installed a pull-up bar wherever we lived. He attached the bar to a big tree and wrapped it with medical tape. Pull-ups are a trademark Marine Corps exercise and made up one-third of the Physical Fitness Test (PFT) Marines took twice a year. I went out to the backyard and stretched my arms and shoulders.

At three feet and 80 pounds, I jumped from a step-stool to grasp the bar, feet dangling in the air. I usually kept my backpack on. *1-2-3-4-5-6-7-8-9-10. Whew!* I was proud of my pull-ups—pull-ups just like my dad. He always max'd out the PFT with 20 (and could keep going after that). I dropped from the bar. My hands stung from my palms pinching against the bar during the Marine Corps ritual. I dropped from the bar and felt my pulse slow back to normal. Morning routine complete.

Sometimes I walked to school with a friend. We talked about ten-year-old things: who was going to get his name on the board with the most checkmarks, what kind of candy we would sneak from our fanny-packs during class, what happened on the latest episode of G.I. Joe, etc.

We always passed by his house on the way to school, and one day we made a brief stop there. We didn't have much time before class, and I was worried about being late. I followed him inside and stood in the entryway.

Then I started hearing strange noises. His older brother was in the living room watching something on television. I glanced at the screen and saw a man and woman doing things I had never seen done before. They sounded like they were in pain. Something wasn't right.

SOMETHING WASN'T RIGHT. *I SHOULDN'T BE SEEING THIS.*

I shouldn't be seeing this. I stared for a few seconds and then trembled at a frightening thought. *If my mom finds out what I've seen, I'll be in big trouble.* I didn't even know what it was that I had seen. I was thrust into a world where I didn't belong. I stepped back outside.

"What? C'mon, what's the big deal?" my friend prodded.

"I shouldn't watch that. I'll be in trouble if my mom finds out," I replied with head and eyes down, convinced of her omniscience. Mothers have a way of knowing. We left his house and went to school, but I only learned one thing that day: the power of video.

THE PORN PROBLEM

At the time of this writing, the second-highest-grossing movie in America celebrated male strippers and "the art of partying, picking up women, and making easy money."[2] It brought in over 39 million dollars. A recent series of erotic novels surpassed the Harry Potter series as the fastest selling paperbacks of all time[3] indicating that one thing Americans like more than teenage magical wizardry is indulgent sexual fantasy.

America's appetite for sex has become an obsession with porn. Years ago it took a certain amount of effort for a child to gain access to graphic images. The explorative child stood a moderate chance of stumbling upon this contraband with a determined search effort around their parents' bed or dresser drawer. Aside from that, the only danger area was the blacked out magazine rack at the checkout counter where magazines were sold.

Now porn comes looking for you. It is not knocking on your door—it is already in your living room. It can be one click away from your child's Minecraft app. One mistype entering a web address on your child's iTouch can give them an unexpected eyeful. Sexually charged advertisements are attached like parasites to everyday websites with moving images, popup windows, and anything else to get your attention and money. Websites display teasers on their homepages before asking if the viewers are of legal age. Only 3% of such websites require proof-of-age before granting access to sexually explicit material and two-thirds of pornographic websites do not include any adult-content warnings.[4]

Kids are sexting, streaming themselves over the Internet, and easily accessing high resolution adult "entertainment." The days of staring through scrambled signals of hotel cable television for that fleeting shot of cleavage are long gone. Kids have instant access to explicit material on their mobile device from almost anywhere in the world, 24 hours a day.

Just how widespread is the penchant for porn? Here are a few statistics:

-9 out of 10 children aged between the ages of 8 and 16 have viewed pornography on the Internet, in most cases unintentionally. (London School of Economics, 2002)

-47% of families in the United States report that pornography is a problem in their home. (National Coalition for the Protection of Children & Families, 2010)

-49% of female college students surveyed find pornography acceptable. (Brigham Young University, 2007)

-One in four internet users look at a pornographic website in any given month. Men look at pornography online more than they look at any other subject. And 66% of 18-34-year-old men visit a pornographic site every month. (Social Costs of Pornography, 2010)

-Approximately 75% of pornographic websites display visual teasers on the homepages before asking if the viewers are of legal age; only 3% of such websites require proof-of-age before granting access to sexually explicit material, and two-thirds of pornographic websites do not include any adult-content warnings. (Social Costs of Pornography, 2010)

Some parents might still be convinced that Johnny and Suzie are still their little angels. Those banking on a lack of evidence as the basis of their peace of mind should consider the following:

-70% percent of teens "hide their online behavior" from parents[5]

-32 % of teens clear the browser history to hide what they do online from their parents. (Harris Interactive-McAfee, 2008)

-16 % have created private e-mail addresses or social networking profiles to hide what they do online from their parents (Harris Interactive-McAfee, 2008)[6]

Children and parents fail to realize that one of their most basic natural instincts is being exploited by profiteers. Each stumble down into the flames worsens an already debilitating limp, strengthening the lie that we are too weak to walk in the light of heaven. Parents need to educate themselves. Let's take a closer look at what's really going on when users indulge in pornography.

DOPAMINE AND DESIRE

Have you ever wondered what makes you feel pleasure? Have you ever wondered why thrilling activities and rich desserts make you feel good? Merriam-Webster's online dictionary defines pleasure as "a state of gratification."[7] Gratification is associated with the concept of "reward" which is defined as "a stimulus administered to an organism following a correct or desired response that increases the probability of occurrence of the response."[8] In other words, if after an act I receive a stimulus that makes me want to do it more, that stimulus is a reward. If we want to learn about pleasure, we need to learn about what kind of stimuli are giving us rewards.

In his book *The Compass of Pleasure*, David J. Linden describes what happens in the brain when we feel pleasure: "Experiences that cause the dopamine-containing neurons of the ventral tegmental area (VTA) to be active and thereby release dopamine in their targets (the nucleus accumbens, the prefrontal cortex, the dorsal striatum, and the amygdale) will be felt as pleasurable."[9] I don't know what any of that means, but I'm pretty sure he's saying pleasure lives in our brain.

When you study pleasure, reward, and addiction, one word persists: dopamine. Dopamine is a neurotransmitter that is released when electrical spikes reach the axon terminals of neurons that are active in the VTA. Electrical and chemical events allow the dopamine to enter the synaptic cleft where they bind to dopamine receptors.[10] This in turn creates further chemical signals within the brain associated with pleasure. Interestingly, the dopamine is then recycled back to the axon terminals via a dopamine transporter to be released again later.[11] This cycle has been called the "pleasure circuit" or "reward circuit," and according to Dr. Linden, it is responsible for why you feel good when you exercise, eat fatty foods, have sex, and give to charity. But is it possible to feel *too* good?

The pleasure circuitry in rats is similar to that of humans. Dr. Linden describes the results of one experiment where rat brains were given unlimited access to dopamine: "Rats allowed to self-administer cocaine and amphetamines will ignore food, water, sex, their personal hygiene, and even their young offspring in favor of the drug. With such behavior these 'rat addicts' are a horrifyingly accurate reflection of the ruined lives of human drug addicts."[12]

Regrettably, this kind of experiment has also been conducted on humans. Dr. Linden describes the result of a study conducted on a psychiatric patient called "B-19" in 1972. Three months after electrodes were implanted in deep regions of his brain, he was allowed free access to the stimulator. He describes the results as recorded in the *Journal of Behavioral Therapy and Experimental Psychiatry*: 'During these sessions, B-19 stimulated himself to a point that, both behaviorally and introspectively, he was experiencing an almost overwhelming euphoria and elation and had to be disconnected despite his vigorous protests."[13] He would not—could not—stop stimulating himself.

YOUR BRAIN ON PORN

Dr. Philip Zimbardo explains the effects of pornography on the brain: "Pornography is a dopamine-producing machine. . . . Its presence helps initiate feelings of enjoyment and pleasure. . . . Once a person develops an addiction, the dopamine pathways become pathological. . . . When excessive porn viewing becomes addictive, the brain lights up as if it were on heroin."[14]

What happens when habitual use becomes a full blown addiction? "As addiction develops and tolerance, dependence, and cravings emerge, the euphoria produced by the drug gradually drains away. Pleasure is replaced by desire; liking becomes wanting."[15] Zimbardo references the works of Gary and Marnia Wilson and their website *Your Brain On Porn* (yourbrainonporn.com). Wilson writes: "Internet porn is now a powerful memory that calls to you at a subconscious level—because it's the most reliable source of dopamine. . . . This is what happens with all addictions. The more you overstimulate the reward circuitry by jacking up your dopamine . . . the less it responds."[16]

> WHEN THE REWARD CIRCUITRY IS ELEVATED FOR TOO LONG, IT EVENTUALLY BLOWS OUT.

The regulation of dopamine in our brain is a natural process that keeps us from starving, drives us towards relationships with others, and encourages altruism. But when the reward circuitry is elevated for too long, it eventually blows out.

Abusing your reward circuitry will not only put you at risk for a dangerous addiction, but it will also taint otherwise normal parts of your life that have become associated with the addictive behavior. Dr. Linden warns, "The sensory cues and actions that preceded and overlapped with those pleasurable experiences will be remembered and associated with positive feelings."[17]

In other words, whatever else you are doing, seeing, smelling, tasting, or touching when you feel pleasure will also become linked with pleasure. If you normally eat triple chocolate cake in front of the television, watching television may become a trigger for eating triple chocolate cake. If you engage in certain addictive behaviors in isolation, then finding yourself in isolation may become a trigger for desiring that behavior. And of course, many people "only smoke when they drink." The nicotine has become powerfully associated with alcohol.

Addictive behaviors not only have a powerful stimulating effect on the brain, they are actually changing brain pathology. Linden continues, "Habitual drug use produces a long-lasting rewiring of the addict's brain, which is manifested at the level of biochemistry, electrical function, and even neuronal structure."[18] Drugs and porn are rewiring the brain, and porn stars are going mainstream. Your kids may be watching them guest-star on their favorite sitcom, play a leading role on the next summer blockbuster, or tweet about their latest scandal. Jeffrey Satinover M.D., PhD, testified before Congress:

> With the advent of the computer, the delivery system for this addictive stimulus has become nearly resistance-free. It is as though we have devised a form of heroin 100 times more powerful than before, usable in the privacy of one's own home and injected directly to the brain through the eyes. It's now available in unlimited supply via a self-replicating distribution network, glorified as art and protected by the Constitution.[19]

Be careful when told to "enjoy [insert highly addictive behavior here] in moderation." Calling porn "erotica" doesn't make it any less addictive or destructive. Why would you crack the door for temptation and sin? Instead, follow the instructions from Ephesians 4:27 and "Do not give the devil a foothold."

The fallout from porn extends far beyond one individual's brain. The desire for porn can destroy careers, drain finances, ruin families, and end marriages. Even those downplaying porn as an "instructional aid" to help enhance their own monogamous sex life are playing with fire and should remember Proverbs 6:27 (if you play with fire, you're going to get burned).

Some like to say, "Who cares where you get the appetite as long as you come home for dinner?" This question is brought to you by the people who balk, "I'd rather be in hell. All my buddies will be there drinking beer!" Such people have tragically misguided understandings of both sex and hell. Hell is a place of conscious eternal torment. There will be great gnashing of teeth when they discover that cold beer and porn are nowhere to be found.

Marriage is the only context in which sexual love is legitimized, and porn exploits the natural instinct for that love. If your marriage is strong, and you understand the dangers of pornography, you have a chance at escaping the virtual sirens beckoning you to their bosom. But you must decide how you will view marriage before you can strengthen it.

It's time to look at marriage through the lens of various worldviews.

---

[1] Laura Berman, M.D., "When Your Man Is Too into Pornography," accessed July 19, 2012,
http://www.drlauraberman.com/sexual-health/addiction/pornography

-addiction.

[2] Warner Bros. Ent., "Magic Mike," accessed July 15, 2012, http://magicmikemovie.warnerbros.com/#.

[3] Kathryn Casey, "Is 'Fifty Shades of Grey' Dangerous?" Forbes, June 23, 2012, http://www.forbes.com/sites/crime/2012/06/23/is-fifty-shades -of-grey-dangerous.

[4] Bsecure online, "Statistics," Bsecure Technologies, accessed July 15, 2012, http://www.bsecure.com/Resources/Statistics.aspx.

[5] John D. Sutter, "Survey: 70% of teens hide online behavior from parents," Cable News Network, accessed July 19, 2012, http://www.cnn.com/2012/06/25/tech/web/mcafee-teen-online -survey/index.html?iref=allsearch.

[6] Ibid.

[7] Merriam-Webster, "Pleasure," accessed July 19, 2012, http://www.merriam-webster.com/dictionary/pleasure.

[8] Ibid., "Reward," accessed July 19, 2012.

[9] David J. Linden, *The Compass of Pleasure: How Our Brains Make Fatty Foods, Orgasm, Exercise, Marijuana, Generosity, Vodka, Learning, and Gambling Feel So Good*, (New York: Penguin Group, 2011), Kindle ed., loc. 293.

[10] Ibid., loc. 255.

[11] Ibid., loc. 304.

[12] Ibid., loc. 313.

[13] Ibid., loc. 213.

[14] Zimbardo, Philip G.; Duncan, Nikita, *The Demise of Guys: Why Boys Are Struggling and What We Can Do About It* (New York: TED, 2012), Kindle ed., loc. 769.

[15] Linden, *The Compass of Pleasure*, loc. 754.

[16] Zimbardo, *The Demise of Guys*, loc. 914.

[17] Linden, *The Compass of Pleasure*, loc. 294.

[18] Ibid., loc. 770.

[19] Jeffrey Satinover, M.S., M.D., "Jeffrey Satinover Statement to Congress on Pornography," Woodbury Reports, Inc., May 9, 2008, http://www.strugglingteens.com/news/RelatedNews/JeffreySatinover .pdf.

CHAPTER 18

YOUR WINGMAN FOR LIFE

Naval Air Weapons Station China Lake, California
September 1990

"After all, we are advocating the destruction of the
centrality of marriage and the nuclear family unit. . ."[1]

—ACTIVIST

"A man will leave his father and mother to be united to his
wife, and they will become one flesh" (Gen. 2:24).

—MOSES

I WOKE UP EARLY TO the sun shining through my hotel room window. I left the drapes open to assist with an early wakeup for a full day of sightseeing. I didn't expect to see anyone at breakfast; the squadron dinner no doubt included a second push, a push that I skipped with the knowledge (and experience to confirm) that nothing good happens after 10:00 p.m.

To my surprise, I ran into one of our new squadron members in the dining area. The weekend was his first social exposure event with the squadron. The quality of his "bar act" was yet to be determined. We found a table and began our getting-to-know-you breakfast.

"So, how did last night end up?" I asked him.

"It was fine," he replied—the standard guy-answer.

"Everybody make it back okay?" I hadn't received any texts, but it's always good to get a head count in the morning after a night on the town.

"I think so, but I'm not sure. I left pretty soon after the push to the strip club," he said.

That got me thinking. It explained why he was up so early. He looked as refreshed as I felt. I wondered what he thought about strip clubs. Did he pull a Houdini* in order to save face and follow his conscience? Was he worried about the temptation to feast on the exploitation of the feminine form? Is this a battle he frequently fought, to keep his thoughts pure in the company of the profane?

I had a glimmer of hope. This guy could have potential. He had the courage to go against the crowd. He could be one of our next great leaders in the ranks, a man known for standing on his principles. The military, like so many organizations full of young (and old) men bursting with testosterone and hooked on adrenaline, desperately needs leaders willing to abstain from, and speak out against the problems of sexual sin. I probed further with renewed hope to see what I could confirm.

"Oh," I said, "are strip clubs not your kind of thing?" I waited for his response, letting him summon the courage to disclose his judgment against men who delight in the exploitation of women.

"Oh, no," he replied, "I took two girls back to my room."

I took a bite of toast.

LOVE, TRUE LOVE

---

* Slang term for disappearing from a situation unnoticed.

It is clear God's intent for sexual love is to be expressed within the bounds of holy matrimony. But how an institution treats marriage reveals the level of sacredness (if any at all) attributed to sexual love.

In evaluating different religions, scrutiny is appropriate toward their founders. After all, the extent to which religions are created out of desire for money, power, and entertainment is proportional to the deception dealt by their founders. But before we look at how each religion's founding father (or mother) treated the institution in practice, we will briefly look at marriage in theory.

MARRIAGE IN THEORY

In Buddhism, marriage is a secular affair and is not considered a sacrament.[2] Marriage is neither encouraged nor discouraged. In Hinduism, *vivāha* describes the eight different types of marriage in the Vedic tradition, and marriage is one of the sixteen sacraments that elevate the husband and wife to a higher spiritual existence. Mormons affirm the sacredness of marriage, the importance of family, and the sanctity of life. The Jehovah's Witness official media web site describes marriage as a serious, lifelong commitment and an exclusive relationship requiring love and respect.[3]

Christian Science denies the reality of sin, death, and evil. You will be hard-pressed to find officially sanctioned views on sex and marriage without registering for their website. Nevertheless, the point is moot. If everything is spirit, and "matter has no life, hence . . . no real existence"[4] as the Eddy holy book *Science and Health with Key to the Scriptures* claims, then white gowns, flower girls, and gold rings are merely sophomoric traditions performed in spiritual naiveté.

Ex-New Ager and author of *Inside the New Age Nightmare* Randall Baer describes the marriage arrangement under his jettisoned worldview: "In New Age morality, there are no prohibitions against divorce. Whether a married couple stays together is based mainly upon 'soul growth compatibility.' That is, if after a time, two souls who are married start to grow in different directions, then it is appropriate, if desired, to dissolve the marriage and find other more spiritually compatible soul mates."[5] This fits their credo to "create your own reality according to what feels right for you." For the New Ager, "whether a person chooses to be homosexual, bisexual, monogamous, polygamous, or whatever is okay as long as 'it is right for you' or 'it is done with love and no one's hurt.'"[6]

Author Brad Scott left the movement and wrote about his experiences in *Embraced by the Darkness*. He predicts life in a future state of planetary evolution and consciousness: "More and more people would never marry because they would see no spiritual advantage in it. They would leap into and out of relationships to find their 'soul mates' or burn up their karma with one insignificant other after another, all in the name of their single-minded effort to liberate themselves from the clutches of maya."[7]

IN A FUTURE STATE OF PLANETARY EVOLUTION AND CONSCIOUSNESS, MORE AND MORE PEOPLE WOULD NEVER MARRY.

No worldview can guarantee the *reality* of commitment, fidelity, sacrifice, or unconditional love in marriage. But New Age thought fails to even deem these traits desirable. In fact, there's not much reason to get married at all. It must be unsettling to know any moment your spouse might trade you in for a fresh spirit.

The weight of an organization rests upon its leader. We've seen how a few worldviews treat marriage in theory. Next we'll look at how well their leaders upheld the spirit of the institution.

MARRIAGE IN PRACTICE

Helena Petrovna Blavatsky has been described as the mother of all Spiritualism. Peter Washington's biography *Madame Blavatsky's Baboon* details the life of the matriarch of Theosophy and foremother of the New Age Movement. Blavatsky was first married in 1848 at the age of seventeen to Nikifor Blavatsky. He was the Vice-Governor of Yerevan in the Caucasus and many years her senior. "At least one biographer," writes Walter Martin, author of *Kingdom of the Cults*, "asserts that she married General Blavatsky merely to spite her acid-tongued governess, who, in a moment of sarcasm, declared that even the noble old gentleman would not marry a shrew like Helena."[8] The marriage failed and she fled the arrangement after only three months. Washington notes that she "may or may not have had other lovers," and that she "sometimes denied the liaisons and sometimes hinted that they were true."[9] In 1875, while still married to her living husband, Madame Blavatsky married again to Georgian Michael Betanelly. Soon after, she concocted schemes to informally dissolve the relationship.[10]

Joseph Smith, founder of the Church of Jesus Christ of Latter Day Saints (LDS), had multiple wives before polygamy became church doctrine. Polygamy was later abolished in 1890 by LDS president Wilford Woodruff.[11] Smith married somewhere between thirty and forty women, some of whom already had husbands when they were "sealed" to the prophet.

Charles Taze Russell was the founder of the Jehovah's Witnesses. Maria Ackley married him in 1879 and later left him in 1897. She sued for separation in 1903, and the ordeal was finalized in 1906. Their court proceedings ended in 1909 when Russell gave her a settlement of around $6,000 dollars to avoid alimony. J.F. Rutherford, the organization's second patriarch, married Mary Malcolm Fetzertook in 1891. They later separated after Rutherford became the president of the Watchtower Society after Russell's death in 1942.[12]

Regarding the deity of Hinduism, Ravi Zacharias points out how the "playfulness of Krishna and his exploits with the milkmaids in the Bhagavad-Gita is . . . an embarrassment to many Hindu scholars."[13] Regarding Islam, Zacharias continues, "Mohammed's marriages to eleven wives have been a fascinating subject for Muslim scholars to explain."[14]

Siddhartha Gautama (later known as "the Buddha") abandoned his wife and son to seek enlightenment, and Bhagwan Shree Rajneesh was a sex guru who never married. Spiritualism is to Rajneesh as addiction is to dopamine. Whenever you begin to study one, you inevitably run into the other.

Mary Baker Eddy, founder of Christian Science, married three times. Her first husband died of yellow fever, she divorced the second, and her third died of coronary thrombosis (though she was convinced he died of mentally delivered arsenic poisoning, whatever that means).[15]

Then we have Jesus, the only spiritual leader who lived a sinless life and actually claimed to be God. Despite Dan Brown's imaginative tales told in *The Da Vinci Code*, there is no historical evidence that Jesus ever married. In 2012, a curious fragment of papyrus sent the nation abuzz with speculation about a reference to Jesus' "wife." No sooner than the report trended did skepticism emerge after experts intimated a clever forgery in a lucrative antiquities industry. His example of commitment and sacrificial love was expressed toward all of humanity rather than to one woman (or thirty).

The holy institution of marriage as modeled by Jesus to his church helps us understand the relationship between man and God. In Ephesians 5:22-33, Paul used the analogy of marriage to describe the sacrificial love that Christ has for the church. Jesus is the bridegroom and the church is his bride. Husbands are to "love their wives as Christ loved the church and gave himself up for her." Jesus also explains through Paul in 1 Corinthians 7:8, that while it is good to be married, it is also good to be single (which affords more devoted time to study and worship).

Believing religious leaders' claims of divine commission is easy if you ignore the historical record. But history reveals most were full of sin like me and you, and many of them failed at marriage.

I'm not claiming that a failed marriage invalidates religious doctrine, nor am I claiming religious doctrine on marriage invalidates theology. I am simply

NONE OF THESE RELIGIOUS LEADERS PROVE WORTHY OF WORSHIP . . . EXCEPT ONE.

pointing out that these men and women— worshipped almost as if they were God—experienced very human failure. None of these religious leaders prove worthy of worship . . . except one.

Jesus showed us why it is good to "wait" for marriage. Perhaps he could have chosen to marry on earth (I'll leave that debate to seminary students), but he decided to wait for the consummation of a *spiritual* union with his Church. Christians aren't embarrassed of their leader; they want you to investigate him as much as possible! Look for dirt; dig deep; ask the hard questions. They do so with confidence because throughout his birth, death, and resurrection, his purity remains.

Jesus' repute is universally acknowledged. He is the only human in history who never fails—at anything. His love is limitless and his anger toward sin is perfectly just. He knows what to say and do in every situation, and he never lies. Jesus is the actualization of what eight-fold-path-followers can only chase as chimerical ideals. It has become popular to say that "everything is one," but it is not.

ALL IS NOT ONE

Pantheists preach of "unlimited potential" and the "oneness of everything." They say things like "the universe has consciousness" and "everybody creates." Since they are often untroubled by contradictions, they will tell you that this "All-That-Is" god can be a personal god, but this is not so. David K. Clark in *Apologetics in the New Age* says, "Pantheists . . . generally argue that personhood is simply another of those delimiting concepts that reduce God to the level of our thought." He continues, "Personhood entails twoness, for to be personal is to be in relation to another person. . . . Since pantheism militates against any form of duality, God must *rise above personality* into the impersonal."[16] (Italics mine.)

When I began my search for answers to the big questions in life, I was looking for something extraordinary— something with inconceivable wisdom and undeniable truth. Jesus Christ alone answers the existential and philosophical questions of life with clarity and coherence. Honest seekers are thankful when they discover this for themselves.

But not everyone is a seeker, and not all seekers accept truth immediately. Jesus' siblings were not fully supportive of his ministry during his time on earth. We read in John 7:5, "For even his own brothers did not believe in him." You can find encouragement in this verse first by knowing that Jesus' brothers rejected him before the world rejected Christians, and second, that his brothers did eventually believe. You will be discouraged at times, but you must complete the mission.

One of your most important missions as a leader—a husband, a wife, a parent—is to keep drugs from destroying the people in your charge. Every year millions of Americans become casualties of a substance which has beat out crack and heroin in some studies for the title of "most dangerous" drug.[17]

It's time to talk about alcohol.

[1] Matthew Hays, "Not the marrying kind," *Daily Xtra*, Pink Triangle Press, January 13, 2012, http://dailyxtra.com/canada/news/the-marrying-kind
-51542.

[2] Buddha Dharma Education Association, Inc., "Buddhist Ethics," accessed January 11, 2013, http://www.buddhanet.net
/e-learning/budethics.htm.

[3] Watch Tower Bible and Tract Society of Pennsylvania, "Our Families," accessed September 5, 2012, http://www.jwmedia.org
/aboutjw/article2.htm.

[4] Mary Baker Eddy, *Science and Health with Key to the Scriptures* (Boston: Christian Science Board of Directors, 1994), 584.

[5] Randall N. Baer, *Inside the New Age Nightmare* (Lafayette: Huntington House, Inc., 1989), 54.

[6] Ibid., 88.

[7] Brad Scott, *Embraced by the Darkness* (Wheaton: Crossway, 1996), 164.

[8] Walter Martin, *Kingdom of the Cults* (Bloomington: Bethany House, 1997), Kindle ed., 284.

[9] Peter Washington, *Madame Blavatsky's Baboon: A History of the Mystics, Mediums, and Misfits Who Brought Spiritualism to America* (New York: Schocken Books, 1995), 30-31.

[10] Ibid., 48-49.

[11] Martin, *Kingdom of the Cults*, Kindle ed., 203.

[12] James M. Penton, *Apocalypse Delayed: The Story of Jehovah's Witnesses*, 2nd ed. (Toronto: University of Toronto Press, 1997), 72.

[13] Ravi Zacharias, *Jesus Among Other Gods: The Absolute Claims Of The Christian Message* (Nashville: Thomas Nelson, 2000), Kindle ed., 41.

[14] Ibid.

[15] Martin, *Kingdom of the Cults*, 150.

[16] David K. Clark and Norman L. Geisler, *Apologetics in the New Age: A Christian Critique of Pantheism* (Eugene: Wipf and Stock Publishers, 1990), 119.

[17] CNN wire staff, "Study: Alcohol 'most harmful drug,' followed by crack and heroin," CNN Health, Cable News Network, November 1, 2010, http://www.cnn.com/2010/HEALTH/11/01/alcohol.harm
/index.html.

CHAPTER 19

BORN IN A BAR

MCAS Iwakuni, Japan
April 2008

"Heavy drinking in the military has been an accepted custom and tradition."[1]

—*ENCYCLOPEDIA OF DRUGS, ALCOHOL, AND ADDICTIVE BEHAVIOR*

"Any perception that alcohol is central to our traditions is wrong."[2]

—*COMMANDANT CHARLES C. KRULAK*

THE UNITED STATES MARINE CORPS was born in a bar. On the eve of our nation's independence, a committee of the Continental Congress met at Tun Tavern in Philadelphia, PA, to draft a resolution calling for two battalions of Marines able to fight for independence at sea and on shore, and on November 10, 1775, the Marine Corps was born.[3]

Tun Tavern was a venue for the first recruitment drive and found no shortage of volunteers seeking cold beer and an opportunity to fight. Marines since have enjoyed throwing a few back after a hard day of training. Friday nights at the club have been an historic occasion to build camaraderie between men and women bonded by the brotherhood of service.

There are no laws—military, statutory, or moral—which prohibit responsible drinking by those of legal age. But when a Marine abuses alcohol, they are engaging in conduct prejudicial to good order and discipline. Similarly, when a Christian abuses alcohol, they are engaging in conduct prejudicial to sanctification. In the next two chapters, we will look at drunkenness from both a secular and a Christian perspective.

DRUNKENNESS

Heavy alcohol consumption has become a significant problem in the military. It has affected both service members and their families. It has cost military leaders political capital with host nations overseas and decreased force readiness at home. Dr. Robert Brewer, the Alcohol Program Lead for the National Center for Chronic Disease Prevention and Health Promotion, notes that many binge drinkers are active duty military personnel, along with college students, high school students, and medical students.[4] Health behavior studies have reported increases in heavy alcohol use, and we are at the point where the media is reporting substance abuse in the military as a public health crisis.

> THE MEDIA IS REPORTING SUBSTANCE ABUSE IN THE MILITARY AS A PUBLIC HEALTH CRISIS.

During a discussion about how to improve unit cohesion and morale, one Marine revealed a disturbing mindset about alcohol. We talked about the long hours the Marines were working which often included portions of the weekend. This Marine added her thoughts: "We're working on the jets all day Friday. We might get off around 8:00 p.m. Then we have to show up early the next morning, and some Marines need duty rest. That leaves them only two hours to get drunk on Friday!"

She spoke with genuine concern and annoyance. Her main concern was "when are we going to be able to get drunk?" and they were looking to their leaders for help. Instead they received counseling on why our culture accepts and promotes lifestyles which celebrate irresponsible drinking.

I have seen alcohol damage, destroy, disappoint, disgrace, debilitate, and dishonor those who abuse it. Yet many still look forward to getting tanked. Marine leaders have been looking for a solution. In 1996, General Charles C. Krulak, the 31st Commandant and top leader in the Marine Corps, issued the following statement in a message released to all Marines:

> [This] new comprehensive, aggressive campaign to deglamorize alcohol use…is the beginning of a cultural change that must result in decreased alcohol use throughout the Corps. That doesn't mean a change in Marine Corps tradition…*any perception that alcohol is central to our traditions is wrong.* The harm that alcohol abuse causes, which is reported to me every day, leads me to believe that this perception does exist. This must change. By working together, this campaign will not only benefit the Marine Corps, but also thousands of individual Marines and their family members.[5] (Italics and brackets mine.)

The Commandant, the Marine Corps' highest ranking officer, is sending the right message: "All leaders must guard against reckless behavior—it jeopardizes the health, safety, and combat readiness of our entire force. Risk mitigation is one of the best means available as we fight to eliminate senseless and needless loss of life and injury, both on duty and on liberty."[6]

According to the Commandant, the fact that the Marine Corps was born in a bar should remain a piece of history, not a justification for excessive alcohol consumption. This begs the question: if Marines have been told not to abuse alcohol, then why are some Marines abusing alcohol? Somewhere between the Commandant and the corporal is a disconnect between Marine Corps standards and what some Marines believe is acceptable behavior.

COMMANDER'S INTENT

"Commander's intent" is the military concept that allows small-unit leaders flexibility in executing their orders. It's like a common sense clause allowing decision makers to take guidance from the commander and use their own initiative to achieve the higher unit objective. An infantry officer might be given orders to defend a hill, but if the commander's intent is to minimize losses, he might need to fall back to a more advantageous position if overrun. Commander's intent keeps him from blindly defending the hill in the face of certain death.

Another useful analogy is speeding. We are supposed to obey the speed limit, and by exceeding the speed limit, we are breaking the law (in most states). What reasons might you have for speeding? I can think of two. First, you might think the speed limit is inappropriate—you think the speeds are too slow or that it is safer to go with the flow of traffic. Second, you might believe you can exceed the speed limit while satisfying the intent of the law, which is to maintain a safe driving environment.

In the case of teaching Marines about responsible drinking, commander's intent has been omitted or misconstrued when passed down to the lower unit levels. The Commandant's intent for the campaign to deglamorize alcohol is to guard against reckless behavior that jeopardizes the health, safety, and combat readiness of the entire force.

However, somewhere down the line, the commander's intent has been construed to mean "Just don't get into trouble. If you're going to abuse alcohol, have a plan to get home safely, and if your plan fails, make sure your buddy has a backup plan."

IT'S OKAY, I'M JUST DRUNK

Before every holiday weekend, commanders assemble their unit and urge them to "be responsible" by avoiding drowsy driving, using the proper personal protective equipment before various sports and activities, and most important, applying sunscreen! Commanders lavish their Marines with encouragement to be safe and to use good judgment in every situation. Then they address alcohol by urging everyone to drink responsibly.

But what does drinking responsibly mean to a 22-year-old? Years ago, I might have answered: having a designated driver if you plan to get drunk, making sure you have liquor *then* beer (you know how the saying goes), and having a solid rehydration plan. Have a plan: check. Take care of each other: check. Use common sense: check.

Unfortunately, the guidance above can fail because common sense is neither commonly understood nor commonly applied. The end result is leaders who feel like they have covered their bases and Marines with just enough rope to hang themselves. I have seen responsible drinking defined as a self-imposed limitation on time, place and quantity when consuming alcohol. *Perfect! I'll drink only after 5:00 p.m., only at the Officer's Club, and no more than five drinks per hour. Start drafting the citation for my responsible drinking medal!*

Sometimes the effects of "alcohol related incidents" are emphasized rather than the judgment of the people who caused them. The result of alcohol abuse with damaging repercussions: scowls, lectures, stand downs, training, and counseling. The result of alcohol abuse that ends happily ever after: laughter and sighs of relief, "Whew. Thank God no one got hurt or in trouble. The Marines have been working hard. They deserve to cut loose."

The language used when describing non-drinkers hurts the effort. The educational material says "it is *okay* not to drink," as if abstinence from alcohol was an alternative lifestyle choice. Saying something is "okay" carries a connotation of acceptable-but-inferior. It's like telling Marines "it is *okay* to cry." While the statement is true, it doesn't make me want to stand in front of a formation of Marines with a K-Bar in one hand and Kleenex in the other. The presentation of the message conveys a judgment on the action, and the judgment is: not tough, not cool, not Marine.

A better way to deglamorize alcohol is to replace "it is okay not to drink" with "it is *not* okay to get drunk." In this way, the leader condemns the problematic act (getting drunk) instead of merely affirming the nonproblematic avoidance of the act (staying sober). Abstinence is a responsible choice and can reflect wisdom and strength of character, and with all the dangers associated with alcohol abuse, abstinence guarantees protection from its pitfalls. As long as teetotalers are viewed as social odd-balls, Marines will receive abstinence as awkwardly as it is suggested.

I have never heard a commander tell his men simply not to get "drunk." I wonder, why not? Plenty have warned not to get drunk *and do something stupid.* Why do leaders think people can get drunk and refrain from being stupid?

> THAT IS NOT WHAT OUR COMMANDANT CONDONES, NOR WHAT OUR NATION EXPECTS.

I suspect there are still corporals, captains, and colonels who believe it is okay to get drunk as long as nothing bad happens (or gets reported). That not what our Commandant condones, nor what our nation expects from its defenders having been reposed with special trust and confidence.

In the world of international security studies, there is a concept known as soft power where one country attempts to make their values and goals desirable to another country.

This is similar to the lifestyle evangelism method of sharing Christ's truth with the world. This involves building relationships and simply modeling the Christian lifestyle.[7] The emphasis is not on preaching or explaining, but simply showing others what a life transformed by Jesus looks like. Soft power and lifestyle evangelism are both ways of walking the walk.

Diplomacy is an additional instrument of national power involving compromise and persuasion. Similarly, apologetics is another important aspect of evangelism and involves defending the faith. In order to give a good reason for the hope that we have (as Peter encourages us in 1 Peter 3:15), we must be able to not only explain what we believe, but why we believe it.

Diplomacy and apologetics are both ways of talking the talk. Many Christians can walk the walk, but can't talk the talk. This creates significant problems for people who need barriers removed before the path to their heart will be open. In the campaign to deglamorize alcohol, many leaders are talking the talk, but not walking the walk.

MIXED MESSAGES
Clear guidance and prohibitions from a commanding officer are powerful weapons available to a Marine fighting against peer pressure. However, some leaders might fear the hypocrisy of prohibiting activities they once enjoyed. This line of thinking strips the leader of a necessary authority. It is similar to a parent thinking that they can't prohibit a child from smoking because they once smoked. The results can be tragic.

"Work hard, play hard" is an oft-used rationalization used to muzzle the whispers of conscience when we debase ourselves. "Don't do anything I wouldn't do (wink, wink)," is used to provide obligatory guidance to junior Marines without feeling indicted by the Ghost of Military Past. This leaves the young Marines confused about what is really off-limits and what is not. It also leaves them with less top cover when their buddies suggest taking the low road.

Temptation breeds rationalization. *I know technically it is wrong, but it is not affecting anyone but me. Nobody's perfect. Aren't we allowed some mistakes? I'm really a good person and this isn't that big of a deal in the grand scheme of things. Plus, I'm sure God will forgive me . . . .*

This kind of thinking leads to a moral fork in the road. Do you give in to temptation in a moment of weakness, only to later find yourself in a predictable state of shame and disappointment? Or do you remain steadfast with the strength of the Spirit and preserve your integrity and relationship with the Lord?

But I know God will forgive me . . . .

There is a warning in 1 Corinthians 10:9 against testing the Lord, and verses 12-13 lay out the following advice: "So, if you think you are standing firm, be careful that you don't fall! No temptation has overtaken you except what is common to mankind. And God is faithful; he will not let you be tempted beyond what you can bear. But when you are tempted, he will also provide a way out so that you can endure it."

WHAT KIND OF SPIRIT MESSES WITH TEMPTATION? A DEAD ONE.

I thought of my father's words about what kind of pilot messes with the weather. *What kind of spirit messes with temptation? A dead one.* When dabbling with the thought of sinning, we need to find the way out that God has provided. When you find the exit, run for the door and remember what happened to Lot's wife when she looked back! Unfortunately, some people have not found the exit, others aren't looking, and some are standing in the way.

We cannot afford for our leaders to passively condone drunkenness. Our leaders need to acknowledge that getting drunk is alcohol abuse, and it's wrong to intentionally get wasted. The attempt to deglamorize alcohol is not about crushing fun; the goal is to keep Marines ready, their families healthy, and their reputations untarnished. Commanding Officers have every right to tell their Marines not to get drunk. In fact, they have an obligation.

Christians have an obligation, too. Their "freedom in Christ" allows for drinking, but when they drink to get drunk, they're missing the mark.

It's time to look at drunkenness from the Biblical perspective.

---

[1] Gale Cengage, "Military, Drug And Alcohol Abuse In The United States," *Encyclopedia of Drugs, Alcohol, and Addictive Behavior Vol. 2,* ed. Rosalyn Carson-DeWitt (New York: Macmillan Reference USA, 2001), eNotes.com, April 13, 2013, http://www.enotes.com/military-drug -alcohol-abuse-united-states-reference.

[2] ALMAR 151/96, April 15, 1996.

[3] United States Marine Corps, "Timeline," Marines.com, April 1, 2012, http://www.marines.com/history-heritage/timeline.

[4] Dr. Sanjay Gupta, "Americans Binge drinking More," CNN Health, Cable News Network, January 10, 2012, http://thechart.blogs.cnn.com/2012/01/10/americans-binge-drinking -more/?hpt=hp_t3).

[5] ALMAR 151/96, 15 April 1996.

[6] Lt. Matt Allen, "21st Century Sailor and Marine Initiative Highlighted in Afghanistan," Navy.mil, March 19, 2012, http://www.navy.mil/search/display.asp?story_id=65956.

[7] D. Story, *Engaging the Closed Minded: Presenting Your Faith to the Confirmed Unbeliever* (Grand Rapids: Kregel Publications, 1999) 11.

CHAPTER 20

DOWN TO THE DREGS

MCAS Iwakuni, Japan
February 2009

"Let me get wine! Let us drink our fill of beer! And tomorrow will be like today, or even far better" (Isaiah 56:12).

—ISAIAH

"Wine is a mocker and beer a brawler; whoever is led astray by them is not wise"
(Prov. 20:1)."

—SOLOMON

A CHRISTIAN CANNOT FORM A Biblical opinion on drinking without referencing the Bible. No need to panic; the New Testament does not prohibit drinking alcohol outright. There are some cases in the Old Testament where people voluntarily abstained from drinking alcohol; however, "Thou shalt not drink" never made the list of commandments (although countless other prohibitions are established by Biblical principles external to the Ten Commandments).

In the Old Testament, grain and new wine frequently represent abundance and the favor of God. Wine is described in a pleasurable light throughout the Song of

Solomon, and Jesus thought wine worthy of a miracle when he attended a wedding in Cana. Wine was also used to treat wounds (Luke 10:34), sooth the effects of maladies (1 Tim. 5:23), and help illustrate analogies (Matt. 9:17). Even the priest of God Most High, Melchizedek, brought out bread and wine to bless Abraham in the Book of Genesis.

However, this is an area where we should temper our freedom in Christ with good judgment. The farmer in the parable of the rich fool in Luke, chapter 12, thought we should eat, drink, and be merry amid an abundance of possessions and beverages. Getting drunk might lead to embarrassing and damaging circumstances, but isn't that part of the whole experience? Isn't that where legends are born, whose liquid courage and epic feats of strength become immortalized in the telling and re-telling of their tales? In order to validate the worth of drunkenness, it is wise to look at some of the oldest stories being retold today.

You only have to get to the ninth chapter of Genesis to find the first train wreck. Noah got drunk, naked, and fell asleep. By seeing his father's nakedness, his son destroyed the sanctity of the family, and the strength of the father was made a mockery.[1] Ten chapters later, both of Lot's daughters manipulated their father by getting him drunk, committing incest, and bearing his children in order to preserve the family line. In 2 Samuel, chapter 13, King David's son, Absalom, enraged at his brother Amnon for raping his sister Tamar, ordered his men to wait until Amnon was in "high spirits from drinking wine" before murdering him.

It is worth asking: does God give us any examples where *good* things happen in a drunken state? From what I have seen, mixing blurred vision, impaired judgment, and unrestraint within an inculpable ethic concocts an unstable brew with a bitter aftertaste.

THE UNBRIDLED PURSUIT OF PLEASURE WILL LEAD TO MONETARY AND SPIRITUAL IMPOVERISHMENT.

Let's look at what God has revealed to us about drunkenness. "Wine is a mocker and beer a brawler; whoever is led astray by them is not wise" (Prov. 20:1). In other words, a fool allows himself to be led astray by alcohol. "Whoever loves pleasure will become poor; whoever loves wine and oil will never be rich" (Prov. 21:17). Instant gratification and the unbridled pursuit of pleasure will lead to monetary and spiritual impoverishment. "Do not join those who drink too much wine or gorge themselves on meat, for drunkards and gluttons become poor, and drowsiness clothes them in rags" (Prov. 23:20-21). We are to exercise self control and resist peer pressure to join in activities that offend God, shame ourselves, and dishonor our service.

> Who has woe? Who has sorrow? Who has strife? Who has complaints? Who has needless bruises? Who has bloodshot eyes? Those who linger over wine, who go to sample bowls of mixed wine. Do not gaze at wine when it is red, when it sparkles in the cup, when it goes down smoothly! In the end it bites like a snake and poisons like a viper. Your eyes will see strange sights and your mind will imagine confusing things. You will be like one sleeping on the high seas, lying on top of the rigging. "They hit me," you will say, "but I'm not hurt! They beat me, but I don't feel it! When will I wake up so I can find another drink?" (Prov. 23:29-35).

Drunkenness is damaging mentally, physically, socially, and spiritually. "It is not for kings, Lemuel—it is not for kings to drink wine, nor for rulers to crave beer, lest they drink and forget what has been decreed, and deprive all the oppressed of their rights" (Prov. 31:4-7). Those appointed by God to leadership positions have a greater responsibility to avoid harmful activities.

"They cast lots for my people and traded boys for prostitutes; they sold girls for wine to drink" (Joel 3:3). Enslaving desires for alcohol can lead to other immoral behavior. When we allow vices and addictions to interfere with legitimate duties and obligations, the addiction can take over. "People are slaves to whatever has mastered them" (2 Pet. 2:19). The masters of alcohol, nicotine, and pornography are ruthless and unforgiving; they do not discriminate and hold millions under their control.

"Let us therefore make every effort to do what leads to peace and to mutual edification. Do not destroy the work of God for the sake of food. All food is clean, but it is wrong for a person to eat anything that causes someone else to stumble. It is better not to eat meat or drink wine or to do anything else that will cause your brother or sister to fall" (Rom. 14:19-21). Even if I drink responsibly, other Biblical principles require me to exercise restraint in some circumstances.

"In the hand of the Lord is a cup full of foaming wine mixed with spices; he pours it out, and all the wicked of the earth drink it down to its very dregs" (Ps. 75:8). Here the cup of wine represents judgment. The Book of Galatians describes drunkenness as an act of sinful behavior. Those who indulge in a life of sin will drink from the Lord's cup of judgment:

> Woe to those who are heroes at drinking wine and champions at mixing drinks, who acquit the guilty for a bribe, but deny justice to the innocent. Therefore, as tongues of fire lick up straw and as dry grass sinks down in the flames, so their roots will decay and their flowers blow away like dust; for they have rejected the law of the Lord Almighty and spurned the word of the Holy One of Israel. Therefore the Lord's anger burns against his people; his hand is raised and he strikes them down. The

mountains shake, and the dead bodies are like refuse in the streets (Isa. 5:22-25).

Refuse is defined either as trash or garbage, or the useless or worthless part of something. Woe to those who are heroes at drinking wine? My, how far we have come. Today's refrain is more like "hooray to those who are heroes at floating kegs and downing shots!" A fighter pilot's "bar act" (combined with other factors) can influence a pilot's fate—if he lets it.

"Do not get drunk on wine, which leads to debauchery. Instead, be filled with the Spirit" (Eph. 5:18). It doesn't get clearer than that. Instead we are to abide by the instructions Paul gave in his letter to the Romans: "Let us behave decently, as in the daytime, not in carousing and drunkenness, not in sexual immorality and debauchery, not in dissension and jealousy. Rather, clothe yourselves with the Lord Jesus Christ, and do not think about how to gratify the desires of the flesh" (Rom. 13:13-14). Drunkenness didn't end well in Biblical times, and it doesn't end well today. Being a Christian does not mean we will not sin; it means owning up to it when we stumble. The difference between stumbling into sin and *living in* sin is monumental, and once the process of sanctification has begun, a Christian will recognize sin in places where he was once blind. If a Christian is drinking with the intention to get drunk, they are not stumbling—they are already on the ground.

DRUNKENNESS DIDN'T END WELL IN BIBLICAL TIMES, AND IT DOESN'T END WELL TODAY.

After warning of false teachers and the love of money in 1 Timothy, chapter 6, Paul gives Timothy advice for responding to charlatans and sinful desires in general: "But you, man of God, flee from all this, and pursue righteousness, godliness, faith, love, endurance and gentleness." Notice, he does not say we are to tolerate sin as long as it is not hurting anyone else. He does not say to ignore sin as long as it is not affecting us. He does not say to look the other way, or to turn our back on sin while remaining in its presence. He says to *flee* from sin! The Greek word used in this case can also mean to "escape." This is appropriate given the nature of sin to hold us captive to its seductive promises of pleasure. We are to run from it! Flee from it! Escape it any way we can!

A LITMUS TEST

Drunkenness is clearly prohibited as evidenced by the scripture above, but if you're still not convinced, we can ask some simple questions to determine whether an act is in accordance with Biblical principles. John Feinberg in his book *Ethics for a Brave New World* helps us exercise discernment in cases not explicitly covered in the Bible. If unsure whether you should engage in a particular act, ask yourself the following questions: "Am I fully persuaded that it is right? . . . Can I do it as unto the Lord? . . . Can I do it without it being a stumbling block to my brother or sister in Christ? . . . Does it bring peace? . . . Does it edify my brother? . . . Is it profitable? . . . Does it enslave me? . . . Does it bring glory to God?"[2]

You may be able to drink responsibly, but if you're at a work-sponsored function and one of your Christian colleagues is a recovering alcoholic, the prudent action may be to abstain for the night lest your actions cause him to stumble.

In his letter to the Corinthians, the apostle Paul writes in chapter 10, verse 23: "'I have the right to do anything,' you say—but not everything is beneficial. 'I have the right to do anything'—but not everything is constructive. No one should seek their own good, but the good of others." This addresses how we are to use our freedom in Christ.

Christians have the right to drink responsibly; however, conscience or principle will demand that some Christians choose abstinence.

After seeing how drunkenness is viewed from both a secular and Christian perspective, we must demand our leaders call drunkenness by its name—alcohol abuse—and condemn it as wrong. The burden is not on the teetotaler to prove his camaraderie—it falls on the head of our leaders to set both the expectations and the example.

Leaders must be consistent and ready to challenge policies drafted with a distorted view of the world. Leaders who fail this test fail their team.

Men and women will look to their leaders for answers. And they must always be ready.

---

[1] J. F. Walvoord and R. B. Zuck, *The Bible Knowledge Commentary: An Exposition of the Scriptures* (Wheaton: Victor Books, 1983), Gen. 9:18–23.

[2] Feinman, John S.; Feinman, Paul D., *Ethics for a Brave New World* (Wheaton: Crossway Books, 1993), 44-45.

PART III
ALWAYS BE
READY

CHAPTER 21

PUTTING OUT
CHAFF

Clearwater, Florida
December 2010

*"We are going to go right on trying to discredit you in the
eyes of your children, trying to strip your fundamentalist
religious community of dignity, trying to make your views
seem silly rather than discussable."*[1]

— RICHARD RORTY

*"Turn away from godless chatter and the opposing ideas of
what is falsely called knowledge, which some have professed
and in so doing have wandered from the faith"*
(1 Tim. 1:20-21).

—THE APOSTLE PAUL

FIGHTER PILOTS PUT OUT COUNTERMEASURES called chaff to
confuse enemy radar systems. Thin pieces of aluminum or
metalized plastic are ejected from the aircraft and bloom into
a reflective chaff cloud. Chaff muddles the picture as the
radar operator attempts to track the target.

Chaff is a decoy intended to fool the unsuspecting into
thinking they have found what they are looking for. A
successful radar operator must learn how to distinguish
between chaff and real targets. The Bible uses a different

kind of chaff—that of wheat grain—in harvesting analogies to distinguish nourishment from waste.

Some worldviews are like chaff. Seekers believe they have found what they are looking for, but they have actually locked on to an imitation. They mistake nourishment for something indigestible. We must learn to separate the wheat from the chaff—truth from fiction—when investigating the various worldviews.

WHAT'S THIS RELIGION BUSINESS?

During a trip to Florida, I took a detour through the town of Clearwater, the Mecca of Scientology. After walking one lap around the deserted streets surrounding their self-described Super Power Building, I had a clear case of the heeby-jeebies. Author Janet Reitman spent five years compiling information to write an extensive modern history of Scientology. She described science fiction writer L. Ron Hubbard, founder of one of the most litigious religious organizations in the world, as "the Madame Blavatsky of 1950."[2]

Scientology is a religion whose Messiah offered not only healing, but mental and spiritual upgrades as well. Like a fantasy role-playing game, you trade your currency for tools and experience in order to level-up. Hubbard understood the power of manipulation and the profit in gullibility. The keepers of Scientology reportedly only share their secret theology with the elite (though it is readily available on the Internet), and most services come with a fee.

Later that year, I had the opportunity to speak with a Scientologist manning a small booth outside a local Walmart, sporting the trademark E-meter and stack of books. This individual, whom I'll call Rod, became a Scientologist in the 1970s.

I spoke with him for about thirty minutes, asking honest questions, and sharing my Christian faith in the process. Rod was very proud of their state-of-the-art facilities. He bragged how people plan on coming in for ten minutes and stay there for five hours—even "forgetting to pick up little Suzie from school!" When I asked him what you had to believe to be a Scientologist and how it works, he replied, "It works because it *works*! It has nothing to do with belief. Scientology is beyond belief."

I couldn't argue with his last point.

I recalled Reitman's expose on the organization's complicated system of manufacturing, services, and licensing. It brought in loads of cash, and Hubbard bragged of his millions stashed in a Swiss bank account. Fortunately, you no longer have to take out a second mortgage to be let in on Scientology's big secret. All you need is an internet connection or a book from one of the organization's disgruntled former members.

It will come as no surprise that the religion founded by a science fiction writer contains a creation story via handwritten space opera on a single page. If you're into aliens and spacecraft and volcanoes, you will find the story entertaining. I will spare the details and simply say that Scientology posits the existence of spiritual parasites attached to our bodies, and the goal of Scientology is to clear the body of those parasites. This should enable you to now do all the great things promised by the nice guy in the booth or the cute girl in the bookstore.

QUESTIONS BEGINNING WITH "WHY" ULTIMATELY LEAD TO THE SPIRITUAL REALM.

When an evangelist explains Scientology as non-religious or pan-denominational, you should take it with a grain of salt. No, a whole pillar.

BREAKING THE SHACKLES OF NATURALISM

Questions beginning with "why" ultimately lead to the spiritual realm. Science can explain how the earth orbits the sun, but it cannot tell us why electrons obey the laws of physics.[3] Science helps describe the relationship between matter, space, and time in the natural world, but philosophy is man's quest to answer questions about First Things. What existed before the universe? Why does the universe exist?

In a secular society science is king, but the king's authority has boundaries. His power resides only within his kingdom. The kingdom of science is the natural world.

When a scientist forays into the field of metaphysics, he must doff his crown. The reductionist nature of science can strengthen an inclination toward naturalism, but penetrating the depths of the cosmos and the human cell reveals that only a mind is capable of creating our universe. Antony Flew reminds us that even famed theoretical physicists Heisenberg and Planck believed in a "divine Mind."[4] After breaking free from the shackles of naturalism, exploring the spiritual realm no longer seems a worthless exercise.

THE POWER TO HEAL CAN BE AN IRRESISTIBLE ENTICEMENT.

A God this powerful has the power to heal. But some spiritualists would rather convince you to supernaturally heal yourself.

THE ALLURE OF HEALING AND POWER

A search for God will lead you to evaluate the world's major religions, most of which offer healing. Many alternative therapy practitioners offer some kind of power. The promise of power and the prospect of healing are very attractive, and when combined, the power to heal can be an irresistible enticement.

Some religions offer spiritual healing while others emphasize physical or emotional healing. There will always be a demand for healing, and all offers will be voraciously pursued.

The universal desire for healing corresponds to the intuitive notion that our bodies, our minds, and our souls are not as they should be. An ideal world would not be plagued with evil and suffering, but evil and suffering exist. Therefore, the world is not perfect. If it ever was, something has gone terribly wrong.

And so the process of elimination begins. Start with any philosophy claiming that you are perfect, complete, or denies the reality of sickness or evil. Next, throw out any ideas that deny a distinction between good and bad. These assertions are unfounded and counter to human experience.

Next, look for generalizations. Contrary to the platitude that "all religions are basically the same," most major religions make mutually exclusive claims. That means they cannot all be correct. The belief that all religious paths are equally valid is called religious pluralism, and it is self-defeating. If my religion says religious pluralism is false, then the religious pluralist must accept my claim—which claims that his own belief is false! They are doomed to the same fate as the skeptic who must remain skeptical about his skepticism, or the person who doesn't believe in beliefs.

The founders of several major religious movements claimed a healing experience as the genesis of their enlightenment. In the late 19th century, a number of esoteric spiritualists claimed healing power and secret knowledge. I learned about one of these leaders by a fascinating coincidence.

EDDYFICATION

When my Grandpa Norm passed away, my grandmother collected some of his writings. She had them copied, bound, and provided one for each family household. The collection included journal entries from his naval service in WWII, genealogy and family history information, a newspaper article on his hole-in-one, and various other snippets.

While reading a section on his family history, I came across the name of his mother, my great-grandmother Grace Eddy. The name was more familiar now than before. Then I remembered why: I had discovered a possible genealogical link to a well-known figure in the history of American religion.

I took to the Internet that night. The thought of confirming the link was exciting and weird. After two nights of searching and a page full of names, birthdates, and marriages, I confirmed the discovery: my great-great-great-great-great-great aunt by marriage was Mary Baker Eddy, founder of Christian Science.

In the yearbook of religious history, Christian Science should win the superlative for "most confusing title." The website Christianscience.com describes the organization as "based on the Bible and is explained in *Science and Health with Key to the Scriptures* and other writings by Mary Baker Eddy."[5] However, some teachings (e.g. Jesus is not God; and sin, death, and evil do not exist) contradict essential beliefs that comprise the core of orthodox Christianity. Additionally, other beliefs (e.g. there is no literal, physical existence of the material universe) are anything but scientific.[6] The website explains how Christian Science was born after an accident in 1866:

> [Mary Baker Eddy] had a severe fall. After three days her health was not improving, so she asked for her Bible and became completely well after reading two of Jesus' healings. Throughout her life she'd been able to heal others, but now she began to understand the science behind the activity. Often asked how she was able to heal, Eddy explained and documented it in her primary

work, *Science and Health*, and named her discovery Christian Science.[7] (Brackets mine.)

Walter Martin deflates Eddy's claims of divine authorship with evidence she plagiarized from Phineas Parkhurst Quimby, a peer and "mental healer" from whom she also took the term "Christian Science."[8] Eddy was just one of several who adopted the 19th century habit of starting a new religion after healing from an injury.

NEW AGE, OLD IDEAS

Madame Helena P. Blavatsky was the founder of the Theosophical Society and the mother of the New Age Movement which exploded in the 1990s. Armed with a spunky personality and a vivid imagination, the movement was founded more in the fulfillment of her ego than the pursuit of truth.

Madame Blavatsky was a spiritual-seeker-turned-magician. Described by Peter Washington in *Madame Blavatsky's Baboon* as "self-absorbed and egotistical,"[9] she was a master performer who masqueraded as a spiritual medium and delighted in chicanery. Despite her dream of creating a single wisdom religion for the entire world, she held some worldviews higher than others.

Peter Washington explains how she "took little account" of the world's three Abrahamic religions: Christianity, Judaism, and Islam.[10] Heavily influenced by Buddhist philosophy, Blavatsky' teachings became less inclusive of Christianity and more heavily aligned with eastern occultism. Washington thoroughly exposes her fraudulent behavior in his book befittingly subtitled *A History of the Mystics, Mediums, and Misfits who Brought Spiritualism to America.*

The growing influence of eastern thought in the West is largely due to Blavatsky's influence along with fellow spiritualist Henry Olcott. Together they created great spectacles to satisfy a growing population hungry for esoteric knowledge, ecstatic experiences, and divine wisdom. Unfortunately for her patrons, Madame Blavatsky's parlor experiences—complete with séances, materializing letters, and invisible spirit guides—were exposed as simple parlor tricks.

BLAVATSKY'S PARLOR EXPERIENCES WERE EXPOSED AS SIMPLE PARLOR TRICKS.

Blavatsky became a Buddhist and founded the Theosophical Society in 1875. Theosophy is based upon the philosophy of Monism (all is one) and the theology of Pantheism (all is God). Since everything is one, man is everything, and since everything is God, man is God. Once you've mentally evolved yourself from the product of design to the ultimate divine, why *wouldn't* you claim unlimited potential, total creative power, and secret wisdom?

For the last hundred years, these ideas flourished and became the basis for the numerous beliefs and practices lumped under the overall category of the New Age Movement. Many Christians involved in New Age practices are unaware these activities are spiritually harmful. Walter Martin's extensive list of words and phrases associated with the movement deserve restating here:

Monism, Pantheism, Reincarnation, Karma, Evolution, Personal Transformation, Unlimited Human Potential, Reality Creating, Energy Alignment, Energy Healing, Energy Focusing, Attunement, At-one-ment, Enlightenment, Inner Power, Goddess Within, Mother Earth, Sensory Deprivation, Intuitive Abilities, Near-Death Experiences, Chakras, Gurus, Tarot, Kabbalah,

Pyramids, Crystal, Power, Auras, Color Balancing, Psychic Centering, Extraterrestrials, Brotherhood of Light, Higher Consciousness, Cosmic Consciousness, The Christ, Ascended Masters, Spirit Guides, Mediation, Yoga, Guided Imagery, Visualization, Astral Projection, Silver Cord, Inner Light, Out-of-Body Experiences, Mystics, Metaphysical, Holistic Healing, Therapeutic Touch, Biofeedback, Transpersonal Psychology, Hypnotherapy, Paranormal, Parapsychology, Higher Self…and Values Clarification.[11]

CRICK, CRACK, KUNDALINI?

Eastern religion not only conceived the New Age Movement in the West; it affected other practices as well. Daniel David Palmer was the father of chiropractic medicine. The science and art of spinal adjustment to help heal the body is widely practiced. It is believed to produce health benefits by influencing the body via the nervous system. What is probably less well-known are the metaphysical assumptions of its founder.

Kundalini is a Sanskrit word to describe a corporeal energy which supposedly resides at the base of the spine and can be awakened by practicing certain esoteric disciplines. Palmer believed a guiding energy flows throughout the body, calling it "innate intelligence." Authors Simon Singh and Edzard Ernst, MD, write in *Trick or Treatment*, "Palmer viewed God as the Universal Intelligence, guiding the totality of existence, which meant that innate intelligence represented God's guiding influence within the human body."[12] Subluxations, or displacements of the spine, were thought to interfere with this innate intelligence. He believed spinal adjustments unblocked the flow of this energy, thus allowing it to cure much more than back and neck ailments.[13]

Not all chiropractors subscribe to Palmer's belief in special life-force energy. Chiropractors who rejected the religious component integrated more heavily with mainstream science and took on the label of back specialist.[14] Known as *mixers*, these practitioners are less likely to advertise health benefits far beyond problems directly related to the back and neck.

Believers in Palmer's innate intelligence are known as *straights* and commonly advertise chiropractic's ability to help with asthma, pregnancy, premenstrual syndrome, allergies, osteoporosis, fibromyalgia, colic, carpal tunnel, attention deficit hyperactivity disorder and more. Singh and Ernst conclude that spinal manipulation has no impact on non-musculoskeletal conditions.[15] Before I part with my hard-earned cash, I want to know if the person is cracking my back or channeling my Chi. I think cracking my back just might work.

Some spiritual leaders preach undeniable truths about the world. Others are putting out chaff. Sometimes we must make the painful conclusion that we have been fooled.

More important, we must learn from our mistakes.

---

[1] Richard Rorty, ed. Robert B. Brandom, "Universality and Truth," *Rorty and His Critics* (Oxford: Blackwell, 2000), 22.

[2] Janet Reitman, *Inside Scientology: The Story of America's Most Secretive Religion* (New York: Houghton Mifflin Harcourt Publishing Company, 2011), Kindle ed., 31.

[3] Dinesh D'Souza, *What's So Great About Christianity?* (Washington D.C.: Regnery, 2007), Kindle ed., 136.

[4] Flew and Roy Abraham Varghese, *There Is a God* (New York: Harper Collins Inc., 2007) Kindle ed., 237.

[5] Christian Science Board of Directors, "What is Christian Science?" accessed October 20, 2012, http://christianscience.com/what-is-christian-science.

[6] Walter Martin, *Kingdom of the Cults* (Bloomington: Bethany House, 1997), Kindle ed., 147.

[7] Christian Science Board of Directors, "About the founder, Mary Baker Eddy," accessed October 20, 2012, http://christianscience.com/what-is-christian-science#history-of-cs.

[8] Martin, *Kingdom of the Cults*, 151.

[9] Peter Washington, *Madame Blavatsky's Baboon: A History of the Mystics, Mediums, and Misfits Who Brought Spiritualism to America* (New York: Schocken Books, 1995), 30.

[10] Ibid., 57.

[11] Martin, *Kingdom of the Cults*, 429.

[12] Simon Singh and Edzard Ernst, MD, *Trick or Treatment: The Undeniable Facts About Alternative Medicine* (New York: W. W. Norton & Company, 2008), 161.

[13] Ibid., 159.

[14] Ibid., 166.

[15] Ibid., 179.

Chapter 22

Going to School

"It is only when we forget all our learning that we begin to know."[1]

—HENRY DAVID THOREAU

"Those who cannot remember the past are condemned to repeat it."[2]

—GEORGE SANTAYANA

WHENEVER SOMEONE ASKS ME ABOUT my major field of study in college, I take a deep breath. Then I tell them, "My major was p-wad."

"Your major was what?" they respond.

It was Peace, War, and Defense (PWAD), commonly pronounced "p-wad". I explain how it is a curriculum that includes courses from several disciplines and focuses on the fundamental issues of human conflict and national and global security and defense. That's as far as the conversation usually goes.

During my time at Carolina, I found PWAD studies interesting and sure to help with my professional development as a young officer, but two aspects of this major went underappreciated. First, I did not fully appreciate how important these concepts are to the security of America and a stabilized world. Second, I didn't see the analogy for *spiritual* peace, war, and defense.

Establishing a worldview based on truth will help you teach your children, but that is not where your responsibility ends. Adopting a Christian worldview is a life changing experience. The message of Christ at its core is simple to understand. By his grace—his undeserved favor—you are free from the burden of guilt and sin

LIKE EXECUTING FIGHTER TACTICS, LIVING A HOLY LIFE IS A PERISHABLE SKILL.

if you acknowledge his sacrifice for you on the cross and live as a new creation in Christ. However, living a holy life in a broken world is difficult. The Bible tells you how to live, but you're going to forget a lot of what it says. You must continually stay in the Word. Like executing fighter tactics, living a holy life is a perishable skill. To stay current and proficient you've got to stay in the books—all sixty-six of them.

I finished college in May, 2001. We were not a country at war. The Cold War was over and the economy was booming. After pushing back Saddam Hussein in the first Gulf War, the US military increasingly conducted humanitarian missions in developing nations. Terrorist acts were relatively infrequent and diplomacy ruled the day (augmented by Tomahawk missiles launched at the occasional international thug or Balkan dictator). Like so many others, I took our country's peace for granted.

I had a small perspective of the world. Some college students grieved over genocide, human rights violations, and civil unrest. I was not as troubled. It is easy to become wrapped up in our own lives, either blind or indifferent to the plight of others. I was going to be a fighter pilot. Academic discussion and philosophy disappeared in the rearview mirror on the way to Pensacola.

Ten years later, I began using principles I learned in school to study a different kind of war. Spiritual warfare rages on the battlefield of beliefs where players have differing notions of war and peace. Every day we are bombarded with billions of bits of data. Some data becomes useful information, other data becomes disinformation, and the rest is noise. A Christian worldview helps sort the gold from the garbage. While everyone has the right to believe in garbage, it won't turn it into gold. But the enemy is a master salesman of spiritual pyrite (fool's gold).

FINDING PEACE IN WAR

War is the by-product of a broken world. Similarly, a spirit of rebellion has plagued the Creation since before the beginning. In this chapter, we will look at the nature of spiritual warfare and formulate a plan-of-attack to defeat the Enemy. This will require identifying the enemy, gaining intelligence on his weapons and tactics, determining his center of gravity, finding ways to exploit his critical vulnerabilities, and preparing ourselves for the possibility of capture. We will also need to use a process developed by famous fighter pilot and military strategist Colonel John Boyd.

We're going to learn about the OODA Loop.

OODA LOOP

The OODA Loop is a model of the command and control process used in the military. The acronym stands for observation, orientation, decision, and action—the process by which a commander assesses a situation and executes a response. The model assumes the enemy is using the same process; therefore, whoever completes the cycle more quickly can interrupt the cycle of his opponent.[3]

I've never understood how someone can be willing to believe anything. Without a recognized worldview, I had difficulty sorting out what ideological ballast was required to keep from capsizing. I needed a captain who could teach me to identify deadweight and a crew to help toss it back into the Sea of Nonsense. I could plot a course in any direction, but it was difficult deciding which course to take. A lack of decisiveness led to a failure to act. It was easy to observe, but difficult to orient, and that made deciding impossible. Something was wrong with my OODA Loop.

I identified the problem with my OODA Loop after studying the things of God. I discovered not only was I lost at sea, but I was adrift without a compass. With no land in sight and no north-seeking needle, I had no point of reference. There were only other boats going this way and that way.

Some were too fast to flag down; others were slow and friendly. Some let me board their vessel, but most could not find their compass or didn't know how it worked. A few seafarers were particularly indulgent of worldly pleasures. They were consumed with gratification and the pursuit of happiness, but their painful smiles masked a festering heart disease.

Inside their cabins was shattered glass and bent arrows on broken compasses. Like Captain Quint smashed the *Orca's* radio in Stephen Spielberg's *Jaws*, they had ulterior motives for destroying their only hope of rescue. They had done what the Apostle Paul warned Timothy against in 1 Timothy 1:19 by rejecting faith and good conscience, leaving them shipwrecked.

In the remaining chapters, we will "observe" some different worldviews, attempt to "orient" ourselves on a mountain with many paths, "decide" which path is worth taking, and "act" to make our lives truly reflect what we believe.

CENTER OF GRAVITY

Before you plunge headlong into battle, you should identify the enemy's center of gravity and then find a way to exploit it by attacking his critical vulnerabilities.

The center of gravity is an enemy's important source of strength. The devil's center of gravity is his ability to plant ideas in the minds of men. It began with Eve and the serpent's fork-tongued fabrications. It continues today when his whisperings invoke anxiety about the future and death. When ungodly ideas take root in our minds, we become blind to the reality of God—a pleasing condition to principalities and powers.

In 1999, a film called *The Matrix* told the story of a world where machines breed humans to use as batteries. To prevent an uprising by humans, the machines created a fantasy world which would satisfy the needs of the human mind and keep them blind to the reality of their condition. The protagonist is given the choice between taking

ACCEPTING THE TRUTH OF CHRISTIANITY IS LIKE TAKING THE RED PILL.

two pills. The blue pill will keep him in the dream world, ignorant of reality. The red pill will wake him up to the real world— a world filled with difficult truths to accept and challenges to face.

Accepting the truth of Christianity is like taking the red pill. Once you've taken it, you can begin to see the matrix the enemy has been using to keep you in the dark. The difference is, the devil doesn't want you for your energy; he wants you for his pride. Rejecting Christianity is like taking the blue pill. It means you would rather live in a comfortable fantasy than a difficult reality. Let me give you an example of the kind of idea the enemy uses to keep people choosing the blue pill.

During one conversation about Christianity, I asked someone why they didn't like talking about spiritual things. Their reply was, "Religion and philosophy add nothing to my life." I wondered what the *absence* of religion and philosophy had added to their life—greater still, what it had subtracted.

I don't believe this person had ever approached Christianity with the penitent heart required for accepting its truth. I was reminded of a child who first learns about the birds and the bees. Embarrassed and aloof, a 10-year-old would easily say that kind of stuff adds nothing to their life, because their life revolves around candy and horseplay and discovery. Ironically, the process they claim "adds nothing to their life" is the very process which gave them life. Adults make the same mistake when they reject God, the giver of all life.

The enemy lies to us; in fact, he is called the father of lies (John 8:44). He relishes stirring up thoughts of envy, greed, and lust, but he usually starts with pride. It takes three steps to stumble over the devil. It begins with inception, continues with deception, and ends with rejection.

First is the inception of an ungodly thought (e.g., the notion that stolen waters are sweeter). Next comes the deception of the flesh by bargaining with the spirit; the heart pleads for the mind to allow for indiscretion. Finally, the rejection of the spirit and obeisance to the flesh signals victory for the enemy's spiritual attack. If we have any hope of defeating the enemy, we must find where he is weak, and attack him first. We must find his critical vulnerability.

CRITICAL VULNERABILITIES

A critical vulnerability is defined in the Marine Corps *Warfighting* doctrinal publication as "a vulnerability that, if exploited, will do the most significant damage to the enemy's ability to resist us."[4] Exploiting an enemy's critical vulnerability is a means to weaken his center of gravity. Let me illustrate with a military example.

An enemy center of gravity may be their industrial capability and resupply system. Terrain and political borders could lead to overextended and exposed supply lines, creating a critical vulnerability. By exploiting the supply lines and preventing ammunition, food, and supplies from reaching the front lines; the enemy's center of gravity can be weakened.

Satan's critical vulnerability is pride. Here's the good news: God knew how to exploit it from the beginning. In Genesis 3:15, God told the serpent, "He will crush your head, and you will strike his heel." God was speaking about Jesus, one of the offspring of Eve. This verse foreshadows both the crucifixion and the resurrection. Norman Geisler echoes the explanations of theologian Millard Erickson and John of Damascus, explaining that "Satan struck at the bait of Christ's humanity and was caught on the hook of his deity."[5] Satan thinks he is smart, but God's knowledge and wisdom is perfect.

Satan has another critical vulnerability which would be impossible to recognize in any other wartime scenario: his future is already written. Because of God's revelation to us through the Bible, we know the final outcome. This vital piece of intelligence not only tells us how to fight (Ephesians 6), but it also assures us of victory. The result is a measure of confidence unrivaled by any military commander in the history of the world.

If Satan has been defeated, then how can he still influence us today? Geisler continues, "Satan was defeated officially (legally) by the death of Christ (Rom.3-5). He is defeated practically (applicationally) in our lives when we resist him by the power of the Cross (Rom. 6-7). And he will be defeated finally (ultimately) when Christ returns (Rom. 8) and redeems our bodies from death."[6]

These critical vulnerabilities can all be exploited by accepting God's grace, using the power of prayer, and wielding the sword of the Spirit which is the Word of God. Anxiety over the future is replaced by peace in Christ, fear of death turns to zest for life, and promises from the enemy are exposed as lies.

Next, we must gain as much information as possible about the enemy's weapons. We cannot afford intelligence failures.

It's time to continue our spiritual reconnaissance.

---

[1] Henry David Thoreau, *The Writings of Henry David Thoreau* (Boston: Houghton Mifflin, 1906), 371, http://babel.hathitrust.org/cgi/pt?id=uc1.b3546855;view=2up;seq=400;skin=mobile

[2] George Santayana, *The Life of Reason, vol. 1, Introduction and Reason in Common Sense* (New York: Charles Scribner's Sons, 1927), Hathi Trust Digital Library, 284, http://babel.hathitrust.org/cgi/pt?id=osu.32435028551414;view=1up;seq=308

[3] U.S. Marine Corps, *MCDP 6: Command and Control* (Washington, D.C.: Department of the Navy, 1996), 63.

[4] U.S. Marine Corps, *MCDP 1: Warfighting* (Washington, D.C.: Department of the Navy, 1997), 47.

[5] Millard Erickson, *Christian Theology* (Grand Rapids: Baker Books, 1983), 813, quoted in Norman Geisler, *Systematic Theology*, vol. 4, *Church, Last Things* (Minneapolis: Bethany House, 2004), 275. Derived from John of Damascus, *Exposition of the Orthodox Faith*, 3.27.

[6] Norman Geisler, *Systematic Theology*, vol. 3, *Sin Salvation* (Minneapolis: Bethany House, 2004), 177.

CHAPTER 23

SPIRITUAL RECONNAISSANCE

Tucson, Arizona
November 2012

"It now seems almost certain that. . .[love and kindness]
are not the product of some immaterial substance or spirit
but arise through the natural operations performed by a
highly complex but still purely material brain."[1]

—*VICTOR J. STENGER*

"Whoever does not love does not know God, because God
is love" (1 John 4:8).

—*THE APOSTLE JOHN*

ON NOVEMBER 8, 2012, JARED LOUGHNER was sentenced to life in prison without parole for the attempted murder of Congresswoman Gabrielle Giffords in Tucson, Arizona. A friend of Loughner recounts some of his characteristics: "By the time he was 19 or 20, he was really fascinated with semantics and how the world is really nothing—illusion." According to his friend, Loughner commented, "I'm pretty sure I've come to the conclusion that words mean nothing."[2]

When it comes to word craft, the devil is a master artisan, and deception is his rasp. In order to make his masterpiece, the enemy has hijacked one of our most basic human capacities: language. The devil attempts to change the meaning of words and fosters apathy towards understanding them properly. As you will see, this can have tragic consequences.

When communication has no meaning, humanity itself becomes absurd. When you question the words, you will next question the actions they express. Eventually the only thing left to question will be existence itself, and when existence has no meaning, *WHEN EXISTENCE HAS NO MEANING, THERE IS NO REASON FOR RESTRAINT.* there is no reason for restraint. A world without restraint is a world of violence.

Anyone who has ever played *Scrabble* knows the importance of following the rules. The rules are simple: you must create words to earn points. One way to cheat is by taking points for a letter-combination that is not actually a word. The rules can be enforced by having a dictionary on hand to challenge players who tile the board with nonsense.

The problem with the pursuit of meaningful dialogue today is that people understand words differently, or not at all. When someone has a question, they don't open a dictionary; they use their imagination. They respond with, "I think it means this," or "I believe it means that," or "I define it as this," none of which leads to knowledge. These cheaters quickly tire of skeptical rule-enforcers who question their words, so they find another game where people are not only laying down nonsense, but receiving triple-word-scores for their efforts. Thus marks their departure from reality and rejection of reason. In order for communication to be meaningful, the sender and receiver must have a mutual understanding of terms.

Some are playing this dangerous game with a shameful opportunism. These are the "teachers" of various fields of study who think that stringing together popular buzz words will create a credulous claim. Phrases certain to lure the impressionable often include words like consciousness, awareness, awakening, ego, acceptance, enlightenment, quantum, energy, and potential. Put these words into a hat, add a few conjunctions, and mix them up. Then dump them onto the ground and read the words in no particular order. You will then sound like the New Spiritualists continuing to spread the Gospel of You by recycling Eastern philosophies.

Westerners are intrigued by the paradoxical nature of Eastern philosophy. When an American impersonates a wise man, he will often raise his finger, speak slowly, and begin with, "Confucius say . . . ." He will quote famous koans (e.g. what is the sound of one hand clapping?) and ask questions while claiming there are no answers. He is fascinated by martial arts with its blend of physical and spiritual power. He is attracted to meditation and the notion of searching for peace although he is less familiar with the concept of enlightenment.

But Confucius has a cool accent, Bruce Lee was the man, and hot yoga is hot. Whether Eastern philosophy is true or not, it certainly is fashionable. What's not to like about a world where you can create your own reality; make words mean whatever you want; defeat evil by changing your perception, pursue everything without giving anything in return; and sigh with pity at the less-enlightened, the less-aware, and the less-awake? Itching ears love to be scratched.

The Apostle John warns in 1 John, chapter 4: "Do not believe every spirit, but test the spirits to see whether they are from God, because false prophets have gone out into the world." The New Spirituality says, "Don't be too cerebral. Too much thinking. Not enough feeling. All that matters is what things mean to *you*."

Acts of linguistic terrorism which emphasize the now, the self, and the world do nothing to prepare our grieving souls when they are pierced by evil. If an author writes that there's no such thing as self, then ask him who, exactly wrote those words? If someone says they only believe in "now," then ask them if they ever pack a bag for an overnight trip. If they don't believe in spirit, then ask them if they are any different than a cockroach and why they shouldn't be squashed like one.

I was surprised when on two separate occasions I was recommended the works of a particular spiritual teacher. I was struck by how they described their attraction to him. They focused less on his message, and more on his delivery. Both people specifically mentioned his voice. They fawned over his golden voice, smooth tones, and irresistible charisma. I was reminded of a passage in 2 Timothy: "For the time will come when men will not put up with sound doctrine. Instead, to suit their own desires, they will gather around them a great number of teachers to say what their itching ears want to hear. They will turn their ears away from the truth and turn aside to myths."

Whether words are redefined or simply rearranged, a common thread binds the tapestry woven by the new spiritualists: a lack of falsifiability. You cannot disprove a claim that "every thought creates." Creates what? How about a claim that "life will give you whatever you need?" If you claim life didn't give you what you needed, you'll be told you don't really know what you needed (and then charged a lot of money).

The key to recognizing deception is to realize the very language we use to seek understanding is under attack. You might hear, "You are God. You create. You have no limitations," but what is actually being said is, "I don't care about truth, reason, or coherence anymore. Don't think, lest my lies be exposed. Just feel this, do that, and believe." In contrast, Jesus' message was: believe, for I have done it all, and you will feel my love now and in eternity.

But the Father of Lies is a master of messaging. He's an expert at brand development and has ensured that search engines will point toward his domain. You might not know his name, but he knows yours, and he whispers to you in the moments between right and wrong.

IDENTIFYING THE ENEMY

Sun Tzu was the Chinese General and philosopher who said, "If you know the enemy and know yourself, you need not fear the result of a hundred battles."[3]

THE WAR IS REAL, AND IT IS A CLASH BETWEEN AN UNHOLY TRINITY OF WILLS.

If you've made it this far, hopefully you know thyself as a child created in the image of God. Now it's time to know thy enemy.

It is impossible to prepare for battle if you are ignorant of the war. A spiritual attack can be less conspicuous than rocket attacks from the Gaza Strip. But the war raging today remains largely unnoticed, even by many Christians. But the war is real, and it is a clash between an unholy trinity of wills, all opposed to God and described in Ephesians, chapter 2: the will of the world, the will of your flesh, and the will of the devil.

The first will we are in conflict with is that of the world. Warren Wiersbe describes the world as "the system around us that is opposed to God." The second will we fight is our own. The flesh represents our ungodly desires reignited by sin, even after conversion. Paul describes the fight against the flesh in Romans, chapter 7. The third will we fight is that of the devil.

In order to recruit soldiers for this battle, we must first become leaders that others will follow. We must learn how to be in the world, but not of the world.

WEAPONS OF WAR

We cannot see the devil's will, and we can no better see our own will than the wills of the world. But we can see his handiwork—the instruments, tools, and weapons brandished by these wills opposed to God. The devil's weapons include darkness, destruction, deception, and division. We will look at how the enemy wields these weapons in the context of American culture, and we're going to find him in places you might not expect.

A DARK BOX OF LIGHT

If we want to stay a step ahead of the enemy, we have to begin the Boyd cycle and get our OODA loop going. First we must observe what's going on in the world around us and find our orientation. Where do we observe darkness, division, and destruction? (Keep in mind that deception masks the other three weapons of war.)

I won't focus here on conspicuous darkness surrounding things like violence, selfishness, and immorality. Instead, I will focus on things you don't normally think of as weapons. Like searching for black holes, some darkness must be observed indirectly by examining disturbances that surround it. We must look at seemingly harmless things to detect and expose darkness—like cartoons.

Many adult cartoons are overtly crude and take pride in their status as equal-opportunity offenders. One of the most popular cartoons began with a parody of Jesus and has gained enormous popularity by lampooning everything holy and good. Other cartoons use subtler means to transmit symbols and communicate ideas.

You wouldn't expect darkness in a show called *My Little Pony: Friendship is Magic*. However, you don't have to get past the show's introduction to find the writers smuggling in images and concepts from Chinese philosophy. The concept of shadow and light is present, and the narrator speaks of maintaining balance, describing the "elements of harmony" as the key to unlocking a powerful magic. The animators even include a yin-yang symbol with the sun and moon.

Taoism (or I Ching) is defined in *Merriam Webster's Collegiate Dictionary* as a "religion developed from Taoist philosophy and folk and Buddhist religion and concerned with obtaining long life and good fortune often by magical means."[4] Walter Martin explains how this religion is based on the philosophy that "universal existence is based upon the harmonization and balance of two opposing forces, yang and yin (positive and negative, male and female)."[5] Yin-yangs, harmony, balance—there sure is a lot of Taoism in Ponydom.

Yet the creators used very Christian themes when constructing their creation story: a powerful entity feels resentment toward a higher authority, then devolves into a state of wickedness after challenging that authority, and is subsequently banished by that authority. Yet they did not include symbols representing Christianity—no crosses, fishes, or subliminal allusions to the trinity.

The show has been praised for its appealing animation, relevant storylines, and moral themes. These themes might suffice until the young girl (or middle-aged man, apparently), begins asking questions about morality. In Taoism, right and wrong are misleading; they are human constructs—merely matters of cultural experience and individual perception.

Other cartoons go straight for shock value. By its title, you wouldn't expect a show called *Family Guy* to include perverted voyeurism, spousal abuse, cruelty to animals, racial stereotypes, encouragement of dangerous behavior, drug use, and the suggestion that any sexual activity other than coitus counts as abstinence, all in one episode. People watch these shows to laugh and be entertained, but something is amiss with this kind of comedy. If you believe comedy must be offensive, you'll have to explain to me why Jim Gaffigan and Michael Jr. are so successful.

In his work *Poetics*, Aristotle describes comedy as "an imitation of the characters of a lower type . . . the ludicrous being merely a subdivision of the ugly. It consists in some defect or ugliness which is not painful or destructive."[6] Is there nothing painful in a cartoon character calling his daughter a sexual practice-girl? Is there nothing destructive when the protagonist suggests drug users share needles to save money? Have we as a culture become so desensitized to sex, drugs, and violence, that we actually crave the painful and destructive representations offered by the entertainment industry? *Family Guy* is a poison pill with a candy shell.

These shows are colorful and cute, witty and smart. The writers operate on multiple levels to entertain children and stimulate adults. They tap into popular culture and weigh in on issues with an intellectual immunity reserved for animated icons.

Ravi Zacharias is correct with his observation of how people are affected by television today: "Instead of viewing the world *through* the medium of television, they allowed the medium to define the world for them. . . . Television—and now viral media—is the shaper of everything we think and believe."[7] Cartoons can only be seen with the use of light, yet some of them are full of darkness. When you surround yourself with darkness, it's easy to be deceived.

DIVISION AND DESTRUCTION

The enemy has a successful formula to keep the world under his influence: divide and conquer. The body of Christ has fought against division since Jesus walked the streets of Jerusalem. Not all people believe, and sometimes believers need help with their unbelief

SOMETIMES BELIEVERS NEED HELP WITH THEIR UNBELIEF.

(see Mark 9:24). Disputes break out over Biblical interpretation. Churches split into denominations and sects. Men and women who should be united under a single message of salvation are divided by issues large and small. Some are essential teachings with eternal implications; others are doctrinal disputes about nonessentials with no impact on our relationship with God. While Christians are focused on fighting each other, they lose sight of the enemy.

The enemy is smart, and based on your vantage point, the truth can be difficult to see. Sometimes you must rise above your surroundings to get an accurate view of reality.

One summer, I did just that. Deep within the Alaskan Range, a few thousand feet from the highest mountain peak in North America, the picture formed by competing philosophies about spiritual truth became bigger.

It was time to begin climbing the mountain.

---

[1] Victor J. Stenger, *God: The Failed Hypothesis—How Science Shows That God Does Not* Exist (New York: Prometheus Books, 2008), Kindle ed., loc. 3599.

[2] Nick Baumann, "Exclusive: Loughner Friend Explains Alleged Gunman's Grudge Against Giffords," Mother Jones and the Foundation for National Progress, January 10, 2011, http://www.motherjones.com/politics/2011/01/jared-lee-loughner -friend-voicemail-phone-message.

[3] Sun Tzu, *The Art of War* (Simon &Brown, 2012), 13.

[4] Merriam-Webster, Inc., *Merriam-Webster's Collegiate Dictionary, Eleventh ed.* (Springfield, MA: Merriam-Webster, Inc., 2003), "Taoism."

[5] Walter Martin, Jill Martin Rische and Kevin Rische, *The Kingdom of the Occult* (Nashville: Thomas Nelson, 2008), Kindle ed., 212.

[6] Aristotle, *Poetics* (Acheron Press), Kindle ed., loc. 133-136.

[7] Ravi Zacharias, *Why Jesus?: Rediscovering His Truth in an Age of Mass Marketed Spirituality* (New York: Hachette Book Group, 2012), Kindle ed., 23.

CHAPTER 24

CLIMBING
MOUNTAINS

Ruth Glacier, Mount Denali
July 2012

"I am a convinced universalist. I believe that in the end all
men will be gathered into the love of God."[1]

-WILLIAM BARCLAY

"Very truly I tell you, no one can see the kingdom of God
unless they are born again" (John 3:3).

-JESUS

DURING A SUMMER VACATION, I traveled with my father-in-law and two brothers-in law to fish for salmon and visit the highest mountain in the United States. While standing on a glacier atop Mount Denali (McKinley), I thought of the popular many-paths-to-the-summit-of-a-mountain analogy spiritual pluralists use when preaching that "all paths lead to God." It wasn't until later that I realized how quickly the analogy fails when you account for crevasses.

Mount Denali rises 20,327 feet above sea level. Glacial rivers flow down its peak, past glistening icefalls and around its base into the surrounding valleys. We flew in with an air-taxi service to witnesses the mountain's majesty on one of the few days of the year with clear weather. We launched from a small airstrip in Talkeetna and snapped hundreds of pictures before landing on Ruth Glacier in an area known as the Don Sheldon Amphitheatre.

We exited the plane, and the pilot warned us not to stray from the immediate area. Crevasses hidden beneath the snow-packed surface killed three of the first expert climbers to perish on McKinley.[2]

We stayed within a few hundred feet of the plane and took pictures of the mountains and each other. Pilots landed at this spot daily, and the chances of plunging into a hidden crevasse were probably small, but you never know.

When expert climbers ascend a mountain like Denali, they probe the snow with poles to check for crevasses. It's the only way to detect the deadly drop-offs waiting silently beneath the surface. Similarly, a rock climber always tests their footing before committing their full weight to a hold. Just as taking the wrong physical path has consequences, taking the wrong spiritual path has consequences as well.

TAKING THE WRONG SPIRITUAL PATH HAS CONSEQUENCES.

Choosing a spiritual belief system is indeed like choosing a mountain path—but one covered with deadly crevasses. There are many routes and tracks left from climbers past. The tracks all head in different directions, but passersby assure you they all lead to the top eventually.

In reality, only one path is completely free from deadly crevasses sitting in wait to swallow you whole. As you start along your chosen route, you probe the path ahead for unstable snow. In the beginning, your lack of experience makes it difficult to detect the perilous ice pits. But soon you meet other climbers with better equipment and the experience to successfully avoid them. Each path up the mountain represents a different worldview.

LOGICAL   CONSISTENCY,   EMPIRICAL ADEQUACY, AND EXPERIENTIAL RELEVANCE

Ravi Zacharias explains how worldviews have been tested since antiquity: "Imagination and meditation are not secure ways on which to build a worldview that reflects reality. They may make for a beatific smile but not for a philosophical alternative to truth. A worldview tested by truth will inform imagination and meditation, *not the other way around.* That is why the rigorous way of testing truth has always been through logical consistency, empirical adequacy, and experiential relevance."[3]

The mountain of spirituality is littered with crevasses. Using these tests for truth will keep you safe from harm, and ignoring them will send you to an icy grave.

Logical consistency is represented by how you respond to a change in the snow ahead. If you detect a sagging trench on the snow's surface (a classic sign of a hidden crevasse), but dismiss it as the product of the wind or the melting sun, your belief has failed the test of logical consistency. After all, you have come to like this path with its promises of happiness, prosperity, and comfort. A crevasse on this path would be too . . . inconvenient. There is some cognitive dissonance, but not enough to change your mind. You have already invested time, energy, and money on this route. The sunk cost bias is too great to overcome.

The reassuring guide represents empirical adequacy. He has told you there will be no crevasses on his path, but does not provide any evidence for his claim. He confidently tells you to leave your poles behind. In a soothing and attractive voice, he says the poles will stunt your progress and ruin an otherwise liberating experience with a cold and oppressive rationalism.

You peer down the mountainside to see millions of people following his path, all blindfolded, and none of them have poles. The blindfold represents the blind spot formed by quantum uncertainty. This guide teaches that the odd and underdeveloped field of quantum mechanics should make you question the existence of any crevasses you *think* you see. Odder still, the only thing exempt from quantum uncertainty are his teachings. He declared the snow to be solid and crevasses-free, and they have put their trust in him. With an unreasonable faith, one by one his followers plunge like lemmings into an icy oubliette.

Experiential relevance is demonstrated when the followers raise their blindfolds to see parallel climbers on other paths drop under the snow, never to resurface. Their experience of watching other climbers disappear challenges the veracity of their guide's claims.

The guide, now nervous, tells them to turn around. "Look at where you have been. Look how far you have come. Look at the wonderful feelings and experiences you have had along the way. Surely, there will be no crevasses. But if you do fall into a crevasse, some climbers find the descent exhilarating and the solitude sublime," he says.

You eventually find yourself wedged at the bottom of two ice walls. Still conscious and with bated breath, you whisper to yourself, "I'm okay. . . . The guide told me I'll be okay." But as you assess the situation, your confidence wanes. You are hundreds of feet below the surface, surrounded by darkness and squeezed in a behemoth glacial vice. Worse yet, you have massive injuries and lack the tools for a self-rescue.

You turn on your headlamp and find a familiar face lodged ten feet away. It's the guide. His remarkably white teeth peer through a frozen smile. He's dead, and suddenly you feel very alone. You realize the teacher was pointing you in the wrong direction. In fact, he was walking backwards up a mountain he hardly knew.

CONQUERING THE MOUNTAIN

You might be wondering how Christians are any different than the guide and his followers. Christians are confident their worldview is built upon a solid foundation. Every step of the Christian path promises the strength to support your full weight, baggage and all. The difference is that Christians encourage you to ditch the blindfolds, take the poles, watch the snow, and learn from those falling down around you.

When worldviews lack logical consistency, empirical adequacy, and experiential relevance, those with the most to gain will discourage you from challenging the claims of its founder. Examples include Muslim sensitivity to criticism of their prophet, Jehovah's Witness' de-emphasis on Russell, and Scientology's insistence on recognizing an inflated version of Hubbard.

Unfortunately, spiritual danger is less recognized and more ignored than in previous times. When a climber discovers a crevasse, he changes his course because he doesn't want to die. But when a person discovers spiritual danger in a pleasurable experience, they question the reality of the danger, rather than the consequence of the experience. They don't want to avoid spiritual death; they want to disprove its existence. The brain's addictive chemical cocktails dangle pleasure above reason and keep us enslaved to the sin of selfishness.

> YOU WILL BE DRAWN TO THE CARPENTER FROM NAZARETH.

But if you believe in the existence of things unseen, if you are committed to conquering the mountain of truth by rejecting what is false, and if you put the benefit of others over your own personal gratification, you will be drawn to the carpenter from Nazareth who makes all things new.

THE WONDER OF RATIONALITY

We are all looking for peace (world peace, spiritual peace, and if you have small children, a few minutes of peace in the bathroom), but we must not settle for a counterfeit peace at the expense of reason. Human beings were created with rationality and placed in a rational universe.

You don't have to be an emotionless Vulcan when you evaluate worldviews. Feelings and the joy of sensational experiences have their place. When experiences are built on a foundation of truth, their effects will linger after the moment has passed. If the experience is built upon a lie, the affect will spike like a child's blood-sugar on Halloween night and then plummet to a dangerous and confusing low.

The plummet is coming, and the stubborn will enter a free-fall of fear when the breathing tube comes out and the priest comes in. What a tragedy it would be to utter the same words as Napoleon during his exile at St. Helena: "What an abyss between my deep misery and the eternal kingdom of Christ."[4] Let us follow Napoleon's example, and allow Christ to bridge the gap by accepting him before we pass through the ultimate one-way decision gate.

I used to be annoyed by Christians like Karry's aunt and her parents. Now I have joined them. In him, I will put my trust. On him, I will depend. Through him, I will persevere. From him, I have meaning, purpose, and destiny. By him, I see my own brokenness. Out of him, comes forgiveness and love.

I am a follower of Jesus, saved by grace. I am a slave of Christ—owned by the Father and purchased with the blood of his Son. I am saved.

I was finally at peace. Imagine my surprise to learn another war was just beginning.

---

[1] William Barclay, *A Spiritual Autobiography* (Grand Rapids: William B. Eerdmans Publishing Co., 1977), 65-67.
[2] James M. Tabor, *Forever on the Mountain*, (New York: W. W. Norton & Company, 2007), 13.

[3] Ravi Zacharias, *Why Jesus? Rediscovering His Truth in an Age of Mass Marketed Spirituality* (New York: Faith Words, 2012), 32-33. These three tests for truth are also mentioned in Zacharias' book *The End of Reason*. The construct originates from USC philosophy professor, speaker, and author Dallas Willard in his book *Does God Exist?*

[4] John S.C. Abbott, *Napoleon Bonaparte,* A Public Domain Book, Kindle ed., 68.

CHAPTER 25
NEVER SURRENDER

Camp Bastion, Afghanistan
September 2012

*"The only demons we must fear are those that lurk inside
every human mind: ignorance, hatred, greed, and faith,
which is surely the devil's masterpiece."*[1]

—SAM HARRIS

*"If you do not stand firm in your faith,
you will not stand at all" (Isa. 7:9).*

—ISAIAH

ON SEPTEMBER 14, 2012, LIEUTENANT Colonel Christopher Raible ran toward the sound of chaos. The Commanding Officer of Marine Attack Squadron 211 grabbed a handgun, hopped in a vehicle and sped toward the flightline where fifteen insurgents dressed as US soldiers launched an assault to destroy Americans and their aircraft. They had infiltrated Camp Bastion, a British facility in Afghanistan's Helmand province, and were advancing on the squadron's AV-8B Harrier jets. Raible started gaining accountability for his Marines and issuing orders. As he ran to another building to account for more of his men, he was felled by an explosion. He and Marine Sergeant Bradley Atwell were killed in the attack.[2]

War rages today as it has for centuries and as it will in the future. Emerging technologies may change the character of war, but the nature of war remains constant: ugly, violent, and necessary as long as evil remains a reality of the human heart. But for every enemy driven by hatred and cowardice, there will be men like Lieutenant Colonel Raible and Sergeant Atwell willing to face them with bravery and courage.

There are several questions to ask as you stand before the enemy. Is your faith strong enough to withstand his attacks? Will you obey God's command to share your faith with others? Are you willing to leave your foxhole and expose yourself to enemy fire?

We can learn a lot about spiritual warfare by studying physical warfare. Prussian war theorist Carl von Clausewitz is best known for his definition of war as the continuation of politics by other means. He also describes war as a clash between two opposing wills.

However, one of Clausewitz's most valuable insights is "friction," a term described as those things, both physical and psychological, that impede the smooth execution of military operations. Clausewitz wrote, "Friction, as we choose to call it, is the force that makes the apparently easy so difficult."[3]

He recognized the uncertainty presented by incomplete, inaccurate, or contradictory information, referring to it as the "fog of war." Friction, uncertainty, a clash between opposing wills—these characteristics describe spiritual warfare equally well. Therefore, you must prepare for the prospect of capture during the fight for your eternal destiny.

YOU MUST PREPARE FOR THE PROSPECT OF CAPTURE.

CODE OF THE US FIGHTING FORCE

All Soldiers, Seamen, Airmen, and Marines are instructed on a code of conduct before being sent into harm's way. On August 17, 1955, President Eisenhower established the Code of Conduct for war prisoners through Executive Order 10631.[4] I find it worthwhile to study this code for several reasons. First, when making an analogy with spiritual warfare, it serves as a useful tool for keeping faith when we make contact with the enemy. Second, the Code of Conduct is built upon principles which are also contained in the Bible. The code states:

> Your obligations as a US citizen and a member of the armed forces result from the traditional values that underlie the American experience as a nation. These values are best expressed in the US Constitution and Bill of Rights, which you have sworn to uphold and defend. You would have these obligations—to your country, your service and unit and your fellow Americans—even if the Code of Conduct had never been formulated as a high standard of general behavior.[5]

Notice these values "underlie" or form the foundation of the American experience. That is different from the more recent and backwards notion that the American experience shapes the values of our nation. The Code says these values are "expressed" in the US Constitution and Bill of Rights, not that they are "created" by these documents. In fact, the Code makes no mention of where these values come from. Could this be a tacit recognition of the inseparability of God and morality?

The Code continues: "To sustain these personal values throughout captivity requires that you understand and believe strongly in our free and democratic institutions, love your country, trust in the justice of our cause, keep faithful and loyal to your fellow prisoners and hold firmly to your religious and moral beliefs in time of trial."[6]

The combination of religious and moral beliefs is no accident. This is not to say you must believe in God to act morally. Rather, you must believe in God to explain our knowledge of morality.

Man is not the maker of truth. The men and women of the armed forces are expected to recognize the objective truth of "these obligations" in the context of wartime conduct. Why then are moral obligations in the context of protecting the unborn vulnerable to subjective interpretations of legislators and judges? Either the unborn are persons or they are not. That truth must be discovered by man, and in this case, the Supreme Court justices. Their decision for or against will either be correct or incorrect, but it cannot be both.

> I. I am an American, fighting in the forces which guard my country and our way of life. I am prepared to give my life in their defense.

Article I highlights that our country and way of life is always guarded against the enemy. The Code acknowledges the reality of conflict and evil—that things are not as they should be. Soldiers are prepared to give the ultimate price: their life. Our lives should only be given for something of ultimate worth—in this case, freedom. Freedom from oppression is an example of a universal objective moral value.

> II. I will never surrender of my own free will. If in command, I will never surrender the members of my command while they still have the means to resist.

We must be actively involved in the battle against the enemy. Although we may tire, we must never quit. A commander will never surrender his members just as a pastor will never surrender his flock while they remain in his pasture.

> III. If I am captured I will continue to resist by all means available. I will make every effort to escape and aid others to escape. I will accept neither parole nor special favors from the enemy.

For the soldier, the preface is "if I am captured." For the Christian, it could read "*when* I am captured," for we become prisoners when we sin. And let those holier-than-thou be reminded of 1 John, chapter 1, verse 8: "If we claim to be without sin, we deceive ourselves and the truth is not in us." While the explanation for our wrongdoing is debated, the phenomenon is undeniable: we all sin (or, "do wrong" for those uncomfortable with spiritual code-talk). Whether our inheritance of Adam's sin can be explained by epigenetics or something more mysterious is irrelevant. What is relevant is to confess that we can never be perfect, no matter how hard we pray or how many vices we shun. God ordained perfection for one man only, and we are not him.

When we are captured by sin, we must continue to resist, lest our stumble become a headlong plunge into spiritual relapse. The soldier must use all means available, but the Christian must use the only man capable: Jesus Christ. In order to escape, we must repent. In order to aid others in escape, we must fulfill the Great Commission by sharing the Gospel with everyone. We must not accept parole. Wartime captors say, "Favors and freedom I will give thee if you swear allegiance to our state, our cause, our Great Leader."

JESUS RESISTED. THE SOLDIER IS TO RESIST. WE MUST RESIST.

Remember Satan's temptation of Jesus in Matthew 4:9, "All this I will give you . . . if you will bow down and worship me."

Jesus resisted. The soldier is to resist. We must resist. The special favors promised by the enemy are a trade: your rightness in the eyes of God for the momentary comfort of illegitimate pleasure. Our conscience is quick to judge our actions when enjoyment comes at the expense of trust, honor, or loyalty.

> IV. If I become a prisoner of war, I will keep faith with my fellow prisoners. I will give no information or take part in any action which might be harmful to my comrades. If I am senior, I will take command. If not, I will obey the lawful orders of those appointed over me and will back them up in every way.

One way to keep faith with our fellow prisoners is to go to church with our fellow sinners. Increasing numbers of Americans love God but are leaving the church. Too many are on a never-ending hunt for the perfect pastor, the perfect music, the perfect dress code, the perfect style—the perfect pipe dream. Is your refusal to fellowship with other Christian believers becoming harmful to your comrades (your parents, your friends, your children)? Let us not give up meeting together, as the author of Hebrews exhorts, lest we cause our comrades to stumble.

In captivity, the senior member will take command. Let the elders in the church likewise take command and fulfill their obligation to lead the young. They must be encouraged to finish the race by imparting wisdom to the young and impressionable. And let our youth obey the command in Romans 13:1 to submit to authorities, "for there is no authority except that which God has established."

> V. When questioned, should I become a prisoner of war,
> I am required to give name, rank, service number, and
> date of birth. I will evade answering further questions
> to the utmost of my ability. I will make no oral or
> written statements disloyal to my country and its allies
> or harmful to their cause.

In the prisoner's camp, the soldier responds to interrogation with three items only: name, rank, and serial number. These items correspond to identity, authority, and loyalty. The devil attacks these same ideas in attempts to deceive, confuse, and win over the unarmored heart. He challenges our identity as children of God by asserting we can "be like God." He challenges our authority—given to us in the name of Jesus—by claiming to have authority over him. "All this I will give you," he tempted Jesus in the desert and whispers to us today. He tests our loyalty by prodding, "Did God *really* say?" And while Paul says in Romans 2:11, "God shows no favoritism," the devil strokes our egos with seniority and power. Let our response to demonic interrogation be: "I am a Christian, saved by the grace of God, loyal to his son, and equal among my brethren in the eyes of the Lord."

The prisoner is to avoid answering questions to the best of his ability. Similarly, we are to avoid becoming caught up with dishonest questions goading us to cast our pearls before swine. We should follow the advice in Proverbs 26:4 and refrain from answering a fool according to his folly. Paul writes in 2 Timothy 2:23, "Don't have anything to do with foolish and stupid arguments, because you know they produce quarrels."

Finally, the prisoner must remain loyal to his country and its allies. As the soldier must not make seditious statements, we must not blaspheme our Lord. Job's wife told him to curse God and die in order to end his suffering. But like Job, we must stand firm in our faith when the going gets tough.

> VI. I will never forget that I am an American, fighting for freedom, responsible for my actions, and dedicated to the principles which made my country free. I will trust in my God and in the United States of America.

Christians must never forget that they are fighting for truth, responsible for their message, and dedicated to the God who created them free. If we read the message of the Code of Conduct in the spirit of Biblical truth, we *will* be prepared to defend our faith during spiritual interrogation.

DECIDE AND ACT

We must continue to fend off spiritual attacks until Christ's final return. The instances of inception and deception will not cease. But the process of sanctification will make it more difficult to reject the Holy Spirit. Instead of rejecting the spirit, you will grow stronger in rejecting enticements from the flesh and the world. This is where we come to the "decide" step of the OODA loop process. In the words of the character Walter Donovan in *Indiana Jones and the Last Crusade*, "It's time to ask yourself what you believe."[7]

We've observed the enemy (the Devil, the flesh, and the world), and studied his weapons (darkness, deception, division, and destruction), and found our orientation in the middle of it all. Look any direction and you will find the enemy wielding his weapons of war. In the words of legendary Marine Lieutenant General "Chesty" Puller at the Battle of Chosin Resevoir, "We're surrounded. That simplifies things." Now we must take the last step. Like Lieutenant Colonel Raible, we must remain alert, recognize the enemy, and take action when he attacks.

The enemy cannot prevent you from developing a worldview; he can only work to keep it unrecognized and ever-drifting with the current of a culture unmoored. Is human monogamy God's plan for marriage, or just evolution's way of protecting vulnerable offspring? Are humans special or just another animal with different DNA? Is it reasonable to believe something can come from nothing? Is it inspiring to speak of hope today if there is no hope in eternity? Are you willing to bet your soul, that you don't have a soul? What will you teach your children?

Without understanding your worldview, you cannot provide justifiable answers for these questions, disqualifying you from providing hope to the hurting and crippling your ability to lead with conviction.

If you allow Christ to change you from the inside out, everything becomes new. You will lead better, and you will love better—your spouse, your children, and your brothers and sisters both in and out of Christ. You will not be deceived, and you will receive the power to "fight the good fight, holding on to faith and a good conscience" (1 Tim. 1:18-19).

If you seek God, you will find him. If you seek truth, you will not be deceived. If you remain ready to defend your faith, you will fulfill one of God's commandments, help Christians better understand their own faith, assist with the soul-saving work of God, counter the negative image of Christianity in the media and culture, defend against apostasy, expose false teachings, counter the rise of immorality, and help defuse the anti-Christian hostility prevalent in many academic institutions.

THERE WAS ONLY ONE HINDRANCE TO ACCEPTING THE WORD OF GOD: PRIDE.

I had observed enough. I had seen all I needed to see. By admitting my own brokenness and believing in the saving power of the gospel of Jesus, I had found the one true compass which points to the ultimate power and authority in the universe. There was only one hindrance to accepting the word of God: pride.

Believing you are too smart or too enlightened to accept a worldview filled with miracles, wonder, and hope is the ultimate self-delusion. It is the fulfillment of God's pronouncement in Romans, chapter 1: "Although they claimed to be wise, they became fools. . . . They exchange the truth about God for a lie" (Rom. 1:22-25). I was a man without excuse, for God's eternal power and divine qualities truly can be seen by the things he has made, if we have eyes to see. Standing on this third rock from the sun, I discovered the truth in the Rock of the Son. From a firm foundation with an unbreakable cornerstone, I could finally take a leap of faith.

In the 2013 film *Ender's Game* based on the novel by Orson Scott Card, Colonel Hyrum Graff responds to veteran bug-killer Mazer Rackham's assessment that young Ender Wiggin is not ready to command his troops in the final battle to save their civilization. Colonel Graff responds: "You're never ready. You go when you're ready enough."[8]

Faith is not supposed to be certain. "Faith is confidence in what we hope for and assurance about what we do not see" (Heb. 11:1). You're never ready to believe with certainty. You believe when you're ready enough. The time had come to decide exactly what, or whom, I was living for.

---

[1] Sam Harris, *The End of Faith* (New York: W. W. Norton & Company, Inc., 2005), Kindle Ed., 226.

[2] Ernesto Londoño, "Slain Marine commander's actions in Afghanistan called heroic," The Washington Post, September 22, 2012, http://www.washingtonpost.com/world/national-security/2012/09/21/f4703c76-042d-11e2-91e7-2962c74e7738_story.html?hpid=z2.

[3] Carl von Clausewitz, *On War*, trans. Michael Howard and Peter Paret (Princeton: Princeton University Press, 1976), 121.

[4] James Beasely Simpson, *Best Quotes of '54, '55, '56* (New York: Thomas Y. Crowell Company, 1957), 224, quoted in W. J. Federer, *Great Quotations: A Collection of Passages, Phrases, and Quotations Influencing Early and Modern World History Referenced according to their Sources in Literature, Memoirs, Letters, Governmental Documents, Speeches, Charters, Court Decisions and Constitutions* (St. Louis: AmeriSearch, 2001).

[5] Dwight D. Eisenhower, "Code of Conduct for Members of the United States Armed Forces," Executive Order 10631, Wikisource, last modified February 2, 2013, http://en.wikisource.org/wiki/Executive_Order_10631.

[6] Ibid.

[7] Julian Glover, *Indiana Jones and the Last Crusade*, directed by Steven Spielberg (Hollywood, CA: Paramount, 1989), DVD.

[8] *Ender's Game*, directed by Gavin Hood (2013; Universal City, CA: Summit Entertainment, 2013).

CHAPTER 26
LOVE ON THE NISHIKI

Kintai-kyo, Iwakuni, Japan
July 31, 2010

"Most of what we currently hold sacred is not sacred for
any reason other than that it was thought sacred yesterday."

—*SAM HARRIS*

"God's temple is sacred, and you together are that temple"
(1 Cor. 3:17).

—*THE APOSTLE PAUL*

KAERIMASU MEANS "TO RETURN." IT was 2010 and I was back in Iwakuni—the same base where I met Karry fifteen years earlier. We had been married nine years, moved seven times, adopted, and later gave away, two cats and two dogs, killed a dozen plants (both of us), endured one deployment, and birthed four children (mostly Karry . . .).

My search for truth began in our bedroom in San Diego and continued in a "can" at Al Asad, in the Marine barracks at Kaneohe Bay, on a cot in a tent in Pohang, on the beaches of U-tapao, under the lights of "Walking Street" in Pattaya, on a dusty trail in Katherine Gorge, behind a blackout curtain in Alaska, and had arrived on the fourth floor of a six-story midrise where we geared up for a trip back to the Nishiki River.

We packed a cooler, bathing suits, and my camera and headed down to the car. We drove down the street past the single story house where I lived in the summer of '95. There was a new placard hanging from the torii and a different car in the driveway, but the front yard grew the same grass I used to mow with my shirt off, wondering if Karry would notice. The backyard had the same row of bushy trees I used to cross to see her after school.

The base had changed, yet remained deeply familiar. A new runway built on reclaimed land was finished during our time there. I had the privilege of being the first F/A-18D Hornet pilot to land on it with my commanding officer as my WSO. At the Torii Pines golf course, I must have sliced hundreds of balls onto the flight line from a par-3, unaware I would one day fly the same Hornets I was potentially FOD-ing* out. There were many other renovations, expansions, and additions, but MCAS Iwakuni still had the same small town feel. It was a small slice of America nestled between the lotus fields of rural Japan.

We left the base and drove down the uncomfortably narrow roads leading to *Kintai-kyo*, the bridge where we fell in love under summer fireworks 15 years before. It was a perfect July afternoon, sunny with unusually clear skies. My friend Mike was waiting for me and a few others. After his service in the Marines, Mike moved to Iwakuni and went into full-time ministry. It had been seven years since we graduated together from TBS, and running into him on this small base on the southern tip of Honshu was a pleasant surprise.

During a meeting after services one Sunday, I told Mike, "I know someone who wants to be baptized."

---

* FOD: Foreign Object Damage. Also used to describe any object with the potential to damage an aircraft, particularly the engines.

"Oh?"

I left silence in the air and anticipation on his face. I remembered my pugil stick setup question in Norfolk and wondered if he would guess who I had in mind.

"Who is it?" he probed.

I thought about my father's question from OCS, "How bad do I really want this?" Now I was asking, "How truly do I really believe this?" *Do I really need to do this? Aren't you supposed to get baptized as a baby? Why does it feel embarrassing? What about all these other people! Have they been baptized or are they too chicken, too afraid to go on record? Do I really believe all the things I'm trying to believe? What if I change my mind?* I remembered 2 Peter 2:21, "It would have been better for them not to have known the way of righteousness, than to have known it and then to turn their backs on the sacred command that was passed on to them." I was tired of returning to my vomit. This dog needed transformation.

"It's me," I confessed.

He smiled.

A few weeks later, we were back on the bank of the Nishiki River. I waded out to where Mike stood in waist high water. The cool, clear water moved briskly downstream where fish were gobbled by Cormorant birds under torchlight on summer nights. Karry and the kids looked on with a handful of other church members. The time had come.

"We sure have come a long way, haven't we?" Mike grasped my shoulder with a firm, brotherly grip.

"Yep. We sure have," I said with my father's brevity. Nothing more was said. There didn't need to be.

He looked me in the eye, "Do you accept Jesus Christ as your Lord and Savior?"

"Yes, I do."

"I baptize you in the name of the Father, the Son, and the Holy Spirit," he said as he lowered me into the water. I thought about the helo-dunker and the inevitable stinging sinuses from a water inversion. I plugged my nose. The water engulfed my body until I was completely submerged. I had always loved water, but never before had I appreciated its cleansing powers. As the water had the power to clean my body, Jesus Christ has the power to cleanse my soul.

Mike lifted me up out of the water, the air colder now. Water dripped from every part of my body—cold, cleansing, wonderful water. I wasn't expecting to see a dove, or feel a whoosh, but you never know. I felt at ease, at peace. And that was it—nothing supernatural, nothing contrived or forced. It was another opportunity to say, "Lord, I'm doing what you told me to do."

I FOUND LOVE TWICE ON THE NISHIKI RIVER. THE FIRST WAS MY LOVE FOR KARRY. THE SECOND WAS GOD'S LOVE FOR ME.

I found love twice on the Nishiki River. The first was my love for Karry. The second was God's love for me.

A HEART ISSUE

When my questions were answered, I believed. My heart was ready and I was waiting for someone to give me answers, and I found them in Jesus. But people have their own reasons for rejecting God. Whether they admit it or not, the reasons are rarely intellectual. Even when the intellectual questions are sufficiently answered, they still refuse to believe. For most, it is not a head issue, it is a heart issue—a moral issue.

A quote derived from the works of G.K. Chesterton rings true: "When people stop believing in God, they don't believe in nothing—they believe in anything." When Jesus came, he taught the little children. When he comes again, he will descend with a double-edged sword, and on his robe will be written:

KING OF KINGS, AND LORD OF LORDS

Yes, my life is remarkable enough for a book. My life is part of God's story. Yours is, too. It's time to make a decision. You're ready enough.

CHAPTER 27

THE BEST DAY

Phoenix, Arizona
April 16, 2015

*"The hour of departure has arrived and we go our ways; I
to die, and you to live. Which is better? God only knows."*

—SOCRATES

*"He will swallow up death forever. The Sovereign Lord
will wipe away the tears from all faces" (Isa. 25:8).*

—ISAIAH

PRECIOUS LITTLE BOONE, BORN ALIVE with a beating heart, so
small and so still when we held him. We prayed that we would
know what to do when he came.

The doctor handed me surgical scissors to cut Boone's
two-vessel umbilical cord, to sever the life-line between
mother and child. She grasped it between her finger and
thumb and felt the pulse of his mother's heart. He wasn't
breathing.

What will you do, Boone? Will you stay with us, or will you go?
I could ask him to wake up.

*Wake up, Boone, and see the eyes of your father. Wake up and
listen clearly to the voices once muffled by the womb. Wake up and feel
more of the love we promised you from the day you were conceived.*

Wake up, Boone, and look at the world and all its beauty. Wake up so you can marvel at God's work and all the people he has made. Wake up and see the good, a reflection of him in all creation.

Wake up and hear the laughter of your brothers, the sound of your sister helping you learn to walk. Wake up and witness the symphony of life in all its glory.

But how could I rouse Boone from his peace in the arms of the Lord just because I wanted more time with him? Our worst day was the result of fear. Fear of death and the unknown. How could I ask him to fight when the cards of life were stacked against him—to fight for nourishment, for every breath, and for every drop of blood pumped from a heart that wasn't whole?

I couldn't, and I didn't.

When Jesus appeared after his crucifixion, the apostles knew that death had been defeated. What was once the worst day became the best. We, too, had the comfort of knowing that death is not the end. It is the beginning of new life.

Boone Shepherd Ladd never left the arms of the Lord, yet we held him for a lifetime.

But that's another story.

EPILOGUE

Death Valley Crash Site
August 14ᵗʰ, 1990

ARNOLD WAS OUT OF CONTROL.

Seconds later, he gained enough nose authority to hold his position for a few more seconds. He had to make a choice: hold his position and risk going further out of control, or attempt to sink/fly down the mountain slope toward the thicker air. The pilot on the hoist barely cleared the treetops when he pointed downhill and began an "air taxi" maneuver to reduce power required and regain more tail rotor authority. Finally under control and with the pilot safely on board, he headed to the staging area to drop him off with the base safety officer.

The corpsman radioed for a litter and splint bag which they retrieved from the staging area and then delivered to the other mishap pilot via the hoist. It would take 15 minutes to prepare the aircrew for transportation in the litter and move him about 30 meters to a suitable pickup point. They were starting to get low on fuel. Arnold called back to base and requested a second SAR bird so they could transfer the aircrew if the situation required.

They were about 250 pounds lighter due to fuel-burn once the litter was ready for hoist. They brought him aboard without incident and brought him to the staging area. When the second SAR bird, "Coso-24," arrived on the scene, Arnold directed him to land at the staging area and pick up both the mishap pilots while he returned to pick up the corpsman. He found another rock outcropping and picked up the corpsman via another one-skid operation before one last trip to the staging area to pick up the safety officer and their rescue gear. He joined up with Coso-24 and they headed back towards the Naval Weapons Center. Due to the aircrew injuries, Coso-24 flew directly to Ridgecrest Regional Hospital where reporters were waiting to interview the pilot that had just rescued the downed pilots. Arnold flew directly back to base and shut down.

A few days later the aviation maintenance officer (AMO) asked him to come over to the hangar.

"Arnold, come over here for a minute." He said as he led them out onto the ramp toward the HH-1K. They stood next to the helo and the AMO pointed up toward the blades.

"See that?"

Arnold looked up at the underside of the rotors to see gouges and grooves.

"That must have been some rescue. How low did you get?" he asked in amazement. *Apparently low enough to prune some trees*, Arnold thought to himself. He never had a chance to speak with the pilots that he rescued. In fact, he never remembered speaking with any of his rescued aircrew, nor would he hear from them again. It was all in a day's work and he loved his job.

But the same work that gave him such satisfaction in serving his country also troubled him with unanswered questions. In his twenty years of flying, he lost many buddies to aviation related mishaps. Young men in the prime of their lives left behind young wives and small children. Most had not died in combat, but on routine training missions. *What kind of world must this be where such pointless deaths occur? With so much evil and suffering in the world, who could possibly believe in the*

existence of a loving God? How could such tragedies be anything but random and purposeless? Familiar voices whispered across the plain between life and death: *what a horrible, tragic, pointless waste*
. . .

But this story is bigger than a single rescue mission in the California desert. Something greater is going on here. "I wonder," reflects author James Tabor upon seven stranded climbers on Mount McKinley, "when players in a tragedy realize that the story is about their own destruction."[1] Perhaps the worst mistake a rescuer can make is not crashing over the crash site, but failing to realize when he needs rescuing himself. There are many ways to go down and not all of them are sudden and violent. It may result from a slow settling into the familiar forest of a broken world.

The moral fabric of our society did not go up in flames. Rather, it was slowly picked apart one fiber at a time—one rationalization at a time—leaving its signs of wear and tear unnoticed. Like the revelation of the branch-stricken rotor blades, oftentimes it takes someone to pull you aside and point their finger up to reveal just how much danger you've been in. Arnold didn't get the recognition that night for the bravery he displayed on that mountain. His sons learned of his heroism from a typewritten award drafted twenty-two years before they heard his story:

```
            Chief of Naval Operations

   The  President  of  the  United  States
   takes  pleasure  in  presenting  the  AIR
   MEDAL  (with  Bronze  Star  for  the  First
   Award)  to

                  MAJOR
               JOHN C. LADD
           UNITED STATES MARINE CORPS
```

For service as set forth in the
following

CITATION:

For meritorious achievement while
participating in aerial flight as
Aircraft Commander flying a HH-1K
Search and Rescue (SAR) Helicopter
while serving with the Naval Weapons
Center, China Lake, California on 14
August 1990. Major Ladd was assigned
as SAR Mission Commander to rescue two
downed F/A-18 Hornet aircrew, one of
whom had sustained major disabling
injuries. The Rescue attempt in steep
mountainous terrain with high
Aircraft gross weight required the
utmost skill in operating the
Aircraft at the edge of its
performance limits with no margin for
error. With a major forest fire and
thunderstorms threateningly close,
Major Ladd calmly and skillfully
maneuvered his Aircraft overhead the
survivors as he struggled to maintain
directional control. Utilizing
superb, aggressive airmanship, he
held his laboring craft in a steady
hover as the victims were safely
hoisted aboard without a moment to
spare. Major Ladd's leadership,
airmanship, and loyal dedication to
duty reflected credit upon himself

```
and were in keeping with the highest
traditions of the Marine Corps and the
United States Naval Service.
```

```
For the President,
```

```
F. B. KELSO, II
Admiral, United States Navy
Chief of Naval Operations
```

There are many ways to die. There's only one way to really live.

I don't know exactly where my father stands with God. But recently, and for the first time, he spoke to me in Scripture. He didn't quote the book or verse; he probably didn't know if it was from the Old or New Testament. But he knew it was God's wisdom he was passing to his son. It was short and quick, but spoken with love in a deliberate gesture to touch my soul.

It worked.

Everyone has looked up. Many have seen. Some have even believed. Fewer still will finish the race. In the parable of the wedding feast in Matthew 22:14 Jesus says, "Many are called, but few are chosen."

Will you be *one of the few*?

---

[1] James M. Tabor, *Forever on the Mountain* (New York: W. W. Norton & Company, 2007), 191.

Get updates on future projects at

WWW.JASONBLADD.COM/BLOG

Acknowledgments

IT TAKES MANY TO WRITE about the few. Thanks first to God for giving us life and art and the burden to help others. Thank you to Karry for your love, patience, and asking the question that started it all. Thank you to my parents and Kevin for the wonderful childhood, and to the Babbitts for making me part of the family.

For inspiration, thank you to the team at RZIM for speaking to the heart and challenging the mind. For encouragement, thanks to Jack Hawkins for preaching the sermons when my ears were first truly opened and to Steve Brown for bringing the memories of Iwakuni into the marriage which bound Karry and I together. Thanks to Lenor for planting the seed to start writing, Danielle DuRant for the initial guidance, Steve Wyatt for the early advising, to Jane Anderson for managing the Launch Team, and to Joel and Cora Bauer for their faith in my work.

Thank you to my many advisors: Steven Garofalo, Jason Brigadier, Rye Barcott, Michael Silva, Jacob Yoffee, Louis D'Elia, Mike Marshall, Annie Marshall, Brian Miller, Tom Morkes, Troy McLaughlin, Joe Courtemanche, Tom Farrington, and R.R.; all have helped make this book better.

Thanks to my editing team— Linda Maciulis, Melissa Cain Travis, Andrew Tuttle, Susan Irene Fox, Sandra T. Lloyd, and Julie Gwinn for your expertise and advising—true molders of the clay. Thanks to TVS Design Craft for the cover design, Satoshi Hirokawa for the photos, Jacob Yoffee and David Diperstein for the pre-order campaign trailer, and the Launch Team for helping me spread the Word.

And finally, thanks to the supporters and patrons who made the pre-order campaign on Publishizer.com a success.

You are the few.

4-Star Supporters

MARK & ANN BABBITT

3-Star Supporters

Jared Cagle

1-STAR SUPPORTERS

STEVE SHIPLEY

DEBBIE MCCAFFREY

NIJOLE LADD

CHRIS LADD

PATRONS

MEGHAN REID

MIKE WEST

NICHOLAS MINKO

RAWY SHEDIAC

RYE BARCOTT

BRIAN MILLER

SATOSHI HIROKAWA

FLOYD WINN

JOEL BAUER

CORA BAUER

BIBLIOGRAPHY

Abbott, John S.C. Napoleon Bonaparte. Public Domain.

Allen, Matt. *Navy.mil*. March 19, 2012. http://www.navy.mil /submit/display.asp?story_id=65956.

Aristotle. *Poetics*. Kindle edition. Public Domain.

Augustine. *The Confessions of Saint Augustine*. 401.

Baer, Randall N. *Inside the New Age Nightmare*. Lafayette: Huntington House, 1989.

Barrie, J.M. *The Little White Bird*. Nisyros Publishers, 2013.

Baumann, Nick. *Mother Jones*. January 10, 2011. http://www .motherjones.com/politics/2011/01/jared-lee-loughner -friend-voicemail-phone-message.

Berman, Laura. *Love and Sex with Dr. Berman*. http://www .drlauraberman.com/sexual-health/addiction/pornography -addiction (accessed July 19, 2012).

Blackmun, Harold A. *FindLaw.* http://caselaw.lp.findlaw.com /cgi-bin/getcase.pl?court=us&vol=410&invol=113 (accessed April 26, 2013).

Blackmun, Harold A., Warren E. Burger, William O. Douglas, Byron R. White, Potter Stewart, William H. Rehnquist, William J. Brennan, Thurgood Marshall, and Lewis F. Powell, Jr. "U.S. Supreme Court ROE v. WADE, 410 U.S. 113 (1973)." *FindLaw.* http://caselaw.lp.findlaw.com/cgi-bin /getcase.pl?court=us&vol=410&invol=113 (accessed April 26, 2013).

Boyd, Gregory A. *Letters From a Skeptic.* Colorado Springs: David C. Cook, 2008.

Brewer, David J., John M. Harlan, Horace G. Gray, Henry B. Brown, George Shiras, Jr., Byron R. White, and Joseph McKenna. "COTTING v. GODARD, 183 U.S. 79 (1901)." *FindLaw.* http://caselaw.lp.findlaw.com/cgi-bin/getcase .pl?court=us&vol=183&invol=79 (accessed April 26, 2013).

Breznican, Anthony. *USA Today.* April 23, 2006. http://www.usatoday.com/life/movies/news/2006-04-23-united93-main _x.htm (accessed April 26, 2013).

Bsecure Online. *Statistics.* http://www.bsecure.com /Resources/Statistics.aspx (accessed July 14, 2012).

Buddha Dharma Education Association, Inc. *Buddhanet.* http://www.buddhanet.net/e-learning/budethics.htm (accessed January 11, 2013).

Carlin, George. *Brain Droppings.* New York: Hyperion, 1997.

Casey, Kathryn. *Is "Fifty Shades of Grey" Dangerous?* June 23, 2012. http://www.forbes.com/sites/crime/2012/06/23 /is-fifty-shades-of-grey-dangerous.

Cengage, Gale. *eNotes.com.* April 13, 2013. http://www.enotes .com/military-drug-alcohol-abuse-united-states-reference.

Chesterton, Gilbert K. *The Everlasting Man.* Radford: Wilder Publications, 2008.

Christian Science Board of Directors. *What is Christian Science?* http://christianscience.com/what-is-christian-science (accessed October 20, 2012).

Claire, Rodger. *Raid on the Sun: Inside Israel's Secret Campaign that Denied Saddam the Bomb.* New York: Broadway Books, 2004.

Clark, David K. and Normal L. Geisler. *Apologetics in the New Age: A Christian Critique of Pantheism.* Eugene: Wipf and Stock Publishers, 1990.

Clausewitz, Carl von. *On War.* Princeton: Princeton University Press, 2008.

—. *On War.* Princeton: Princeton University Press, 1976.

Cox, Steven L. and Kendell H. Easley. *Holman Christian Standard Bible: Harmony of the Gospels.* Nashville: Holman Bible Publishers, 2007.

Craig, William Lane. *Reasonable Faith.* http://www .reasonablefaith.org/hawkings-curious-objections-to-divine -creation (accessed April 24, 2013).

Crowe, Russell. *Gladiator,* directed by Ridley Scott. Universal City, CA: DreamWorks LLC and Universal Studios, 2000.

Davies, Paul. *ASU Cosmos.* http://cosmos.asu.edu /publications/papers/OriginsOfLife_I.pdf (accessed August 7, 2012).

Dawkins, Richard. *The Blind Watchmaker.* London: Penguin, 1986.

—. *The Blind Watchmaker.* New York: Penguin Books, 1986.

—. *The God Delusion.* New York: Houghton Mifflin, 2006.

D'Souza, Dinesh. *What's So Great About Christianity?* Washington, DC: Regnery Publishing, Inc., 2007.

Eddy, Mary Baker. *Science and Health with Key to the Scriptures.* Boston: Christian Science Board of Directors, 1994.

Eisenhower, Dwight D. "Code of Conduct for Members of the United States Armed Forces." *Wikisource.* http://en .wikisource .org/wiki/Executive_Order_10631 (accessed April 26, 2013).

Erickson, Millard. *Christian Theology*. Grand Rapids: Baker Books, 1983.

Federer, J. *Great Quotations: A Collection of Passages, Phrases, and Quotations Influencing Early and Modern World History*. St. Louis: AmeriSearch, 2001.

Feinberg, J.S., P.D. Feinberg and A. Huxley. *Ethics for a Brave New World*. Wheaton: Crossway, 1996.

Flew, Antony and Roy Abraham Varghese. *There Is a God*. New York: Harper Collins, 2007.

Ford, Harrison. *Ender's Game*. Directed by Gavin Hood. Universal City, CA, Summit Entertainment, 2013.

Gacek, Christopher M. "Conceiving 'Pregnancy' U.S. Medical Dictionaries and Their Definitions of 'Conception' and 'Pregnancy'." *Family Research Council*. April 2009. http://www .frc.org/insight/conceiving-pregnancy-us-medical-dictionaries -and-their-definitions-of-conception-and-pregnancy (accessed April 26 2013).

Garret, Benjamin C. and John Hart. *The A to Z of Nuclear, Biological, and Chemical Warfare*. Lanham: Scarecrow Press, 2007.

Geisler, Norman L. and Frank Turek. *I Don't Have Enough Faith to Be an Atheist*. Wheaton: Crossway, 2004.

Geisler, Norman L. *Baker Encyclopedia of Apologetics*. Grand Rapids: Baker Academic, 1999.

Geisler, Norman. *Systematic Theology, vol. 2, God Creation.* Minneapolis: Bethany House, 2003.

—. *Systematic Theology, vol. 3, Sin, Salvation.* Minneapolis: Bethany House, 2004.

—. *Systematic Theology, vol. 4, Church, Last Things.* Minneapolis: Bethany House, 2004.

Gitt, Werner. *In the Beginning Was Information.* Green Forrest: Master Books, 2005.

Giubilini, Alberto and Francesca Minerva. *Journal of Medical Ethics.* http://jme.bmj.com/content/early/2012/04/12/medethic s -2011-100411.full.pdf+htm (accessed April 2013, 2012).

Glover, Julian and Kevork Malikvan. *Indiana Jones and the Last Crusade.* DVD. Directed by Steven Spielberg. Paramount Home Video, 1989.

Greene, Brian. *The Fabric of the Cosmos: Space, Time, and the Texture of Reality.* New York: Random House, 2004.

Gupta, Sanjay. *CNN Health.* January 10, 2012. http://thechart .blogs.cnn.com/2012/01/10/americans-binge-drinking-more /?hpt=hp_t3).

Harris, Sam. *The End of Faith: Religion, Terror, and the Future of Reason.* New York: W. W. Norton & Company, Kindle Edition, 2005.

Hawking, Stephen. *A Brief History of Time.* New York: Bantam Books, 1996.

Hawking, Stephen and Leonard Mlodinow. *The Grand Design*. New York: Bantam, 2010.

Hume, David. *An Enquiry Concerning Human Understanding*. Public Domain, 1902.

Irwin, William M., Mark T. Conrad, and Aeon J. Skoble. *The Simpsons and Philosophy: The D'oh! Of Homer*. Chicago: Open Court, 2008.

LaVey, Anton Szandor. *The Satanic Bible*. New York: Avon, 1969.

Lewis, C.S. *Mere Christianity*. New York: Harper Collins, 1980.

—. *The Weight of Glory*. Grand Rapids: Zondervan, 2001.

Linden, David J. *The Compass of Pleasure: How Our Brains Make Fatty Foods, Orgasm, Exercise, Marijuana, Generosity, Vodka, Learning, and Gambling Feel So Good*. New York: Penguin Group, 2011.

Londono, Ernesto. *Slain Marine commander's actions in Afghanistan called heroic*. September 22, 2012. http://www.washingtonpost.com/world/national-security /2012 /09/21 /f4703c76-042d-11e2-91e7-2962c74e7738_story.html?hpid =z2.

MacArthur, John F. *The Gospel According to Jesus*. Grand Rapids: Zondervan, 2008.

Martin, Walter. *Kingdom of the Cults*. Bloomington: Bethany House, 1997.

Martin, Walter, Jill Martin Rische and Kevin Rische. *The Kingdom of the Occult.* Nashville: Thomas Nelson, 208.

Nash, Ronald. *Worldviews in Conflict.* Grand Rapids: Zondervan, 1992.

Neufeld, Gordon. *Hold On to Your Kids: Why Parents Need to Matter More Than Peers.* New York: Ballantine, 2005.

Newport, Frank. *Gallup.com.* June 30, 2011. http://www .gallup.com /poll/147887/Americans-Continue-Believe-God .aspx (accessed April 14, 2013).

Packer, J.I. *Growing in Christ.* Wheaton: Crossway Books, 1996.

Pascal, Blaise. *Pascal's Pensées.* New York: E.P. Dutton & Co., Inc., 1958.

Penton, James M. *Apocalypse Delayed: The Story of Jehovah's Witnesses, 2nd ed.* Toronto: University of Toronto Press, 1997.

Phillips, Michael M. *The Gift of Valor.* 2005 : Broadway Books, New York.

Quinn, Aidan. *Legends of the Fall.* Directed by Edward Zwick. Performed by Aidan Quinn. Columbia TriStar Home Video, 2000, 1994.

Reitman, Janet. *Inside Scientology: The Story of America's Most Secretive Religion.* New York: Houghton Mifflin Harcourt, 2011.

Rorty, Richard. *Rorty and His Critics.* Oxford: Blackwell, 2000.

Russell, Bertrand. *PhilosophicalSociety.com.* http://www .philosophicalsociety.com/Archives/A%20Free %20Man's %20Worship.htm (accessed April 11, 2013).

Satinover, Jeffrey. "Struggling Teens." *Woodbury Reports, Inc.* May 9, 2008. http://www.strugglingteens.com/news /RelatedNews/JeffreySatinover.pdf (accessed April 27, 2013).

Schaeffer, Francis A. *How Should We Then Live? (L'Abri 50th Anniversary Edition): The Rise and Decline of Western Thought and Culture.* Wheaton: Crossway, 2005.

Scott, Brad. *Embraced by the Darkness.* Wheaton: Crossway, 1996.

Simpson, James Beasely. *Best Quotes of '54, '55, '56.* New York: Thomas Y. Crowell Company, 1957.

Singh, Simon and Edzard Ernst. *Trick or Treatment: The Undeniable Facts About Alternative Medicine.* New York: W.W. Norton & Company, 2008.

Stenger, Victor J. *God: The Failed Hypothesis--How Science Shows That God Does Not Exist.* New York: Prometheus Books, 2008.

Story, D. *Engaging the Closed Minded: Presenting Your Faith to the Confirmed Unbeliever.* Grand Rapids: Kregel Publications, 1999.

Strobel, Lee. *The Case for Faith: A Journalist Investigates the Toughest Objections to Christianity.* Grand Rapids: Zondervan, 2000.

Sutter, John D. *CNN.* http://www.cnn.com/2012/06/25 /tech/web/mcafee-teen-online-survey/index.html?iref =allsearch (accessed July 19, 2012).

Tabor, James M. *Forever on the Mountain.* New York: W.W. Norton & Company, 2007.

Tan, Paul Lee. *Encyclopedia of 7,700 Illustrations: Signs of the Times.* Garland: Bible Communications, Inc., 1996.

Taylor, C.L. and L.B. Taylor Jr. *Chemical and Biological Warfare.* New York: Franklin Watts, 1985.

The Holy Bible: New International Version. Grand Rapids: Zondervan, 1996.

The New King James Version. Nashville: Thomas Nelson, 1982.

The Richard Dawkins Foundation for Reason and Science. *RichardDawkins.net.* May 10, 2006. http://old.richarddawkins .net /articles /89.

U.S. Marine Corps. *MCDP 1: Warfighting.* Washington, D.C.: Department of the Navy, 1997.

—. "MCDP 6: Command and Control." Washington, D.C.: Department of the Navy, 1996.

United States Marine Corps. *Marines.com.* April 1, 2012.
http://www.marines.com/history-heritage/timeline.

Walvoord, J.F. and R. B. Zuck. *The Bible Knowledge
Commentary: An Exposition of the Scriptures.* Wheaton: Victor
Books, 1983.

Warner Bros. Ent. *Magic Mike.* http://magicmikemovie
.warnerbros .com/# (accessed July 15, 2012).

Washington, Peter. *Madame Blavatsky's Baboon: A History of
the Mystics, Mediums, and Misfits Who Brought Spiritualism to
America* . New York: Schocken Books, 1995.

Watch Tower Bible and Tract Society of Pennsylvania. *"Our
Families".* http://www.jw-media.org/aboutjw/article21.htm
(accessed September 5, 2012).

Wiersbe, Warren W. *The Bible Exposition Commentary.*
Wheaton: Victor Books, 1996.

Wikipedia. *Al Bundy.*
http://en.wikipedia.org/wiki/Al_Bundy (accessed August
5, 2012).

Wikiquote. *G.K.Chesterton.* http://en.wikiquote.org/wiki
/G._K._Chesterton (accessed April 26, 2013).

Zacharias, Ravi. *Has Christianity Failed You?* Grand Rapids:
Zondervan, 2010.

—. *Jesus Among Other Gods: The Absolute Claims Of The
Christian Message* . Nashville: Thomas Nelson, 2000.

—. *The End of Reason: A Response to the New Atheists.* Grand Rapids: Zondervan, 2008.

—. *Why Jesus? Rediscovering His Truth in an Age of Mass Marketed Spirituality.* New York: Faith Words, 2012.

Zimbardo, Philip G, and Nikita Duncan. *The Demise of Guys: Why Boys Are Struggling and What We Can Do About It.* New York: TED, 2012.

Zimbardo, Philip G. and Nikita Duncan. *CNN.com.* May 24, 2012. http://www.cnn.com/2012/05/23/health/living-well /demise-of-guys/index.html (accessed May 27, 2012).

INDEX

Made in the USA
Charleston, SC
29 October 2015